Love, Equally

The Journey to Marriage Equality

Written by:
Bob Young & John C. Hughes
Research by:
Aaron Peplowski

Front cover photos, left to right:
Jamie, Leif, Erik, Trygve, Eric, and Anders Pedersen, *Jamie Pedersen*
Daphne Draayer, Mary Yu, and Vanessa Williams, *Barb Kinney*
Shauna, Maureen, and Amy Walsh, *Shauna Walsh*
Jeff Hedgepeth and John Medlin with Fudge, *Jeff Hedgepeth*
Margarethe Cammermeyer and Diane Divelbess, *Margarethe Cammermeyer*
Manny Santiago, *Manny Santiago*
Jane Abbott Lighty, Pete-e Petersen, and Anne Levinson, *Anne Levinson*

Back cover photos, left to right:
Hands, *Barb Kinney* (top)
Cal Anderson, *Washington State Archives*
Pete Francis, *Pete Francis*
Maureen Walsh, *TVW*
Jeff Hedgepeth, Marsha Botzer, and Sara Elward, *Associated Press*
Chris Gregoire and Mary Margaret Haugen, *The Seattle Times*
John Singer and Paul Barwick, *MOHAI, Seattle Post-Intelligencer Collection*
Laurie Jinkins, *Laurie Jinkins*

Cover by Amber Raney
Book design by Aaron Peplowski
Printed in the United States of America by Gorham Printing, Centralia, Washington.

WASHINGTON
Secretary of State
Legacy Washington

For the thousands and thousands of Washingtonians from all walks of life who persevered to make marriage equality a reality.

CONTENTS

INTRODUCTION

Our State Was a Trailblazer

On February 1, 2012, I was a member of the Washington State Senate, representing the 44th District in rural Snohomish County. The issue before the Senate that historic day was same-sex marriage. Three years earlier, when Washington voters ratified a referendum on domestic partnerships for same-sex couples, my district had voted no. Now, the visitor galleries were packed as senators weighed in on the contentious issue. I asked to be recognized to explain why my conscience compelled me to vote for marriage equality. I said I had received dozens of emails and phone calls, as well as visits from constituents—even text messages as the debate got under way. They were telling me to vote no.

"So, let me tell you why I'm supporting this bill: I've served in the Army for over 20 years. During that time, I've deployed to two combat zones. Now I'm in the National Guard. This weekend I have drill. I'm going to see many of my fellow soldiers. Some will be wearing the Combat Action Badge or the Combat Infantryman's Badge indicating they were in close combat with the enemy. Many still deal with PTSD. And some of those soldiers I've served with are gay. How could I look them in the eye this weekend if I voted no on this bill? How could I stand next to them if I voted no on this bill? How could I deny a right

As one of the senators who supported marriage equality, I'm at right as Governor Gregoire addresses the audience after signing the legislation. Future Speaker Laurie Jinkins is to my right, and Senator Jamie Pedersen is to Gregoire's right. *Legislative Support Services*

that I enjoy to my brothers and sisters who are willing to take a bullet for me and fight beside me in any combat situation?

"The current estimate is that about 66,000 gays are in the armed forces today. Some of them gave the ultimate sacrifice for their country—much like Army Corporal Andrew Wilfahrt, a gay soldier from Minnesota, who died one year ago in Afghanistan. [A hidden mortar round detonated as his squad crossed a bridge. Three other explosives daisy-chained together failed to detonate. So in death, Wilfahrt saved several comrades.]

"That was three months after President Obama lifted the 'Don't Ask, Don't Tell' policy.

"There's a line in the Soldier's Creed that I never forget. It's drilled into every soldier's head: 'Never leave a fallen comrade behind.' I will never leave a fallen comrade behind. Not now, not ever. And that's why I'm voting yes on this bill."

On the weekend after the Legislature sent the bill to Governor

Gregoire for her signature, I walked into my unit's orderly room and was greeted by the readiness NCO, a Sergeant First Class who earlier had deployed to Iraq. Everyone knew she was a lesbian—and an exemplary soldier.

"Thank you, sir," she said to me, with a smile of gratitude that melted my heart.

This important book and the "Love, Equally" exhibit at the Office of the Secretary of State spotlight the long and winding road to LGBTQ civil rights in Washington.

In December of 2022, as we marked the 10th anniversary of marriage equality here, Congress approved legislation that provides federal protections for same-sex and interracial marriages, sending the landmark bill to President Biden's desk for his signature. The Respect for Marriage Act received bipartisan support in both the House and Senate. The act requires the federal government and all states to recognize marriages if the pair was wed in a state where the union was legal. It also cements protections for interracial couples, ordering states to recognize marriages regardless of "the sex, race, ethnicity, or national origin of those individuals."

National polls now indicate 70 percent of Americans support same-sex marriage. I'm proud that our state was a trailblazer.

Washington Secretary of State

PETE FRANCIS

PAVING THE WAY

It was September 20, 1971. John Singer and Paul Barwick, charter members of the Seattle chapter of the Gay Liberation Front—the movement's "pushy jerks," as Barwick put it—decided to apply for a marriage license even though they didn't really believe in marriage. They got the idea from Pete Francis, a progressive state senator, who took umbrage at being constantly asked whether he was gay—as if you couldn't be straight if you "stood up for all those homosexuals."

Francis as a freshman legislator in 1969. *Pete Francis*

Lloyd Hara, the youngest auditor in King County history, rejected the application with deeply mixed emotions after consulting the county prosecutor's office. Hara, 31, was a third-generation Japanese American who recoiled at "discrimination against anyone."

Singer, a former VISTA volunteer, and Barwick, a hard-nosed former military policeman, regarded the button-down gay guys in Seattle's Dorian Society "as a bunch of closet cases who were afraid to push." Not so their attorney, Pete Francis, who three years earlier had helped the Dorians incorporate. "A libertarian as much as a liberal," the lanky Stanford Law School graduate "wanted government out of private lives," Gary L. Atkins writes in *Gay Seattle*, an indispensable history of the LGBTQ community.

Facing page: John Singer and Paul Barwick apply for a marriage license at the King County Auditor's Office in 1971. *MOHAI, Seattle Post-Intelligencer Collection*

In nine eventful years as a Washington lawmaker, Francis fought for open government; opposed censorship of books and movies; reformed the juvenile and probate codes; eliminated the legal stigma of "illegitimacy," and repealed the state's draconian sodomy laws. The former Marine Corps captain bowed out in 1977 by championing a bill "to assure to all persons, regardless of their sexual orientation, protection of the laws against discrimination."

A decade later, Cal Anderson became the state's first openly gay legislator, reinvigorating the push for an LGBTQ civil rights law. Pete Francis had helped pave the way.

SEATTLE'S battleground 32nd District, stretching from Ballard to the U District, elected Francis to the House in 1968. "What an amazing, tumultuous year in American politics," Francis remembers, still marveling at his defeat of Joe Mc-Gavick, a Republican with close ties to Governor Dan Evans and Attorney General Slade Gorton.

Two years later, Francis outpolled Mary Ellen McCaffree, another Evans-Gorton ally, to keep a Senate seat to which he had been appointed.*

Pegged by caucus leadership as a go-getter, the 34-year-old freshman immediately introduced a bill to lower the age of "majority" to 18 for "all persons" for the purpose of voting, marriage, execution of wills and contracts, and jury service. Republicans controlled the House, but Francis' bill had bipartisan momentum. It was a recommendation of the Washington State Commission for Youth Involvement, a program Governor Evans established within the Office of the Secretary of State. Sam Reed, a future three-term Republican secretary of state, was then assistant secretary. He has vivid memories of working with Francis to promote the legislation during an era when change was in the air.

The bill failed to advance during the 1969 session. In 1970, however, when Francis ascended to the Democrat-controlled Senate, he shepherded it through a special session. The 18-year-old vote would not be implemented until ratification of the 26th Amendment to the U.S. Constitution in 1971.

The other provisions of Francis' bill became law, notably allowing 18-year-olds to "enter into any marriage contract without parental consent if otherwise qualified by law." Previously, a male Washingtonian under 21 needed parental consent to marry; a young woman was free to marry at 18.

Future governor Booth Gardner and George Fleming, the Senate's second

---

* Francis succeeded Senator Wes Uhlman, who was elected mayor of Seattle in 1969. In the 1970s, Uhlman supported the City Council's anti-discrimination ordinances for gay employment and housing rights and was the first Seattle mayor to declare Gay Pride Week.

Black member, were his important Senate allies on reform legislation, Francis re-members.

JOHN SINGER tried to sublimate his radicalism when he attended meetings of the Dorian Society. Before veering off to help organize a Seattle chapter of the Gay Liberation Front, he heard Pete Francis talk about the revised marriage law. Tellingly, Francis noted, it said otherwise qualified *"persons"* at least 18 years of age could be married. It did not stipulate that marriage meant a man and a woman.

Singer and Barwick's lawsuit against the county auditor would take three years to resolve. A lot happened in the meantime.

Pete Francis, in 1973, became chairman of the Senate Judiciary Committee and plowed ahead with an array of criminal code reform legislation endorsed by the Washington Bar Association. He zeroed in on Washington's 1909 sodomy statute. Under the letter of the law, a man and woman who engaged in oral sex could face prison. Homosexuality was even more "abhorrent." Exactingly graphic, the new law amplified an 1893 statue proscribing any "infamous and detestable crime against nature, either with mankind or with any beast." While most newspapers spared their gentle readers the sordid details of the 1909 statute, the code reviser was duty bound to codify the prohibition of any unlawful carnal knowledge of "any animal or bird," or "any male or female person" anally or "with the mouth or tongue"—consensual or not in the case of humans, and certainly in all ways with regard to hapless beasts and birds. "Attempted" intercourse with "a dead body" also constituted sodomy. And anyone guilty of any of the above was to be imprisoned "for not more than 10 years." Though the 1893 law had called for a maximum sentence of 14 years, the revised law's reduced maximum penalty "was still greater than the punishment for forcibly raping a woman, which earned only half as much time in jail," Atkins observes in *Gay Seattle*.

Thus, anything other than "missionary position" heterosexual coitus by married adults, preferably for procreation—"as God has intended," said a Seattle preacher—was an affront to moral order.

Revising the code would require 300 days of maneuvering over the next two years.

SAME-SEX marriage resurfaced in 1973 when the all-male state Senate debated ratification of the federal Equal Rights Amendment. Washington voters had narrowly approved the state's own ERA on November 7, 1972.

Francis, main sponsor of the bill to implement the federal ERA, was cross-examined by conservatives. A.L. "Slim" Rasmussen, a flinty Tacoma Democrat first elected to the Legislature in 1944, asked if the ERA could be interpreted to allow gay marriage, "which would mean the end of our civilization." (Rasmussen's distaste for "queers" was no secret.) "My silence would be acquiescence," Francis remembers, "so I said, 'No, it means equality of rights could not be denied on account of sex, as in the genders. Men and women will remain men and women. We simply all remain equal before the law.' I also thought to myself, 'It's *already* legal because of the law we passed lowering the age of majority to 18 for all persons.' In any case, I said I didn't think gay marriage would be the end of our civilization, which prompted some to claim I had disgraced the Senate."

After the House overwhelmingly ratified the federal ERA, Senate opponents led by future congressman Jack Metcalf, a "states' rights" Republican from Mukilteo, delayed a vote for nearly five weeks. Lieutenant Governor John Cherberg, the Senate president, finally ruled Metcalf's amendments out of order. "When we finally dislodged the bill from the Rules Committee, we knew we had the 25 votes we needed to prevail," Francis remembers.

With the Senate's concurrence, 29-19, Washington became the 29th state to approve the landmark constitutional amendment on March 22, 1973.

THE MARRIAGE LICENSE lawsuit filed by John Singer and Paul Barwick was not faring as well. King County Superior Court, in 1972, ruled they had provided no evidence that state law permitted the marriage of two people of the same sex, or that their constitutional rights had been abridged. Taking their case to the newly-established Washington Court of Appeals, the appellants now also argued that the trial court's rejection violated the Equal Rights Amendment.

The Court of Appeals, on May 20, 1974, flatly rejected the notion that by replacing "man" and "woman" with "persons" the Legislature had opened the door to same-sex marriage. Exhibit A, the court said, was the law relating to affidavits required for the issuance of a marriage license. It "makes reference to 'the male' and 'the female,' which clearly dispels any suggestion that the legislature intended to authorize same-sex marriages." As for the ERA, the appeals court said no court in the nation had yet ruled on the legality of same-sex marriage in light of the proposed new constitutional amendment. That said, the three-member appellate court took note of the state's contention that "there is no violation of the ERA so long as marriage licenses are denied equally to both male and female pairs"—gays and lesbians alike. Then the judges cut to the chase: Marriage, inextricably, was about procreation, a notion cited as being "as old as the book of Genesis." The court concluded:

> It is apparent that the state's refusal to grant a license al-
> lowing the appellants to marry one another is not based upon
> appellants' status as males, but rather it is based upon the state's
> recognition that our society as a whole views marriage as the
> appropriate and desirable forum for procreation and the rear-
> ing of children. ...The fact remains that marriage exists as a
> protected legal institution primarily because of societal values
> associated with the propagation of the human race. Further, it
> is apparent that no same-sex couple offers the possibility of the
> birth of children by their union. Thus the refusal of the state to
> authorize same-sex marriage results from such impossibility of
> reproduction rather than from an invidious discrimination "on
> account of sex." ...In short, we hold the ERA does not require
> the state to authorize same-sex marriage.

There was a footnote intended as judicious:

> We are not unmindful of the fact that public attitude to-
> ward homosexuals is undergoing substantial, albeit gradual,
> change. ...[W]e express no opinion upon the desirability of re-
> vising our marriage laws to accommodate homosexuals and in-
> clude same-sex relationships within the definition of marriage.
> That is a question for the people to answer through the legis-
> lative process. We merely hold such a legislative change is not
> constitutionally required.

The Washington Supreme Court let the decision stand without review.

FRANCIS WAS BUSY on multiple fronts, pushing to open legislative committee
meetings to the public; championing global population stabilization, and intro-
ducing bills to protect the free speech rights of student journalists. He agreed
with Governor Evans that the drinking age should be lowered to 18, and voted for
19 as a compromise. Francis' attempts to decriminalize prostitution—the oldest
"victimless crime," as he put it—generated the most uproar.

During the 1975 legislative session, he reintroduced measures to revise the
criminal code. Deploying a new six-bill strategy, Francis gave the prostitution
legislation a feminist twist by stipulating that men who patronized prostitutes

should be held as culpable as the women.

The bill repealing the sodomy and adultery laws was the bottleneck. Senator Jack Cunningham, a conservative Republican from Des Moines, thwarted its advance, declaring, "I'm not going to sit back and let you rewrite the Ten Commandments."

Francis jettisoned the prostitution bill, repackaged repeal of the sodomy law and repeatedly out-maneuvered Cunningham. The week-long battle of parliamentary jujitsu ended in a 28-20 victory for Francis. Governor Dan Evans, "no fan of victimless crimes," admired the Judiciary chairman's persistence. He signed the new criminal code into law. Francis' friend Charlie Brydon, a founder of the Dorian Society, hailed the change on July 1, 1976, as "a major advance for gay people in Washington."

Senator Francis with Gov. Dan Evans around 1970. *Ron Allen*

WHEN FRANCIS introduced his gay civil rights bill in 1977, discrimination against homosexuals was front-page news thanks to Anita Bryant, a former Miss America contestant singing the praises of Florida orange juice in prime-time TV commercials. When Dade County, Florida, passed a gay anti-discrimination ordinance, Bryant launched a repeal campaign. Millions of Christian conservatives enlisted in her "Save Our Children" coalition when she charged that homosexuals, unable to "reproduce," had to "recruit our children to perpetuate their lifestyle."

Francis now had 11 solid allies in the House—including four Republicans. They introduced a bill asserting that "sexuality expressed between consenting persons" was a private matter "unrelated to a person's capacity to contribute to the economic, social and cultural welfare of our state."

James Gaylord, a veteran Tacoma high school teacher fired when he admitted he had homosexual "preferences," was one of a parade of witnesses who testified before Francis' Senate Judiciary Committee. Noting that Gaylord's dismissal for "immorality" had been upheld by the Washington Supreme Court, albeit narrowly, Francis observed that by that standard President Jimmy Carter, a graduate of the U.S. Naval Academy, wouldn't be allowed to teach in Washington schools. In an interview with *Playboy* magazine, candidate Carter admitted he had "looked on a lot of women with lust…and committed adultery in my heart many times." Charlie Brydon predicted that if all the gay teachers in the state suddenly came out and were removed from the classroom "the impact would be stunning."

Dave Kopay, an All-American running back at the University of Washington in the 1960s, told of his struggle being closeted during nine years in the National Football League. When he came out after his retirement from the NFL, being gay meant being denied a chance to become a coach, Kopay said. A lawmaker asked Kopay what caused people to be gay. "Do you ask a Black person why he's black?" Kopay said, recalling that a friend who knew his secret once asked, "Don't you wish you could change?" "And I said, 'How can you change what you are?' "

Conservative clergy and editorial writers decried "sanctioning unnatural, anti-social deviant conduct."

During breaks in the contentious hearings, reporters prodded Senator Francis to say whether he was gay. "For years, I wasn't willing to answer that question because I felt like it was nobody's business," he says today, at 88. "I'd say, 'It just doesn't matter. People's private lives are their private lives.' But they'd keep asking. My friend Wayne Ehlers, a former Speaker of the House, lobbied for the Privacy Fund, a gay rights political action committee. He's straight. I'm straight, but we had a lot of gay friends because we care about civil rights and justice. In my life I've come to realize what we need more of is people willing to get outraged at injustices being done to other people. Most people don't get outraged unless it happens to them or their group. It just kills me. I find it extremely hard to read a book like Douglas Blackmon's *Slavery by Another Name*, which details the forced labor of Black convicts in the 20th Century. Our mistreatment of Native Americans just tears me up, too."

THE 1977 gay civil rights bills never advanced beyond the Senate Judiciary and House Social and Health Services committees.

For Francis, it was more of a frustrating swan song than a last hurrah. He resigned from the Senate on January 1, 1978. He was 43, with two sons who'd soon be heading to college. He could be earning "as much as $35,000 a year" if he concentrated on his law clients, editorialists noted, lamenting the loss of such "a bright, articulate legislator." His Senate salary was $3,800 per year. "There's no

Francis today. *Pete Francis*

political position quite as bad from a financial standpoint as that of a state legislator," Francis said.

A year later, he joined Charlie Brydon and a broad coalition of other Seattleites—gay and straight—in a campaign to defeat an initiative aimed at repealing the city's anti-discrimination ordinances. Seattle became the first city in the United States to vote in favor of gay civil rights.

When Cal Anderson joined the Legislature in 1987, he introduced gay civil rights and anti-hate bills every session, his civility and parliamentary skill winning more converts with each passing year. In 1994, a year before his death from complications of AIDS, the legislation passed the House, only to fall a vote short in the Senate. No longer referenced as just "the state's first openly gay legislator," Anderson had become, in a poll of his colleagues, one of the state's most effective lawmakers, Gary Atkins wrote.

It remained for Ed Murray, Anderson's protégé and successor, to advance the rainbow colors. He succeeded, with the help of thousands upon thousands of Washingtonians who came to see, as Francis puts it, "That God must have put gay people on earth for a reason. So let's respect their integrity and autonomy as human beings instead of trying to tell them what to do and who to do it with."

Francis remained committed to human rights issues for the rest of a long career as a lawyer. He's retired now, but not retiring.

On January 31, 2006, Governor Chris Gregoire signed Murray's civil rights bill into law. It added "sexual orientation" to the existing prohibitions of discrimination in employment, housing, lending and insurance. She handed Pete Francis one of the pens.

John C. Hughes

CAL ANDERSON'S LEGACY

"You can't have it all, all at once."

The room Cal Anderson booked for a hearing on his gay civil rights bill could accommodate a hundred people. When upwards of 600 arrived by the busload, a lone security guard called the State Patrol for reinforcements. Conservative Christians rattled the doors and jostled in the hallways, chanting "We want in!" Some carried homemade signs denouncing "the sin of sodomy" and "state-sanctioned perversion." It was March 2, 1993. Anderson, the state's first openly gay lawmaker, and his friend Ed Murray, president of the Privacy Fund, a gay rights political action committee, had expected fireworks, not Armageddon. Charlie Brydon and Don Moreland, two respected older gay activists in Seattle, counseled Anderson that the hearing was a bad idea. "Cal was determined," Murray remembers. In Washington, you could be fired from your job or evicted from an apartment for being gay.

Supporters of House Bill 1443—outnumbered three to one—were rallying on the other side of the building. Scott Plusquellec and Kent Johnson of Seattle Queer Nation marched from Seattle to Olympia to draw attention to the legislation.

Anderson, who would oversee the hearing as chairman of the House State Government Committee, moved it to the House chamber at the Capitol, hoping its gravitas would defuse the tension. It was "an unprecedented location for one of the nastiest legislative hearings in memory," David Postman wrote in Tacoma's *Morning News Tribune.*

Representative Lynn Kessler, with a growing sense of dread, watched the crowd pour into the chamber, occupy the lawmakers' desks and commandeer the galleries. Not your average freshman legislator, Kessler, 51, was a former single mom. As executive director of the United Way of Grays Harbor, she helped provide services to a community devastated by logging cutbacks to preserve habitat

Facing page: Rep. Cal Anderson addresses colleagues in the House. *Washington State Archives*

Anderson with his partner, Eric Ishino, in 1987 when the Seattle Democrat became the state's first openly gay lawmaker. *Washington State Archives*

for the Northern spotted owl. Timber families became an equally endangered species. The centrist Democrat from Hoquiam liked to say her grad-school degree was from "the School of Hard Knocks."

Murray, the lead-off witness, also had roots in coastal Washington's timber communities. His grandparents, Irish immigrants fleeing oppression, "settled in Grays Harbor County, logged it, farmed it and helped build our state," Murray said. "They came to this country to ensure that *all* of their children and grandchildren would have an opportunity for a home, a job, and a chance at the American dream."

Opponents began murmuring their dissent. When the executive director of the State Human Rights Commission spoke 10 seconds longer than what Anderson had said would be the limit for testimony, shouts of "shut up!" rang out. Anderson promised there'd be equal time. But when the next 20 witnesses endorsed his legislation, the ornate chamber echoed with booing, hooting and hissing. Gay rights supporters shouted back.

David Serkin-Poole, a cantor at a Bellevue synagogue, began his testimony by singing beautifully, hauntingly. The chamber grew quiet. He denounced the "abuse" of scripture and shared that he and his partner, Michael Serkin-Poole, had adopted two children. "Get out of here, you freak!" someone shouted.

When John Boonstra, an ecumenical Christian clergyman, endorsed Anderson's bill, the opponents were in full cry. "Read Leviticus!" someone yelled. Then, chillingly, another taunt: "When's the next train to Auschwitz?"

"The hatred was palpable," Kessler remembers. "It went right through my skin to my very being. I'd never heard people talk that way. Yet Cal didn't flinch. Arms crossed on the speaker's dais, he let the opponents talk for nearly an hour." When some strayed into recitations of Biblical abominations, he calmly countered, "Isn't it Leviticus that says, 'Thou shalt love your neighbor like you love yourself'? That's the part I like best!" He told others who preached fire and brimstone to stick to the subject at hand, and responded with dry sarcasm when a Tacoma pastor declared that the "what next?" could be pedophilia, bestiality, even necrophilia. "But he never lost his cool," Kessler says. "It was an impressive display of civility."

Gallingly for Ed Murray, a practicing Roman Catholic, and Lynn Kessler, raised in the faith, the lobbyist for the state's Catholic bishops waffled when it was his turn to testify. "We may not want to be hurried into a broader acceptance of homosexuality," said Ned Dolejsi. "We cannot support the present legislation, but we will not oppose it." "It was a stunning reversal," Gary L. Atkins wrote in his award-winning book, *Gay Seattle*. "After a decade and a half of advocating for the bill, the Catholic bishops had declared neutrality."

"We needed to regroup in a hurry," Murray remembers. "Cal had the votes to move the civil rights bill to the floor of the House, where he was confident of victory. But we knew there could be trouble ahead in the Senate, especially if the bishops weren't with us." Murray arranged a Saturday-night summit with the new Archbishop of Seattle, Thomas Murphy.

Wayne Ehlers, Speaker of the House in the 1980s, was lobbying for the Privacy Fund.* He vividly remembers the meeting at the archbishop's mansion. He and Cal Anderson were "the two Protestants" trying to mind their manners, as Ehlers puts it. Murray, who had explored the priesthood after high school, and Jenny Durkan, an activist lawyer from a prominent Catholic family, were the gay Catholic standard-bearers—tempering their arguments with deference for the archbishop. "Archbishop Murphy said we didn't need a gay rights bill because the federal

---

* When Bobbe Bridge, a future Washington Supreme Court justice, stepped down as the Privacy Fund's lobbyist, seasoned political operatives told Murray that Ehlers was interested in the job. Murray chuckles at his political naiveté back then. He didn't know that in 1991 Ehlers had prodded Governor Booth Gardner to prohibit discrimination in state employment on the basis of sexual orientation. "I called Charlie Brydon and Don Moreland for advice," Murray remembers. "They said, 'Get him! Call him right now!' Wayne was perfect because he had a background in progressive politics. And of course he knew the legislative process. He also had business clients who might become our allies. I couldn't believe he landed in my lap. I wish I'd had a Wayne Ehlers as Speaker when I was in the House!"

Constitution protected all Americans, gay and straight alike," Ehlers recalls, remembering watching Anderson stifle his incredulity. "We explained that it wasn't
true. The archbishop kept asking for more clarification." Wouldn't Anderson's bill
lead to gay marriage? No, they said. If signed into law, the bill would merely make
it illegal to deny gay people employment, housing and other basic civil rights.
Finally, "probably without proper respect" for the archbishop's standing as leader
of Western Washington's one million Catholics, Ehlers reminded Murphy that in
the days of virulent anti-Catholicism in the East and South a clergyman in cleri-
cal collar might have been turned away at a hotel or café in a staunchly Protestant
city. The archbishop smiled thinly. Still, Murray thought things, on the whole, had
gone well. "Cal felt positive," he says. "I felt positive. I think Murphy played us. He
was an operator. It just seemed like we were so close."

And yet so far. Thirteen years away, to be precise.

Anderson's gay civil rights bill passed the House 57-41—six more "yeas" than
three years earlier. Seattle Democrat Gary Locke, who in four years would become
the first Chinese American governor in U.S. history, said it was an important step
along the long, muddy road to civil rights for all Americans, regardless of their
ethnicity, religion or sexual orientation.

The bishops' lobbyist continued to obfuscate. Anderson's bill was sent to the
Senate Ways and Means Committee. For all practical purposes, it remained one
vote short of making it to the floor of the Senate, Ehlers remembers.

A year later, resurgent Republicans seized control of the House, 60-38, and
reduced the Democrats' hold on the state Senate to 25-24. Anderson's landslide
victory for a Senate seat from the 43rd District was a bright spot for the Democrats.

THE INTERESTING thing about "the state's first openly gay lawmaker" was that
some gays didn't think he was gay enough. Cal Anderson was too nice, they said;
too well-spoken—the boy next door in horn-rim glasses, joking that what the
Legislature needed was a "sissy." That Seattle's personable star quarterback, Rus-
sell Wilson, was regarded by some Seahawk teammates as "not black enough" had
the same flavor 20 years later.

On the night before the volatile hearing in Olympia, a group of self-described "queer AIDS activists" spray-painted Anderson's Seattle home with "Budget cuts kill!" and "AIDS money now!" They claimed Anderson "was silent when
the federally funded, state-administered AIDS Prescription Drug Program's budget was cut." Anderson denounced the vandalism as the handiwork of a small

group of activists "who like to stand on the side and scream," but do nothing constructive to help people with AIDS. "They don't have the guts to face me because they're wrong," he said. The Northwest AIDS foundation hailed him as one of its strongest supporters. Few knew, however, that Anderson had been HIV-positive for years.

Cal Anderson, born in 1948, was exactly seven years older than Ed Murray. Anderson became a political junkie as a teenager working on his father's campaign for a city council seat in suburban Tukwila. After high school, he worked for the King County Democratic chairwoman before getting caught in the draft. Anderson ended up as a court reporter in Vietnam during the court martial of a My Lai Massacre defendant. His work was so exemplary that he received two Bronze Stars for meritorious service in a combat zone. Next, he worked for a Seattle city council member before becoming Mayor Charles Royer's appointments secretary. In 1987, when Anderson was appointed at mid-term to fill a vacant seat in the Washington House of Representatives, Ed Murray was a

Cal Anderson and Ed Murray on the campaign trail in the 1980s. *Ed Murray*

32-year-old aide in a legal office and immersed in volunteering for the Democratic Party.

"I told Cal I wanted to help him campaign to keep his seat in the Legislature," Murray remembers. "And he said, 'Well, come on over!' From that evening, Cal literally took over my life. I was willing to work. I was hungry. The gay world was kind of elitist. You had to be a lawyer or a business person. I was just a paralegal. Cal for some reason saw something in me and got me appointed to the mayor's Gay and Lesbian Task Force, along with Harvey Muggy, a huge hero in gay politics on Seattle's Capitol Hill. Cal and I were political nerds interested in the Democratic Party. We loved elective politics, working on campaigns and conventions—all the things that come with making government function. We became good friends. Cal was always accused of being a sell-out because he was the State Party secretary. He worked the system. The wealthy part of the community sniffed that he only had a high school education and worked for the mayor as opposed to being part of the activist wing. He had a terrible time early on. When the AIDS ac-

Anderson not long before his death from complications of AIDS in 1995. *The Seattle Times*

tivists trashed his house that was really uncalled for. They couldn't stand Cal. They couldn't stand me either, but I got less of their animosity than Cal because I came along later."

Smiling at the memories, Murray continues: "Above all, Cal was a politician. He knew how to win. Which meant someone had to lose. He could be nasty at it, too." After his death from complications of AIDS in 47 in 1995, tributes poured in "because he was such a likable, barrier-breaking person. I worry, though, that Cal has turned into a plastic saint. You don't win campaigns, and get things done, and win legislative victories because you're a saint. He was merely a marvelous man—a proud gay man—who deeply believed in respecting the people who opposed him. He believed, despite his own significant ego, that humility was a trait he needed to practice. He had a gift that I learned from him, or at least tried to learn from him. It's the gift of being present."

Murray pauses to collect his emotions. "When you're an elected official, there's a lot of people who want things out of you, whether they're people with a lot of money because they're lobbyists, or because they're marginal and don't have access to power. You can sit there and do your grocery lists or plan your evening and move people in and out of your office. You can also be present. That gift is something Cal had. He was always present."

With Cal gone, "it fell to Ed to carry on," Lynn Kessler says. "He advanced quickly in the Legislature because, like Cal, he was a hard-working legislator who happened to be gay rather than a gay legislator. Behind closed doors he could be mercurial. In public he practiced what Cal preached: Staying calm. And he persevered to achieve more than Cal had ever imagined. Ed always said we had to bring people along—that we had to boil the frog."

This particular frog, metaphorically, was same-sex marriage. Frogs, as everyone knows, are prodigious jumpers. The only way to boil one is little by little. You turn up the heat gradually. When Murray dared to dream that same-sex marriage someday would be legal, he knew one thing for certain: It wouldn't happen in one fell swoop. He'd need to advance the plan by taking the public's temperature and winning converts in the Legislature—first for the civil rights bill.

The frog proved wily.

TWO INITIATIVES in opposition to gay rights—inspired by Oregon culture-war agitator Lon Mabon—failed to collect enough signatures to make the ballot in 1994. Rallying under the "Hands Off Washington" banner, gays and lesbians mobilized

Lon Mabon campaigning against "special rights" in 1993. *Boise State University Library, Special Collections and Archives.*

across the state to thwart the incursion. A statewide poll commissioned by Spokane's daily *Spokesman-Review* found that 51 percent of the respondents were not opposed to expanding civil rights to gays and lesbians. Conservative Eastern Washington, significantly, was evenly split on the issue, while 56 percent of the respondents in Seattle and Tacoma opposed the initiatives. Statewide, 50 percent of the respondents were OK with gay marriage and adoptions. The surprise was that 54 percent of Eastern Washington respondents, notably in populous Spokane County, opposed bans on same-sex marriage and adoptions by gays, topping even the 52 percent in Seattle. The caveat, pollster Del Ali said, was that many voters were reluctant to give honest opinions on a topic as controversial as homosexual rights.

That cautionary note, if heeded, might have dampened the exuberance that propelled an anti-discrimination initiative to the ballot three years later.

"It was really Charlie Brydon who decided we needed to organize against Lon Mabon's homophobia crossing the Columbia," Murray says. "The Privacy Fund should do the inside stuff, we decided, and Hands Off should mobilize statewide. It immediately became a tension—*competitive*. And part of it, I think, was a view that Cal Anderson and I held: 'Why are we shifting all of our energies toward fighting something that hasn't happened?' The 'decline to sign' campaigns were good, we all agreed, but we were losing our energy in getting the community to think about being for something—namely the civil rights bill. Remember this is all happening in a hopeless period of the AIDS crisis, when people are feeling stretched emotionally, politically and financially."

Hawaii's Supreme Court, meantime, had sparked a national debate over gay marriage. It ruled in 1993 that denying same-sex couples the right to marry violated the existing equal-protection laws of the state's constitution. "Gay marriage caught the media's attention in a way civil rights never did," Murray says. "It was much sexier. But in his lifetime Cal Anderson never imagined he'd be able to marry his partner. There were letters in the *Seattle Gay News* from a gay guy running against him because he wouldn't introduce a gay marriage bill, and letters back with Cal's reasoning on why he wouldn't. We were clear in the battle for LGBTQ civil rights that we were not advocating for marriage. I believed there was no way to get to marriage without passing the civil rights bill. From my first involvement in the movement, I'd get calls from people who were being thrown out of their apartments or losing a job because they were gay."

Banning gay marriage was the top legislative priority of "pro-family" religious conservatives during the 1996 legislative session. Congress was preparing to debate a federal Defense of Marriage Act, aka DOMA. Gay rights supporters worried that Bill Clinton, the first president to champion their cause, was about to get "boxed in by his political opponents" after waffling on gays in the military.

IN THE ANNALS of the Washington Legislature, the DOMA debates of the 1996 and 1997 sessions are memorable for their emotional intensity, former longtime legislators and political reporters say.

Some lawmakers sobbed quietly as Representative Debbie Regala, a Democrat from Tacoma, recalled that when she fell in love with a Filipino man in 1968, acquaintances warned that "God never intended for the races to intermarry. That's why he made us different colors." Interracial marriage had been legalized nationwide just the year before when the U.S. Supreme Court ruled that state anti-miscegenation laws were unconstitutional, Regala noted. "How would you feel if there were a law that prohibited you from marrying the person you loved?" Murray fought back tears. He and Regala attended Mass together when the archbishop visited Olympia, choosing seats front and center to make it clear their faith was important to them and, as Regala put it later, "they weren't going anywhere."

Bill Thompson, the Everett Republican who sponsored the House bill to ban same-sex marriage, said the issue was perhaps one of the most important since statehood in 1889. It was crucial for the state to affirm marriage's "fundamental role in the procreation and development of children," he said. Julia Patterson, a Democrat from Des Moines, asked, "What about folks, who for medical reasons, can't have children?" That one went unanswered.

The bill died in the Senate, where Democrats held a one-seat majority.

Thompson said he wasn't going anywhere, either.

Gay-rights activists were jubilant in the spring of 1996 when the U.S. Supreme Court rejected an anti-gay constitutional amendment adopted by 53 percent of Colorado voters. The amendment was an attempt to preempt state or local laws protecting homosexuals from discrimination in jobs and housing. It violated their constitutional right to equal protection under the law, the high court ruled, 6-to-3. Murray called it "an incredible moral victory," adding, "This does not mean gays and lesbians have their rights. It only means they cannot be denied their rights. Half the battle remains to be won."

The second half was a series of setbacks and tactical retreats before the breakthroughs.

Murray and his movement allies temporarily modified their civil-rights-first strategy after Congress passed the Defense of Marriage Act. Clinton, to their chagrin, signed it into law on September 21, 1996. Murray, deep down, knew why: the Arkansas shape-shifter had concluded his campaign-trail promises ran ahead of public opinion.

WINNING CONTROL of the Washington House and Senate that November, Republicans announced plans to introduce new bills to ban same-sex marriage, this time with a referendum clause sending the issue to the voters in the event of a veto by Gary Locke, the incoming governor. Locke had voiced support for gay rights during his campaign against State Representative Ellen Craswell, an evangelical Christian warrior who lost big.

As one of his final acts in office, Governor Mike Lowry, long a passionate supporter of gay rights, sponsored legislation to authorize same-

Governor Mike Lowry, left, with his successor, Gary Locke, sponsored legislation to authorize same-sex marriage as one of his final acts in office in 1996. *Washington State Archives*

sex marriage. Murray and Pat Thibaudeau, the senator from their Capitol Hill district, introduced identical bills—together with gay civil rights legislation.* Murray conceded his gay marriage bill likely would not be acceptable to a majority of the electorate—a sentiment with which Locke agreed—but he predicted a ban "wouldn't pass muster, either." He wasn't willing to cede the legislative arena to the foes of same-sex marriage. "I realize this will be seen as extreme by some, but the anti-same-sex marriage bill is also extreme," Murray told reporters. "Sometimes the only way to answer an extreme measure is to introduce another extreme measure." He said his hope was that citizens might react by urging lawmakers to enact middle-ground legislation like the anti-discrimination bill.

Murray and his partner, Michael Shiosaki, testified before the Senate Law and Justice Committee during its hearing on the 1997 bill to ban same-sex marriage. Murray called the legislation "an insult to hard-working gay and lesbian citizens throughout Washington who pay taxes, care for their families, contribute to their communities and ask only for equal rights in return." Proponents said homosexuals' desire to be married "besmirches a sacred institution that has been the bedrock of civilization for centuries." Opponents observed that with three out of five heterosexual marriages ending in divorce, the bedrock seemed more shaky than sacred. "It would be tough to do worse," *The Olympian* editorialized.

Laurie Jinkins, president of the board of Hands Off Washington, said the conservatives setting the agenda in the Legislature were misreading the mood of the voters—witness Locke's landslide victory in 1996. "Washington remains a progressive state on social issues," said the Tacoma activist destined to become the state's first lesbian Speaker of the House. Republicans make electoral gains on fiscal conservatism, Jinkins said, not on their rigid social agenda.

In his inaugural address, Locke vowed to oppose measures that "divide, disrespect or diminish our humanity." A month later, he vetoed the gay marriage ban approved by the Legislature. Moves to send the issue to the voters failed narrowly in the Senate during the final days of a contentious 105-day session. Three moderate Republicans, fearing more gay-bashing, joined Democrats to head off a referendum.

What happened next created a schism in the ranks of Washington gay rights activists—one that would take years to repair.

Jinkins and Jan Bianchi, the executive director of Hands Off, championed the effort to place a gay-rights measure on the General Election ballot. Hands Off

---

* The bills introduced by Lowry, Murray and Thibaudeau advocated civil marriage contracts providing same-sex couples the same marital benefits granted to heterosexual couples, including the right of inheritance, health coverage and hospital visitation privileges.

strategists, heartened by national polls showing support for laws banning workplace discrimination against gays, drafted an anti-discrimination ballot measure "unlike any of those already on the books in 11 states." Besides banning workplace discrimination against gays, it also "explicitly forbid preferential treatment, quotas or partner benefits." Opponents called it a smokescreen. "They still want your kids, and Initiative 677 is another move toward that goal," they warned in a fundraising letter.

Murray believed the polls were too optimistic and that initiative backers were underestimating the enemy. Hands Off's own early polling revealed that 30 percent of the respondents believed job discrimination against gays was already illegal statewide. Exhausted, Murray had spent two sessions fending off attempts to ban same-sex marriage, hoping better days were ahead for civil rights legislation. This roll of the dice was a crapshoot, he warned. A loss at the polls could energize opponents and set back the cause for years, maybe decades.

On the Monday before the election, newspapers around the state carried ads featuring a "letter" to voters from Oklahoma Congressman Steve Largent, the former star wide receiver for the Seattle Seahawks. "I-677 isn't about fairness," the Republican said. "It's about special rights."

On November 4, 1997, nearly 60 percent of the voters opposed I-677. It failed to carry a single county—not even King, where the vote was at least close. Jinkins said the outcome was not as disheartening as it appeared. The gay rights initiative was collateral damage in the National Rifle Association's battle against a gun-control measure opposed by 70 percent of the voters, she said. NRA supporters overwhelmingly opposed the gay rights initiative, a *Seattle Times* poll revealed. Hands Off, which invested about $750,000 in the campaign, was out-spent and out-gunned. Conservatives immediately went on the attack. "When you see a margin this big, it's sending a powerful message to the Legislature that they should continue to refuse bestowing special status for sexual behavior," said the spokesman for the coalition that opposed the initiative.

The 1998 Legislature promptly enacted a ban on same-sex marriage, overriding another veto. Democrats were peeved when Locke rejected a deal designed to allow the ban to become law without his signature. A decisive number of Democratic legislators joined the veto override, worried that if the issue made the ballot "it would bring out too many conservative voters in swing districts." Politics makes for strange bedfellows. "The Republicans have the votes," said Representative Marlin Appelwick of Seattle, the House minority leader. "As distasteful as this is, it's very practical. …You live to fight another day."

Ed Murray talks strategy with House Majority Leader Lynn Kessler in 2006. *Legislative Support Services*

BY 2003, Ed Murray was no longer the state's only openly-gay legislator. Joe McDermott from West Seattle and Dave Upthegrove of Des Moines arrived in the House in 2001, Vancouver's Jim Moeller two years later. "When I first ran, it was like I was 'Ellen,' " Murray said. "Today, it's like 'Will & Grace.' What's the big deal?" Lynn Kessler, the House majority leader, predicted the new four-member gay caucus would go "a long way to eliminate the mystique and just let them be guys. I don't talk about my sex life, so why should people care about theirs?"

A gay civil rights bill was approved by the House in 2003, 2004 and 2005, only to high-center in the Senate. Republicans let an array of bipartisan legislation die in 2004 by abruptly adjourning to avoid a vote on Murray's bill. Nearly a hundred House bills died as well, including funding for schools and colleges and assistance for small businesses. Murray and Speaker Frank Chopp were livid with Bill Finkbeiner, the Senate majority leader, who insisted, "Our top priority is creating jobs. We didn't want to get sidetracked." In 2005, the civil rights bill sailed through the House with a record 61 votes. It still ran aground in the Senate, though Democrats had gained a 26-23 majority. Three Democrats, Jim Hargrove of Hoquiam, Tim Sheldon of Potlatch, and Marilyn Rasmussen of Eatonville sided with the Republicans, who called the bill "a stepping stone" to gay marriage. Democrats adopted an eleventh-hour amendment proposed by Rasmussen, a practicing Catholic. It clarified that Murray's bill did not endorse homosexuality or gay marriage. Rasmussen then voted "yes." The bill still died by a single vote.

This time, however, Murray was upbeat. In nearly 30 years of trying, a gay civil rights bill had never before achieved an up-or-down vote by the entire state Senate. He and Chris Gregoire, the new governor, also pointed to a poll indicating that 71 percent of respondents statewide now supported equal rights for gays and lesbians.

The gay rights community also demonstrated its growing economic and political power when it shamed Microsoft into rebooting its support for the civil rights bill.

A who's who of the Northwest corporate world had endorsed the bill, including the Boeing Company, Nike, Qwest Communications, Washington Mutual, Hewlett-Packard, and Microsoft cofounder Paul Allen's Vulcan Inc. Microsoft had supported the bill in 2004 and "appeared poised to do so again." Then, at the last minute with the bill hanging in the balance in the state Senate, Microsoft decided to declare neutrality. Critics charged that the software giant—one of the first companies to extend domestic partner benefits to same-sex couples—had bowed to political pressure from a prominent evangelical church in Redmond that had threatened to organize a national boycott of Microsoft products. Microsoft denied its decision was influenced by "external factors," despite admitting to Murray earlier in the month that it was under pressure from the church. "We caught them in an absolute lie," Murray says. In chat rooms, blogs, and emails to media outlets, gay rights supporters worldwide denounced the company. Microsoft's many gay and lesbian employees were outraged. *The Stranger*, Seattle's widely-read, gay-centric weekly newspaper, reamed "the vanguard institution of the new economy" as a garden-variety hypocrite. Microsoft's CEO, Steve Ballmer, surrendered two weeks later. In an e-mail to employees, he wrote, "After looking at the question from all sides, I've concluded that diversity in the workplace is such an important issue for our business that it should be included in our legislative agenda." Gregoire and Murray commended the company for reversing course.

Bill Finkbeiner, meanwhile, was having a genuine change of heart.

FINKBEINER was a pro-business, tax-break Republican from the burgeoning east side of Lake Washington. Some were surprised in 2003 when the mostly conservative Senate Republican caucus picked the 34-year-old former Democrat as majority leader. Finkbeiner was openly pro-choice and a self-described "social moderate" with a feminist wife. Before switching parties, he voted twice for gay rights legislation. *The Stranger* wondered whether the "Republican Fink" would continue to front for a right-wing caucus or vote his conscience and risk his chances for re-election or higher office.

On the first day of the 2006 legislative session, having stepped down as Senate GOP leader, Finkbeiner announced he would support Murray's bill. He was the Republican ally the Democrats desperately needed to put the bill over the top.

"I've had a number of conversations over the past year that have led me to more fully understand the level of discrimination against gays and lesbians," Finkbeiner said. "I now find it is both appropriate and necessary for the state to make it clear that this is not acceptable. This bill failed year after year, even in years when Democrats have held strong majorities, because it motivates some party activists on both sides. And the issue has become one of many 'wedge' issues used to split our communities and divide us—a political football used by both parties. I don't agree with the politicization of people's personal lives and I think it is time to move on."

"Sounds like we've got 25 votes," said Lisa Brown, the majority leader from Spokane. "Let's get going."

Murray was "hopeful but cautious," telling reporters, "People thought last year would be the year. Something has always stopped it."

The bill adding "sexual orientation" to the state law banning discrimination in employment, housing, lending and insurance was passed quickly, overwhelmingly, by the House. It now had 47 sponsors, including Republicans. Murray said they should all remember that it was "Cal Anderson's bill."

On January 27, 2006, Bill Finkbeiner was as good as his word, breaking ranks to ensure its passage. "We don't choose who we love. The

In 2006, Senator Bill Finkbeiner of Kirkland, the former GOP minority leader, reversed his stand from the year before and voted with the Democrats to pass a gay civil rights bill. *Legislative Support Services*

heart chooses who we will love," he said. Governor Gregoire looked on from the wings, hugging everyone within reach as she told reporters she was jubilant to sign the bill into law. Anderson's partner of 10 years, Eric Ishino, said, "I don't doubt that he's really smiling down on us right now."*

Opponents vowed to launch a signature drive for a referendum to overturn the law. Gregoire and Murray predicted they would fail. "We will not allow discrimination here," she said. Murray added, "Before you reach for a pen to sign an initiative to end our rights, call up somebody in your life who is gay or lesbian and talk to them about their reality. And then decide whether you want to pick up that pen."

Reality came into sharp focus during the final floor debate on the civil rights

---

* And in 2012, after the same-sex marriage bill passed in the State Senate, Eric Ishino could barely contain his excitement. "Cal would be proud," he said. "I just never thought in my lifetime that I would see this. But it's OK. We always knew in our heart that we were married."

bill. What Senator Bob Oke said is riveted in the memories of everyone who was there. "It's through God's eyes that I see homosexuality…as an abomination," the Port Orchard Republican said, describing the pain he felt for his daughter, who "has chosen the life of a lesbian." Though he said he loved her deeply, he could not welcome her partner into his home. "That's called tough love."

Finkbeiner recalls the "sense of sadness" that enveloped the chamber. "The thing that makes me feel good about being part of passing that bill is thinking about Cal Anderson and Bob Oke's daughter. So many [gay] people were going through things that were difficult. The way people were treating them at the time is so hard to imagine. Bob Oke was a nice guy. It was just a different time."

Finkbeiner acknowledges that his caucus's opposition to the gay civil rights bill contributed to his decision to step down from leadership. "I felt conflicted personally," he says. Any regrets about casting that historic vote? "No. I remember it being a big relief. And the more time goes by, the better I feel about it. It's amazing how far society in general has moved so quickly." Did his vote play a role in his decision to not seek re-election in 2006? "I don't think so. In fact, I think that vote probably would have helped me win re-election. I'd been in the Legislature for 14 years. At the time I took the vote, I was starting to consider it [retiring] so I think the decision to take that vote helped in some ways. I think I was maybe less concerned about re-election than how I was going to keep working with people in the Legislature."

TIM EYMAN, the state's flamboyant initiative promoter—He wore a Darth Vader costume to a press conference that spring—filed an initiative to overturn the new bill. Frank Sennett, a Spokane columnist, declared that if Eyman really had the courage of his convictions, the ballot measure should say: "The people of Washington hereby permit employers to fire people because they're gay. Go ahead and deny them access to housing, insurance and credit, too. Feel free to ban them from stores and restaurants while you're at it."

Even with the support of the Faith & Freedom Network and the Christian Coalition, Eyman failed to collect enough valid voter signatures to make the 2006 General Election ballot.

A month later, on July 26, 2006, the Washington Supreme Court ruled 5-4 that the state's 1998 Defense of Marriage Act was constitutional. "The Legislature was entitled to believe that limiting marriage to opposite-sex couples furthers the state's legitimate interests in procreation and the well-being of children," Justice Barbara Madsen wrote. That said, she emphasized, "We see no reason, however, why the legislature or the people, acting through the initiative process, would be foreclosed from extending the right to marry to gay and lesbian couples in Washington."

Justices Mary Fairhurst and Bobbe Bridge wrote scathing dissents. The majority, Bridge wrote, contend "it is not our place to require equality for Washington's gay and lesbian citizens." By that reasoning, she said, "there would have been no *Brown v. Board of Education*," the game-changing 1954 U.S. Supreme Court case banning segregated schools. Fairhurst wrote, "There is no rational basis for denying same-sex couples the right to marry. … Unfortunately [those in the majority] are willing to turn a blind eye to DOMA's discrimination because a popular majority still favors that discrimination."

Legal scholars, sociologists and public opinion pollsters questioned how popular the "popular majority" really was. "You've gone in 32 years from something that was more or less a slam dunk to where the court is almost evenly and very bitterly divided," said William B. Rubenstein, a UCLA law professor and author of *Sexual Orientation and the Law*. "The issue is in play."

Ed Murray told angry gay rights supporters at a rally that he would introduce a marriage equality bill in January. He counseled patience, however, saying it would take several sessions to pass. "Today we hurt and today we mourn," he said, "and tomorrow we go back to work."

For her part, the governor made it clear she was still struggling to reconcile her Catholicism with her abhorrence of discrimination. She supported granting same-sex couples the legal rights and responsibilities of marriage without calling it marriage. "I believe the sacrament of marriage is between two people and their faith," Gregoire said. "It is not the business of the state."

Murray won election to the state Senate that fall. "Most people don't give up a powerful job like being chairman of the House Transportation Committee to go off and become a junior senator," he says, "but that's where I needed to be to advance marriage equity."

Evan Wolfson, the former law professor who headed the national "Freedom to Marry" movement, advocated a full-court-press. Murray recommitted to incrementalism as the way forward. He took inspiration from Thurgood Marshall and Ruth Bader Ginsburg. When Marshall was the NAACP's lead lawyer, he picked the easiest desegregation cases first, building momentum, Murray said. Ginsburg's legal strategy for winning gender equality was that barriers should be addressed one achievable step at a time: "You can't have it all, all at once."

Jamie Pedersen, a personable young civil rights attorney, was elected to Mur-

A trio of LGBTQ legislators—Jamie Pedersen, Ed Murray, and Laurie Jinkins—led the fight for marriage equality. *The Seattle Times*

ray's seat in the House, boosting the legislative gay caucus to five members. You could feel the pace of change accelerating, Lynn Kessler remembers. "People were getting to know gay people as co-workers, friends and neighbors. Hearts and minds were changing."

A LANDMARK BILL creating a "domestic partnership" registry for same-sex couples and unmarried heterosexual couples, if one partner was 62 or older, was signed into law by Gregoire on April 21, 2007.* The legislation had sailed through the House and Senate, with conservative legislators disappointed that Christians "were letting the culture collapse around them" by failing to mount a more vigorous dissent. "This is a step, just as the civil rights bill last year was a step," warned Representative Lynn Schindler, a Republican from Spokane Valley. "Therefore I beg of you to think very seriously about the road we are going to be going down and how we are going to be changing the civilization we live in."

Two years later, Gregoire signed an "everything but marriage" bill giving gay and lesbian couples all of the state-mandated benefits granted heterosexual couples. The new law expanded on the domestic partner statutes, notably with

---

* That provision was aimed to assist widows and widowers who balked at remarriage for fear of losing a dead spouse's pension or Social Security benefits. Overall, the new law mandated health-care facility visitation rights; the ability to grant health-care consent for a partner who was not competent; the right to control disposition of a deceased partner's remains, and inheritance rights when the domestic partner died without a will.

regard to adoption and child support rights and obligations, pensions and other public employee benefits, including sick leave and workers' compensation coverage. With increasing numbers of gay and lesbian couples raising children, Laurie Jinkins said the new law was an important legal and social safety net.

Many in the gay rights community now clamored for "everything else." Murray cautioned that same-sex marriage was legal in California for five months until the previous fall when voters passed a ballot measure to overturn the law. Opponents of the new Washington law were already mobilizing to secure a place on the 2009 ballot for a referendum. Yet one prominent opponent of same-sex marriage said he believed the effort was doomed. "Why fight a battle you can't win?" said Joseph Fuiten of the Positive Christian Agenda. "It will undermine our position when it comes to fighting the marriage battle."

On November 3, 2009, Washington voters became the first in the nation to ratify domestic partnerships for same-sex couples. "It's historic," said the field director for the National Gay and Lesbian Task Force. Fifty-three percent of the state's voters backed Referendum 71. Still, the urban-rural/conservative-liberal divide was graphically clear on a map depicting how the state's 39 counties voted: The measure was approved in only 10—all west of the Cascades, with King County's 68 percent (a plurality of 203,200 votes) carrying the day.

Murray says he learned two important lessons from Cal Anderson: perseverance and that "you can't be a single-issue legislator and expect to gain real influence." By 2010, Murray was the Senate's Democratic caucus chairman, working with Majority Leader Lisa Brown, Speaker Frank Chopp, Lynn Kessler and the governor to plug a $2.8 billion budget deficit. In 2011, as chairman of the Senate Ways & Means Committee, Murray nurtured a relationship with Joe Zarelli, the committee's ranking Republican, to craft a genuinely bipartisan budget. Zarelli, a staunch conservative opposed to gay marriage, quipped that if they were the odd couple, he was the tidy one.

CHRIS GREGOIRE began her last year as governor by announcing she would support gay marriage. It was January 4, 2012. "I have been on my own journey. I'll admit that," she told a crowded press conference. "It has been a battle for me with my religion. I've always been uncomfortable with the position I took publicly," balking at unconditional support for gay marriage. "Then I came to realize the religions can decide what they want to do, but it's not OK for the state to discriminate. It is now time for equality for our gay and lesbian citizens, and that means marriage." Murray and Jamie Pedersen led the applause. When the Legis-

Gov. Christine Gregoire with State Senator Mary Margaret Haugen, who cast the crucial 25th vote to ensure passage of marriage equality. *The Seattle Times*

lature convened five days later, they introduced their bills.

"Without Chris in the mix we wouldn't have gotten there," Murray says of the two-term governor. "She did not set the marriage table, but she really knew how to sit down and mediate how to get there. Her mediation skills are second to none. I have never seen a better closer in my political career."

The frog was in trouble.

ON THE MORNING of January 23, Senator Mary Margaret Haugen had something important to tell Ed Murray—something she'd been praying about. They had adjoining offices and talked often because the committees they chaired—Ways & Means and Transportation— were where the action happened. This was an errand of the heart and soul. Three years earlier, when the Camano Island Democrat voted against the "everything but marriage" bill, she made it clear to him it was nothing personal. "You know I love you," she said, taking his hands in hers. Murray said he understood.

Now, after 17 years of activism, he was one vote shy of the 25 votes he needed to advance the gay marriage bill. Murray knew he had enough votes for passage in the House.

Opponents, including evangelical pastors, the Tea Party and a coalition of conservative lawmakers, predicted that as many as 10,000 people would descend on the Capitol Campus that day for a noontime rally against same-sex marriage.

Jim Kastama, a Democrat from Puyallup, had announced his support for Murray's bill a few days before, saying he knew childhood friends in his district "who will never forgive me." That left five uncommitteds, including Mary Margaret, a legislator for 30 years. Murray knew she was deeply conflicted.

"He never asked me for my vote," she remembers. "He knew I was praying about it."

At a packed town hall meeting on Whidbey Island earlier in the month, supporters of Murray's bill booed her, saying she was a "racist" and "homophobe" because she advocated sending the issue to the voters. Murray knew she was neither. With her neatly coifed gray hair and disarming smile, the former school board member was one of the most genuine people he'd ever known—and a formidable legislator who kept promises.

Murray and his partner, Michael Shiosaki, were weighing which of the fence-sitters might commit when Haugen walked in to say she would cast the vote ensuring passage. There was a three-way hug. "It was one of the most amazing moments of my life," Murray remembers. "At that point I felt that I really didn't need to do much more in my life. But it was Mary Margaret's family—and families across the state and the entire country—that changed hearts and minds."

Senator Haugen explains why she decided to support same-sex marriage. *Legislative Support Services*

Haugen hurried off to share the news with a throng of reporters. "I know this announcement makes me the so-called 25th vote that ensures passage," she said. "That's neither here nor there. If I were the first or the seventh or the 28th vote, my position would not be any different. I happen to be the 25th because I insisted on taking this much time to hear from my constituents and to sort it out for myself, as a legislator, and as a wife and mother who cannot deny to others the joys and benefits I enjoy."

Calling it "a profile in courage," Murray praised Haugen for voting her conscience. He predicted the political fallout could be substantial in her divided district.

Haugen wrote a blog post to amplify her decision. "I have very strong Christian beliefs," she wrote, "and personally I have always said that when I accepted the Lord I became more tolerant of others. I stopped judging people and try to live by the Golden Rule. I do not believe it is my job to judge others, regardless of my personal beliefs. I have always believed in traditional marriage between a man and woman. This is what I believe in to this day. But this issue isn't just what I believe. It's about respecting others. It's about whether everyone has the same opportunities for love and companionship and family and security that I have enjoyed."

Governor Gregoire signed the gay marriage bill on February 13, 2012. Endorsed by 53.7 percent of the electorate, it took effect on December 6, with the first marriages on the 9th after the state's three-day waiting period.

Today, at 81, Haugen is even more certain she made the right decision, though Murray believes her vote contributed to her defeat in the next election. "It may have," Haugen says. "There were probably other factors, too. I was kind of tough on the ferry workers. But it was the best vote I ever took because it made people happy. My God, what other thing made so many people happy? [It] changed the lives of so many people. I had people I'd known my entire life tell me to my face that they'd never vote for me again. And you know what? *Their lives are just fine today.*" The italics are hers.

John C. Hughes

MARGARETHE CAMMERMEYER

SILENCE WAS NOT GOLDEN: COLONEL CAMMERMEYER'S WAR

When Army Colonel Margarethe Cammermeyer, 47, a decorated Vietnam veteran, applied for a top-secret clearance in 1989, in hopes of becoming a general, the special agent assigned to her case asked a standard question about sexual orientation. "I am a lesbian," she said, a small clutch in her throat.

With one question and one four-word answer, the military she had loved for 26 years became her adversary. The routine interview was now an interrogation.

During Cammermeyer's childhood in Norway, a Bible study lesson focused on Christ's promise that "the truth will set you free." If that had come to mind when the special agent suddenly looked up from his notepad, it probably wouldn't have dispelled the dread radiating from the pit of her stomach.

Cammermeyer, mother of four, recipient of the Bronze Star as a combat-hospital nurse, was about to become the highest-ranking officer to ever challenge the Pentagon's view that homosexuality was "incompatible" with military service. The military's Cold War stance that gay soldiers, sailors and airmen posed security risks had evolved in the 1980s to a declaration that they were detrimental to "unit cohesion."

Over the next five years, as she fought to be reinstated as chief nurse of the Washington National Guard, Cammermeyer was surprised to become "one of the most famous lesbians in America," portrayed by Glenn Close in an award-winning TV movie and sought after for speeches and rallies nationwide.

In the middle of her battle with the Army, the colonel acquired a seemingly improbable ally. Former U.S. Senator Barry Goldwater, the flinty godfather of the modern conservative movement, wrote an op-ed column that made headlines in 1993. "You don't need to be 'straight' to fight and die for your country," the retired

Facing page: Glenn Close and Col. Cammermeyer in a 1995 publicity photo for *Serving in Silence*, which aired on NBC-TV. Close won an Emmy for her performance. *NBC-TV*

Air Force general said. "You just need to shoot straight." Cammermeyer was a veteran healer—literally and figuratively—rather than a shooter. But she had seen war up close and as personal as it gets during her 14 months in Vietnam. Her skill and patriotism underscored that the military's ban on gays was "a senseless attempt to stall the inevitable," Goldwater wrote, adding:

> After more than 50 years in the military and politics, I am still amazed to see how upset people can get over nothing. Lifting the ban on gays in the military isn't exactly nothing, but it's pretty damned close.
>
> Everyone knows that gays have served honorably in the military since at least the time of Julius Caesar. They'll still be serving long after we're all dead and buried. That should not surprise anyone. But most Americans should be shocked to know that the military has wasted half a billion dollars over the past decade chasing down gays and running them out of the armed services.
>
> It's no great secret that military studies have proved again and again that there's no valid reason for keeping the ban on gays. Some thought gays were crazy, but then found that wasn't true. Then they decided that gays were a security risk, but again the Department of Defense decided that wasn't so—in fact, one study by the Navy in 1956 that was never made public found gays to be good security risks. ...*
>
> When the facts lead to one conclusion, I say it's time to act, not to hide. The country and the military know that eventually the ban will be lifted. The only remaining questions are how much muck we will all be dragged through, and how many brave Americans like ... Margarethe Cammermeyer will have their lives and careers destroyed in a senseless attempt to stall the inevitable?

Victorious in federal court in 1994, Cammermeyer returned to duty and set out to help repeal the Clinton-era "Don't Ask, Don't Tell" policy that created a new moral quandary for LGBTQ service members: Ostensibly, they could stay in the

---

* The Crittenden Report, which summarized a 1957 investigation by a U.S. Navy Board of Inquiry, concluded there was "no sound basis" for the belief that homosexuals—characterized earlier as "sex perverts"—posed a military security risk.

trenches as long as they didn't come out of the closet. Yet between 1993 and 2011, when "Don't Ask, Don't Tell" was repealed, more than 13,000 gays and lesbians were forced out of the military.

During the 17-year battle to repeal the policy, Cammermeyer was one of its most influential foes. At the ceremony where President Obama revoked it, she was asked to lead the Pledge of Allegiance.

Awarded the Bronze Star by the hospital commander at Long Binh, Vietnam, in 1968. *Margarethe Cammermeyer*

"Patriotic Americans in uniform will no longer have to lie about who they are in order to serve the country they love," the president said.

Today, Cammermeyer, her spouse Diane Divelbess and their two rescue dogs live on Whidbey Island. Cammermeyer received a Ph.D. from the University of Washington in 1991 and serves on Whidbey's hospital commission. She's proud to be addressed as "Doctor."

Inducted into the Washington State Nurses' Association Hall of Fame in 2014, the former candidate for Congress uses her web site as a platform to discuss current affairs. She writes inspirational songs and plays the guitar. With 11 grandkids, she's troubled by the state of the world, the "hypocrisy and hate-mongering," and worried about the safety of schoolchildren across America, Vladimir Putin's lethal impunity, and a U.S. Supreme Court dominated by conservatives. If Americans who oppose bigotry are not vigilant, hard-won gay rights victories could be reversed, Cammermeyer says. Voter suppression efforts designed to disenfranchise minority blocs are part of the same agenda, she adds. "How can prolife mean pro-gun?" she asks on her web page, https://www.cammermeyer.com "How does killing Asians or Blacks make a white shooter bigger, better, stronger?"

"We are at a stage of going around in a circle," Cammermeyer warns. "They said Roe v. Wade was 'settled law.' Is marriage equality their next target? Once you've dispensed with precedent all bets are off."

CAMMERMEYER'S journey of self-discovery included shedding the vestiges of her own homophobia. After her divorce from her ex-tank commander husband in 1980, she recoiled at "the idea of being a member of a despised and stigmatized minority." In the fight of her life when she came out, she also worked to combat stereotypes about gays and lesbians: The notion that being LGBTQ is a "lifestyle" choice. Or a mental illness, as her bright, resilient mother nevertheless believed. Or, worse yet, that child molestation is an innate proclivity among gay people. Myths abound, Cammermeyer says. Even smart people are susceptible. Cammermeyer's father, a brilliant scientist, refrained from hugging her two brothers, believing such intimacy could make them gay. "The chains of prejudice are made of igno-

Grethe with her brother, Jan Wilhelm, in traditional Norwegian dress in 1947. *Margarethe Cammermeyer*

Grethe with her parents and brothers in Washington, D.C., in 1959. *Margarethe Cammermeyer*

rance and fear," Cammermeyer says, more resolute than ever at 80, three decades after the courts ordered her reinstatement as a military officer.

"Grethe" (pronounced "Greta") Cammermeyer was born in Nazi-occupied Norway in 1942. Her parents were part of the underground war, sheltering resistance forces. "My very first military operation was a stunning success by all accounts," she wrote in her autobiography, *Serving in Silence.* "My mother smuggled guns past Nazi headquarters in Oslo to a rendezvous with Norwegian resistance fighters. The method of transportation was my baby carriage with, of course, me in it. Apparently I performed my role well."

Her grandfathers were physicians; her father a neuropathologist, her mother a former nurse. Unsurprisingly, Grethe's childhood goal was to become a doctor. The family moved to America in 1951 when her father landed a post at The Armed Forces Institute of Pathology. Later, he joined the National Institutes of Health. Grethe and her kid brothers ended up in five different schools, struggling to learn English. She enrolled at the University of Maryland at 17, finding herself "too tall, too shy, and too Norwegian" to fit in. "I was really struggling," she remembers. "But I couldn't put a name on it. I was trying to have somebody else come down and tell me what I ought to do with my life." She floundered in premed, taking an ar-

Grethe at 15 in 1957 as a member of a semi-professional fast-pitch softball team. *Margarethe Cammermeyer*

ray of grueling courses while partying with new friends. With lousy grades and no scholarship, she reluctantly decided instead to pursue a degree in nursing. In many ways, she says, it's "the crummiest job in the world," replete with "blood, barf and bodily fluids," and subservient to doctors. With time, she would come to understand nursing is "the most important job in the world." Nurses on the front lines of the Covid pandemic personify the perseverance she learned in Vietnam, she says. "Finally, when healing is no longer possible, you're the eyes that say goodbye."

IN THE SPRING of 1961, a few months after becoming a U.S. citizen, Cammermeyer told her parents she was applying for the Army's Student Nurse Program. The silence was deafening. American friends told them the only women who joined the American military were lesbians, "whores" or husband hunt-

Sworn in as a Women's Army Corps recruit in 1961. *Margarethe Cammermeyer*

ers. Taken aback, Cammermeyer remembers "completely rejecting" the
idea she might be gay. Sexually naïve
at 19, she was anything but promiscu-
ous. And she had no interest in marriage. Her goal, even back then, was a
career culminating in a general's star.
Her parents nodded their approval.
She set out to become an exemplary
soldier.

At an Army post in Germany in
1964, Cammermeyer went on a blind
date with a spit-shined, six-foot-six
lieutenant from an armor battalion,
Harvey Hawken. In high heels, she
could nearly look him in the eye. "I
think he was as shocked as I to meet

Grethe and a friend at Fort Sam Houston, Texas, in
1963. *Margarethe Cammermeyer*

someone so tall," she remembers. Eight months later, when he proposed, she was
"absolutely dumbfounded." She vacillated before saying "yes," realizing she was
sacrificing her career, her hopes and dreams, for the role of wife and, surely before
long, mother. Marriage meant children. The military's rule then was that female
soldiers with children under 16 would be discharged. "If the Army had wanted
you to have a baby," the saying went, "it would have issued you one."

In 1966, after her husband's unit was ordered to prepare for deployment to
Vietnam, Grethe volunteered to go, too. When his orders were canceled, they
both knew she had to go alone. It would have been unthinkable to shirk her duty
as a military nurse to care for soldiers injured in combat.

The war games in which young nurses participated at Fort Sam Houston,
Texas, had featured mock casualties. Still, the simulated wounds were so realis-
tic that Grethe remembers being at first "immobilized by the horror." However,
it wasn't until she arrived in Vietnam that what war does to people—invisible
wounds included—became real.

She visited Special Forces camps to practice firing the M1 carbine with Green
Beret medics before settling in at the 24th Evacuation Hospital at Long Binh. Her
tour of duty in Vietnam—from February 1967 to May 1968—coincided with a
rapid buildup of U.S. forces and the highest causalities of the war. When the North
Vietnamese staged their surprise Tet Offensive, mortar and artillery shells often

Grethe receives an award outside the Neuro Intensive Care Ward in Vietnam, 1967. *Margarethe Cammermeyer*

fell near the hospital compound. On the medical ward, she cared for sick teenagers caught up in a war she says "none of us really understood." Sixty-one percent of the casualties were younger than 21.

For a nurse, the hardest part was the Catch 22 of "helping them get well and looking forward to their discharge from the hospital, only to then suddenly realize they were better off being sick and in a safe place. …I hate to think of how many we had 'cured' only to die at a later time, in combat." Later, she became head nurse for the hospital's neurosurgical unit, learning profound lessons about advances in battlefield medicine—and hope: "The flicker of an eyelid, or the squeeze of a hand from a young man who had been motionless before," she wrote in *Serving in Silence*. "The long struggle to finally say a single syllable meant that this soldier might learn to speak again."

Today, reflecting on those tumultuous months in Vietnam, she believes "the resilience of the human spirit exceeds all possible expectations." On Memorial Day weekend 2022, she was contacted by her first patient in Vietnam. "He thanked me for my care and caring. I remembered him because he was the one who made me want to send my patient home rather than back to combat and possible death. He survived and I am humbled.

"Looking back over my life—my childhood in Norway during World War II; my service in Vietnam, and now watching the annihilation of Ukraine—one can only ask: *What for?* Regardless of circumstances NO ONE EVER WINS IN WAR." Those are her capital letters.

In 1987, newly promoted to full colonel, Cammermeyer visited the Vietnam Veterans Memorial in Washington, D.C. Architect Maya Lin's powerfully stark black granite walls are engraved with the names of the 58,220 Americans who died in Vietnam. Nearby that day was a POW/MIA tent manned by "a hardened, grungy old sergeant." He came around the table and stood before her. "Welcome home," he said. As her eyes welled up, he said, "It's OK. Colonels can cry, too."

They embraced and wept together.

GRETHE'S HUSBAND made it to Vietnam, but they were miles apart for the first four months. Later they were stationed together at Long Bihn. Rather than remaining on active duty, Harvey resolved to leave the military and attend grad school in forestry at the University of Washington in his home state. As they made plans to build a dream home at Maple Valley, in the foothills of the Cascades, she was pregnant with the first of her four sons. Instead of becoming head nurse of the intensive-care unit at Madigan Army Medical Center at Fort Lewis, she was forced to take a temporary assignment before leaving the Army in the fall of 1968, just before her son was born. Four years later, when the policy changed, she joined the Army Reserves and became nursing supervisor at the 50th General Hospital out of Fort Lawton in Seattle.

Next came graduate school at the UW School of Nursing on the GI Bill, followed by work with the Veterans Administration. All the while she was juggling her role as mom to three young boys—and, in 1976, a fourth. Grethe resolved that her sons would learn Norwegian, shoring up an important part of her heritage—*their* heritage. "My parents always spoke Norwegian to us at home. But my brothers and I got lazy. We didn't switch over to respond in Norwegian. When I was a senior in high school I suddenly realized it was not going to be as easy for me to speak Norwegian. I decided, 'I have to change this!' So I began always speaking Norwegian to my parents again. When the time came that I had kids, I knew that if they were ever going to learn Norwegian it would have to be the mother language."

That her husband, who had become a State Patrol trooper, was not conversational in Norwegian may have contributed to a growing rift. Slowly, subtly at first, the marriage began to unravel. After Grethe was accepted into the UW's doctoral program in nursing, she says he began to resent her professional ambitions. He blew up one day when she and a group of friends were campaigning for passage of the Equal Rights Amendment. It was out of character. Whatever physical attraction she had for him was withering. That was confusing, too.

As the stress metastasized, Grethe grew suicidal. A wise psychotherapist urged her to look back on her life for clues to her despair. She confessed that as a teenager she had felt different from her peers and wondered if she might be gay. The doctor counseled that an individual's sexuality is often "on a continuum." He said there was no cause for shame.

Looking back, Grethe says her resistance to seeing herself as homosexual was partly denial, partly despair at the state of her marriage.

The divorce proceedings turned ugly. A judge awarded her estranged spouse primary custody of their sons. Grethe was devastated.

The divorce became final in 1980. One of the first things she did was reclaim her maiden name. That she was no longer Mrs. Hawken symbolized the fresh start. "I read an article in the paper that said, 'Why do they call it *maiden* names? Why don't they call it *birth* names?' I like that. As conflicted as I was, it was good to be 'Major or Ms. Cammermeyer.'"

With a lovely soft smile, Grethe says the circle was complete in 2022 when she regained her Norwegian citizenship. "For years there was this part of me that felt as though I had essentially betrayed my Norwegian heritage by relinquishing my citizenship. When the policy changed so that Norwegians could regain their Norwegian citizenship, as a dual citizen, I started that process immediately. I'm Norwegian by birth and temperament, though in my mind I'm also an American—proud of the uniform I wore and proud of what I did serving in the military and fighting the military's ban on lesbians and other gay people. And I won't stop fighting."

With her sons at Matt's wedding in 1990. *Margarethe Cammermeyer*

HER AGONIZED decision to move to California in the wake of the divorce was an attempt to insert more distance between her and her ex, though she felt like a mother abandoning her children.

Cammermeyer became a neuro-oncology specialist at the Veterans Administration Medical Center in San Francisco and transferred to an Army Reserve hospital there. By 1985, as a lieutenant colonel, she became chief nurse of the 352nd Evacuation Hospital at Oakland. It was a challenging, stimulating job, in contrast to the exhaustion she felt after a long day at the VA hospital. Despite the staff's heroic efforts, most brain tumor patients died.

There were accolades, too. Among 34,000 Veterans Administration nurses nationwide, she was chosen VA national Nurse of the Year.

Awards and promotions couldn't offset how much she missed her sons. In 1985, she accepted a job as a night-duty staff nurse at the VA's American Lake Medical Center in Tacoma. Before long, she was regaining her old confidence and ambition. She became the Clinical Nurse Specialist in Epilepsy and Sleep Apnea. In 1987, she was readmitted to the UW's Ph.D. program in nursing. A year later she became chief nurse of the Washington National Guard, back on track to achieve her goal of becoming a general.

If love is all you really need, Cammermeyer's life changed irrevocably in 1988 when she met Diane Divelbess. A widely-exhibited painter and printmaker, Divelbess was on the faculty of the Art Department at California State Polytechnic University at Pomona for 29 years, eight as the department chair. Mutual friends engineered their meeting at a Fourth of July outing on the Oregon coast. If not instant, the attraction was apparent and soon irresistible. Grethe was impressed at how easily Diane interacted with her boys. She had never met a better listener. Or anyone with such a disarming laugh. There was mirth in her voice. Her intelligence was apparent, yet down to earth. Diane was "the last, connecting piece" to the puzzle of Margarethe Cammermeyer's identity: She was in love with another woman.

Diane Divelbess. *Outwords Archive*

A year later, she was in trouble for telling the truth.

WHEN THE Army's special agent asked the question about "sexual orientation," Cammermeyer says she never considering lying. The thought that her military career might be over flashed through her mind. "And yet, I still continued not to believe it because I had a good military record," she told reporters in 1991, understating her achievements. "This was me telling a security clearance investigator the truth. And how could that possibly be used against me by the people I had served for so many years?" After all, the military's long-stated rationale for rooting out closeted gays was that they were susceptible to being blackmailed to divulge secrets to enemy agents. Lately, the argument was that allowing homosexuals—and women in general—in combat-ready units would disrupt "unit cohesion." Soldiers lived in close, often unpleasant quarters, including foxholes, Pentagon spokesmen said. Clashes between gay and straight soldiers could impact morale. "This is the same argument used in every other discriminatory regulation that the military has had," Cammermeyer said. "It was used with women in the military, and it was used with blacks in the military. It's almost the identical wording."

Leonard Matlovich, an Air Force sergeant who served three tours of duty in Vietnam and received the Purple Heart and Bronze Star, was dying of AIDS in 1988 when he designed his own gravestone as a memorial to all gay veterans. It reads: "When I was in the military, they gave me a medal for killing two men and a discharge for loving one."

Grethe's activism made her a celebrity. *Margarethe Cammermeyer*

On July 15, 1991, a four-member board of high-ranking Army and National Guard officers met to review Cammermeyer's case. "I truly believe that you are one of the great Americans, Margarethe," said Colonel Pat "Patsy" Thompson, the board's president. "I've admired you for a long time and the work you've done, and all that you've done for the Army National Guard." Then she revealed the board's decision: Colonel Cammermeyer should be honorably discharged.

The wrenchingly ironic footnote to that story would be revealed 22 years later when Colonel Thompson came out as a lesbian. In *Surviving the Silence*, a documentary about Thompson's own journey of self-discovery, the decorated Army nurse remembers how awful it was to preside over Cammermeyer's discharge proceedings. "Oh no! I can't do this to her," she said to herself. "But I wasn't ready to come out." In 1991, Cammermeyer had no inkling Thompson was also a lesbian. When they met again in 2014, Thompson told Cammermeyer, "I'm sorry I had to do that to you." The revelation was met with no hard feelings, Cammermeyer says, only empathy. "She had carried that burden for all those years. There was also my gratitude because Patsy had given us what amounted to two years of breathing space between the time I revealed I was a lesbian and the discharge hearing. That allowed us to collect the crucial depositions that led to an appeal in civilian courts and draw national attention for my case."

Campaigning for reinstatement in 1993.
Margarethe Cammermeyer

   Cammermeyer had served notice immediately that she would appeal the decision through the federal courts. The reluctant provocateur became an activist. Nor was she alone. Dusty Pruitt, a lesbian who served in the regular Army and Reserves as a chemical weapons expert for 13 years, had come out in 1983. The former captain, also an ordained minister, took her case to the U.S. 9th Circuit Court of Appeals. It ruled in August 1991 that the Army had to reconsider her dismissal. Cammermeyer's spirits were buoyed. A few months later, Thomas Paniccia, a decorated U.S. Air Force staff sergeant, made national headlines when he came out as gay on ABC-TV's "Good Morning America." He too was promptly discharged, one of a thousand LGBTQ soldiers reportedly sacked after *Operation Desert Storm*, notwithstanding that many had served with distinction. Joe Steffan, an exemplary midshipman, was expelled from Annapolis shortly before his graduation in 1987 after he was outed by a fellow cadet as being gay. "To gay and lesbian soldiers, the Pentagon prohibition [on gays in uniform] reflects only deep-seated prejudice," Steffan said. "It's based on the assumption that all homosexuals are sex maniacs and somehow incapable of acting maturely."

   Bill Clinton met Cammermeyer in the summer of 1992 on a campaign stop in Seattle, promising, if elected president, to overturn the military's ban on gay soldiers. She was busy writing *Serving in Silence*, with help from Chris Fisher, an award-winning Seattle writer. Fisher immediately grasped that Cammermeyer's life story could inspire courage and conviction in millions of others.

   When Barbra Streisand wanted to produce Cammermeyer's story as a made-for-television movie with Glenn Close, Cammermeyer was not thrilled. She consented when Streisand said she believed gay rights "was the most important social issue of the decade."

In 1993, Cammermeyer and Tom Paniccia testified before the U.S. Senate Armed Services Committee. They said homophobia was more detrimental to the military than gay soldiers. General H. Norman Schwarzkopf, the Gulf War commander, insisted that homosexuals would damage military morale to the point that America would have "a second-class armed force for quite some time in the future."

AS PRESIDENT, Clinton quickly discovered the Pentagon was a more formidable adversary than he had imagined. When he rolled out "Don't Ask, Don't Tell," in 1993, the Democrat declared, "Under this policy, a person can say, 'I am a homosexual.'" The very next day, Defense Secretary Les Aspin told reporters the Commander in Chief had misspoken. "People are not allowed under this regulation to say 'I am gay,'" Aspin made clear. The Joints Chiefs of Staff had negotiated the terms of surrender.

Clinton insisted "Don't Ask, Don't Tell," a new twist on serving in silence, was "a substantial advance." Cammermeyer viewed it as better-than-nothing incrementalism, perhaps "the beginning of an exoneration." She was frustrated, too. The new policy allowed gays to take their uniforms—but not their sexual identities—out of the closet. "We should scream in outrage at still being classified as second-class citizens," she said. "To essentially have the military looking into the private behaviors of consenting adults is ludicrous, and a little bit sick."

There was another catch: If soldiers declared their homosexuality, they could remain in the military only if they could produce "convincing evidence that they have not engaged in homosexual acts," Aspin said. That, of course, meant proving a negative. "Nobody's ever tried this defense," he acknowledged. "It's a very tough standard to meet." The Defense Secretary noted that under "Don't Ask, Don't Tell," Cammermeyer would not have been asked the question that led to her expulsion from the Army. However, now that she was out, in more ways than one, he felt she would have a tough time getting back in. Cammermeyer shot back, "They have to prove that I'm unfit in some way."

ON JUNE 1, 1994, U.S. District Judge Thomas Zilly ordered the National Guard to reinstate Cammermeyer. "The rationales offered by the government to justify its exclusion of homosexual service members are grounded solely in prejudice," he said. "The government has discriminated against Colonel Cammermeyer solely on the basis of her status as a homosexual." The Justice Department said it was weighing an appeal. The bigger fight was far from over. But Zilly's ruling—the latest in a succession of similar legal victories for LGBTQ service members nationwide—was transparently definitive.* Cammermeyer remembers being "absolutely ecstatic." She let out a jubilant whoop so everyone at the clinic where she was working knew the news was wonderful. She told reporters it all felt "so powerful and so vindicating, not just of my own struggle but thousands of others. It's not the military that's wrong, but policies within the system," she said. "It's been a wonderful career, and now I'm looking forward to finishing it."

She happily returned to the Washington State National Guard. And when she retired from active duty in 1997, she redoubled her campaign to repeal "Don't Ask, Don't Tell." It would take another 15 years. Another Washingtonian played a key role. Air Force Major Margaret "Margie" Witt, a decorated operating room nurse from Tacoma, was suspended from duty in 2004 for being a lesbian. She fought back with a federal lawsuit challenging the constitutionality of "Don't Ask, Don't Tell." And in 2008 won a key decision in the 9th Circuit Court of Appeals. Late in 2010, momentum for change undeniable, the U.S. Senate overturned the policy on a 65-31 vote.

Certification and implementation took another nine months. On September 20, 2011, President Obama signed the repeal into law. LGBTQ service members previously discharged were offered re-enlistment. Margaret Witt and Margarethe Cammermeyer were on hand. Grethe led the Pledge of Allegiance.

THE 1995 television adaptation of *Serving in Silence* that aired on NBC had propelled Cammermeyer to even more national prominence. Glenn Close won the 1995 Emmy for outstanding lead actress in a miniseries or movie, and Judy Davis, who portrayed Diane, Grethe's spouse, received the award for best supporting actress. Alison Cross, who wrote the screenplay, won an Emmy as well. Cammermeyer was on the set for virtually the entire shoot. Though seven inches shorter, Close has Cammermeyer's chin and complexion. Her concern for attention to military detail and deportment impressed Grethe from day one. "I like to say that she became a colonel in a week, and it took me 20 years to get there," Grethe says.

"The day we arrived in Vancouver, Glenn came right over, introduced herself and said, 'My father wants to talk to you!' She handed me her cell phone and I had a wonderful conversation with her father, who was a physician. We ended up talking about military hospital issues. So I immediately felt like I had con-

---

*After dickering with Cammermeyer's attorneys over stipulations for her reinstatement, the Pentagon's legal eagles retreated. In 1997, the Justice Department denied a motion to vacate Zilly's decision.

nected with Glenn and her family. I had immense respect for the work she had done as one of our greatest actors. Now, I felt as if I immediately knew her. My role was to make sure her salute was just right, and that she could walk and talk like a soldier, and not like Glenn Close. At one point during the filming they were doing a scene in Volunteer Park. It was a Gay Pride event. Glenn was portraying me being introduced. Just before the shooting was set to begin, she took me aside and said, 'I'm trying to get a real sense of how you were feeling at the time.' And I said, 'Imagine you have just been stripped of your identity. The Army you love has thrown you out. Imagine being totally lost in the world and then coming to a place where you are absolutely embraced by 20,000 people. For

The cover of *Serving in Silence*, Grethe's autobiography. *Margarethe Cammermeyer*

me, it was a moment that touched me tremendously.' Well, she went out and did that scene as though she had been in my shoes. She nailed it. Judy Davis was an extraordinary actress as well. So we were very pleased with the end product."

DESPITE THE POSITIVE response to her book and the televised movie, Cammermeyer's speeches sometimes caused vociferous debate. When she spoke to a Women's History Month assembly at Olympia High School in the spring of 1995—at the invitation of Attorney General Chris Gregoire's daughter Courtney and other leaders of the Student Activist Club—50 students boycotted the event. A hundred others had been kept home by parents outraged that the school board would not cancel the event.

Cammermeyer's talk emphasized the changing roles of women in the military. But the students moderating the program prodded her to say whether she had any regrets about coming out. "I've had a loss of privacy," she said, "but it would be hard to say that you would ever regret being honest. …You are the leaders of tomorrow. You are more sexually active and more sexually wise than my generation. That's not a value judgment—just a statement of fact." The 600 students on hand accorded her a standing ovation. Nineteen state legislators signed a letter chastising the school board. Public schools shouldn't be "platforms to educate youth on the virtues of standing up for one's homosexuality," they said. Letters praising the board's support for free speech—and Cammermeyer's patriotism—dominated the response on *The Olympian's* opinion page.

Cammermeyer was back two weeks later after a hate crime that would lead to tragedy. She joined Olympia Mayor Bob Jacobs at a rally in support of two students called "fags" and assaulted on the school grounds during spring break by teenagers from Rochester, a nearby town. One of the victims was 17-year-old Bill Clayton, an openly bisexual Olympia High School junior who had advocated for Cammermeyer's appearance at the assembly. To cope with an earlier assault, Clayton had just completed two years of therapy. "For this to happen threw him back to a place he didn't feel safe at all," said his mother, Gabrielle Clayton. "It threw him into a severe depression." Bill took his own life a month later, a few days after being released from a Seattle hospital.

"It was just a terrible time," Cammermeyer remembers. "My appearance at the school generated such an uproar that you would have thought I was going to pollute the world—a military nurse. There were police all over the place, with cordoned-off areas like they were expecting a major upheaval. What I emphasized was the progressive role of women in the military. Afterwards there was a backlash at the students who had helped organize the events. Then came the heartbreak of losing Bill Clayton. He was just a charming, fragile young man. I reached out to him at the hospital by phone and told him I was there for him."

CAMMERMEYER'S public events, notably her appearances before congressional committees, gave her a "bully pulpit"—one of her favorite Theodore Rooseveltisms—to run for Congress in 1998. Three other lesbians, Tammy Baldwin, a Wisconsin state legislator; Christine Kehoe, a San Diego councilwoman, and Susan Tracy, a former Massachusetts state legislator, also ran for Congress that year, boosted by the Gay and Lesbian Victory Fund. All four Democrats would win nomination in swing districts represented by Republicans but carried by Clinton in 1996. They were out and proud, to be sure, Cammermeyer remembers, yet "anything but" one-dimensional candidates. Baldwin, now a U.S. Senator, became the first openly gay woman elected to Congress.

Cammermeyer's opponent in the 2nd Congressional District north of Seattle was two-term Congressman Jack Metcalf, a veteran politician long opposed to gay civil rights. Billing himself as "Jack the Giant Killer," the 70-year-old former Everett teacher had twice challenged U.S. Senator Warren G. Magnuson. Trounced both times, he went on to win an open seat in Congress in 1994, and cultivated the support of building trades unions, including Boeing's machinists.

Grethe and Diane on a trip to Norway in 1991. *Margarethe Cammermeyer*

Endorsed by *The Seattle Times* as a "compelling" candidate with "extraordinary gifts," Cammermeyer easily won the Democratic primary. Early on, Metcalf styled her as "a spokesperson for the lesbian lifestyle." He sent 47,000 conservatives a letter asking for donations if they shared "values like honoring the traditional family structure." By September, however, sharp blowback prompted Metcalf to declare she was "a smart, honorable" person with an "exemplary" military record. They signed what amounted to a nonaggression pact—a Pew Foundation Clean Campaign agreement—promising there would be no personal attacks. "Jack, candidly, was slipping," she remembers. "It was his chief of staff who spoke at most of the debates and appearances. But he kept his word. From then on he was gentlemanly. It was actually really classy. I think it was the only, or at least one of the few, congressional races in the country where both candidates had agreed to the Pew agreement to campaign with civility."

Candidate Cammermeyer never felt the need to repeat the four words that changed her life: "I am a lesbian." Her stump speech invariably began like this:

> *I am not a politician. I'm an everyday person who has a health-care background. I am a mother, a grandmother and a nurse who served in Vietnam. I have had the best and worst of social experience. My passions are education, health care and fighting discrimination.*

A few days before the General Election, Metcalf's campaign manager said their latest polls gave him a 20-point lead. Cammermeyer knew better, but realized she was still the underdog.

He won a third term with 55 percent of the vote.

Grethe and Diane with the Obamas in 2015. *Margarethe Cammermeyer*

"Homophobia was an issue, of course," Cammermeyer says, noting that nearly 60 percent of Washington voters had rejected a sexual orientation anti-discrimination initiative the year before. "I also didn't have 40 years of political savvy, entrenched fundraising and his union support. Yet I lost by essentially five percentage points. Pretty good for a beginner. But I had the wisdom not to run again, because what you learn is what political campaigning is really all about. It's about money—raising funds to get your propaganda out there—not so much about the issues, which are what should be of relevance to society as a whole. Complacency is what concerns me now. The fact that there is no sense of vision. Remember when Barack Obama announced his candidacy with a new burst of idealism and commitment? It was a little bit like John F. Kennedy in 1960. It was this infusion of fresh hope for the future. Things are now so polarized, right and left, that we have lost the centrists. We need change agents! I tell people to become informed. Vote. Run for public office. Live your truth."

CAMMERMEYER says two dates only six years apart prove that change agents can shift the tectonic plates of social history in record time. On July 26, 2006, the Washington Supreme Court—which today has two lesbian justices—issued a deeply conflicted 5-4 decision that the Legislature's 1998 Defense of Marriage Act was constitutional. Then, on November 6, 2012, the script flipped: Nearly 54 percent of Washington voters endorsed same-sex marriage. Opponents had attempted to overturn a legislative mandate signed into law by Governor Chris Gregoire.

The vote on Referendum 74 nevertheless reflected a still-widening divide between conservative counties east of the Cascades, as well as many rural counties on the west side. Marriage equality, crucially, was backed by 67 percent of King County voters, yet overall by only 10 of the state's 39 counties. Backsliding worries

Grethe and Diane Divelbess are married in 2012. *Margarethe Cammermeyer*

Dr. Cammermeyer.

The first same-sex marriages in Washington took place on December 9. Grethe and Diane converted their annual Christmas party into a nuptial-fest. Nine other couples happily accepted their invitation to be married that night. "The mayor of Coupeville, Nancy Conard, was the presiding officer. Each of us went into the downstairs library of our home and had our private wedding. I had made Norwegian wedding cake for each couple and ordered some wine glasses engraved with the date. And then we celebrated together."

Grethe finds it curious that homophobes and others who buy into stereotypes about LGBTQ people are so fixated on what happens in the bedroom that they can't grasp that most married gay couples are just like straight married couples. When the novelty of new intimacy wears off, they read books, pop popcorn and watch *Jeopardy!*. "At least early on, my embarrassment was that I thought if some-body was homosexual all you thought about was sex," Grethe says. "Diane and I aren't clingy. We're just married. If I'm at home I'm either working outside or in my office. She sits in her reading chair and reads poetry and pays attention to the news. You couldn't have two more opposite people. You've got a right brain person and a left brain person. Diane is an artist. She is also a religious scholar. Personality wise, what we have in common is that we have our values. We have our respect for one another. We have our professions." Grethe, who has a mellifluous, folky singing voice, plays guitar and writes songs. Some are inspirational, some whim-

Grethe happy at home in 2022. She was the first woman and first nurse to receive the UW's Distinguished Veteran Award. *Margarethe Cammermeyer*

sical. One, *The Tortoise and the Hare*, examines all the ways they're different. "I write that I love the smell of formaldehyde and ammonia and her mentholatum makes me barf!"

Love apparently conquers all. *Love equally.*

Well into their relationship, Grethe and Diane were at a reunion of family and friends. Her father had long since come to admire Diane. Grethe worried he still harbored misgivings about her being gay. Now, standing "as if to make a toast," he declared to the group that he found their household "perfectly normal."

"Diane's eyes twinkled," Grethe remembers. "I was amazed." Then, using the Norwegian word for "papa," Grethe said, 'Far, please pass the salt.'

"I felt nothing more needed to be said by anyone—and Father seemed to agree."

Which seems like a perfect ending.

John C. Hughes

Valerie Mariano

"Make a difference"

Brigadier General Dan Dent, the commander of the Washington Army National Guard, said Valerie P. Mariano's promotion to Chief Warrant Officer 5 in 2021 italicized the fact that she was an elite soldier. The warrant officer corps of the U.S. Army—a cadre of technical experts—accounts for just two percent of the force. And only one-tenth of one percent make it to CWO-5.

"The strength of her smile is only matched by the strength of her shoulders," Dent said.

What went unsaid—because it was no longer of consequence—is that Mariano was one of thousands of LGBTQ service men and women serving their country.

Mariano's 43-year military career began in 1979 as a weekend warrior when she enlisted in the Hawaii National Guard as a high school senior. Next came four years in the regular Army. Then back to the Guard. She retired from the Active Guard Reserve on January 31, 2023. Her career was marked by pride of service and diligent soldiering. Yet even after "Don't Ask, Don't Tell, Don't Pursue"—the full name of the policy—was instituted in 1993, Mariano and thousands of other gay soldiers, sailors and airmen still had to watch their backs. With one slip-up—revealing a "tendency" or "intent to engage in homosexual activities"—at the wrong time in the wrong place, they could face discharge proceedings. The Pentagon maintained their presence "would create an unacceptable risk to the high standards of morale, good order and discipline, and unit cohesion that are the essence of military capability."

Between 1993 and 2011, when "Don't Ask, Don't Tell" was repealed, there was a lot of "pursuing" by the Army's Criminal Investigation Division, the dreaded "CID." More than 13,000 LGBTQ service men and women were dismissed from the service.

Facing page: CWO-5 Valerie Mariano. *Washington National Guard*

After repeal, a survey released by the RAND Corporation in 2018 found that 6.1 percent (79,000) of the estimated 1.3 million persons then serving in the U.S. military self-identified as LGBTQ. The U.S. Navy had the highest concentration of gay people, 9.1%; the Army, 5.5%; Air Force, 5.3%; Coast Guard, 5.2%, and Marine Corps, 4.4%. Lesbians or trans women accounted for 16.6% of the total service members, gay or bisexual men 4.2%.

MARIANO, WHO CAME OUT when she was 14, remembers her six years in the Hawaii National Guard as a back-in-the-closet, yet less stressful time. "Wearing men's Aloha shirts" and "not much caring" what others thought, she concentrated on being an exceptional soldier.

Mariano's personality—a blend of laid-back Hawaiian and attention-to-detail Asian—springs from her gene pool. Her father was half-Hawaiian, half-Filipino; her mother is half Japanese and half Chinese.

"Being in Hawaii was a benefit because [gay] soldiers weren't as shunned as on the mainland," Mariano remembers. In Korea, however, during a 1986-87 tour of duty with the regular Army, her lesbian roommates warned "Mum's the word" whenever they headed out for a night of club hopping. "Be careful of the CID!" they said. "They're having a witch hunt. Don't say anything careless. Don't do anything stupid."

After three years at Fort Lewis near Tacoma, Mariano joined the Washington Army National Guard. It was 1990. She was still mum, but less fearful "and more myself" because "your personal life isn't exposed as much as on the active-duty side. You didn't have to see me much except for one weekend a month." Before long, however, she transitioned to a fulltime role in the Guard. Over the next 12 years, Mariano advanced steadily in the enlisted ranks to master sergeant/ first sergeant before graduating from Warrant Officer Candidate School in 2002.

"It's part of leadership's responsibilities to know your soldiers and their families. It was different as I moved up, but everybody knew my sexual affiliation. I just didn't talk about it. And no one ever did anything. My position was, 'I'm here to do a job and not to win a popularity contest.' I was educating myself on doing a good job; knowing all the rules and regulations. Doing everything by the book. If you were a good soldier, that's what mattered most."

Beginning as a unit supply specialist, Mariano's career as a military logistician was marked by increasing responsibilities in materiel management. She closed out her career as a property book officer for Joint Force Headquarters, accounting for federal government equipment supplied to the Guard to perform its mission—everything from handguns to tanks.

When "Don't Ask, Don't Tell," was adopted, Mariano thought it was half a loaf, but better than crumbs: "I was like, 'OK. Someday there might be a change. In the meantime, I'm still just going to be me and do what I do.'"

One of Mariano's heroes is Colonel Margarethe Cammermeyer, the Washington National Guard's former chief nurse. The Vietnam veteran was discharged in 1991, after admitting to being a lesbian when applying for a top-secret clearance. Cammermeyer fought back, her plight gaining national attention. And in 1994, a U.S. District Court judge ordered the Guard to reinstate her. "The rationales offered by the government to justify its exclusion of homosexual service members are grounded solely in prejudice," said Judge Thomas Zilly.

The battle to repeal "Don't Ask, Don't Tell," was waged for another 17 years.

Meeting Colonel Cammermeyer is high on Mariano's bucket list. "I want to thank her for her service, her courage and persistence.

"I couldn't believe it when 'Don't Ask' was repealed. I didn't know how to accept it because I'd played this role for so long," Mariano says. "I didn't know how to truly fully express myself. I still don't. There's my other self, but not my military self. But I'm one and the same. I feel like I'm a survivor because I've lasted this long. I actually saw the day when it's acceptable to be who you are and not have that compromise your ability, your right and responsibility to serve your country.

"First and foremost, the men and women—gay and straight—who join the military are there as a service to our country. And to do that you have to persevere and be technically proficient. My mantra is, 'Don't be mediocre. Be exceptional. Make a difference.'" Things today are demonstrably different in the Washington National Guard. Its Public Affairs Office celebrated Pride Month in June 2021 with a "Pride in Service" podcast featuring Chief Mariano, as well as a transgender female lieutenant—a recruiter, no less; a lesbian captain, and a former counter-intelligence warrant officer discharged under "Don't Ask, Don't Tell," after 12 years of service when he finally came out. He now works in the state's Emergency Management Division.

After 25 years as a couple, Mariano and her wife, Theresa Quinn, were married in Seattle in 2017. "We made it a special occasion, yet simple, with family members and my hair dresser—someone I've known for 20 years. She too is married to another woman. Her son, who I watched grow up, officiated. The world has changed."

John C. Hughes

MARSHA BOTZER

"THE WAY TO BE HAPPY IS TO
HELP MAKE OTHERS SO."

Marsha Botzer's pioneering journey comes down to a single gesture—a raised closed hand. And it's not so much a fist. Her graceful fingers are joined not to signal defiance, but alliance. It's her guiding philosophy. As Washington's most renowned trans activist, Botzer has embraced a belief that nothing is as rewarding as people working together for a goal bigger than themselves. It's why she founded the Ingersoll Gender Center, joined so many affinity groups in the last four decades, proved herself on so many committees, and like a missionary, shared her story with audiences from Brussels to Beijing. It goes like this:

After Queen Anne High School, Class of 1965, and before she learned anything about gender identity or transitions, Botzer went into construction work. She got swept up in the possibilities of solidarity among the plumbers and pipefitters in her local union. On a trip to Europe, she took in the historic Paris street-protests of 1968 and made her way to Venice where, among a circle of hippies, she overheard a few life-changing words. Back in the states, she returned to hard labor. She called doctors about the idea of what we now call gender confirmation care. Some hung up on her.

To help others with similar struggles, back in the days before Chaz Bono tangoed on "Dancing with the Stars" and Amy Schneider set records on *Jeopardy!* Botzer created the Ingersoll Gender Center in Seattle to offer support services. She spent summer vacations as a guide for people having transition surgeries in a historic Colorado mining town called Trinidad. She rose to the top of prominent LGBTQ groups, including the National Gay and Lesbian Task Force and Obama Pride 2008.

It's almost exhausting to consider her credentials, never mind the 400 hours

Facing page: In decades of award-winning activism, Botzer has learned this: "When it's won, it isn't."
Washington State LGBTQ Commission

Marsha Botzer flashes her signature gesture of solidarity at Seattle's Pride Parade. *Ed Murray*

of personal electrolysis she endured, well over 2500 consecutive weeks (and counting) Ingersoll's support group has met, and her role at 75 as co-chair of Washington state's relatively new LGBTQ Commission.

The deliberate and philosophical Botzer accidentally discovered her favorite quote. It's by Robert Ingersoll, who lived in the 19th century and had nothing to do with gender issues, as far as she knows. It goes: "The time to be happy is now. The place to be happy is here. And the way to be happy is to help make others so."

There was a time when people couldn't find therapists to discuss their sense of being a different gender than the one assigned at birth. Botzer went back to school to earn a master's degree in clinical psychology so she could assist them. There was a time when those feelings were not recognized by the medical establishment. The American Psychiatric Association now describes gender dysphoria as the "psychological distress that results from an incongruence between one's sex assigned at birth and one's gender identity."

Now, identity is acknowledged. Now, therapy abounds. Fortune 500 companies tout their anti-discrimination policies for trans employees. President Joe Biden chose Rachel Levine as his assistant secretary of health—the highest post in federal government attained by a trans person.

But Levine still faced what Senator Patty Murray called "ideological and harmful misrepresentations" in her 2021 confirmation hearings. And that was just the spear tip of a right-wing thrust. When arch-conservatives knew the marriage-equality battle was lost, they pivoted, says Sasha Issenberg, author of *The Engagement*, a history of the strategic battles over same-sex marriage. "Religious conservatives had lost their position of strength for a variety of reasons—opinion change, demographic changes. And then they decided that they were going to go to trans issues instead."

In 2022, their offensive swept across states in a historic wave of bills that would restrict rights, curtail gender studies, and investigate families with trans children for child abuse. Trans people remain the "bete noire" to many, Botzer says. And one thing she has learned in her activism is: "When it's won, it isn't."

Botzer founded the Ingersoll Gender Center in 1977. Medical research 45 years later concludes that gender identity "is not a pathology, or crazy," she says. "It's diversity." *Ingersoll Gender Center*

DISPARAGING TRANS people became a litmus test for GOP candidates in 2022 elections. Challengers vying to oust incumbent Republican Jaime Herrera Beutler in southwest Washington's 3rd Congressional District targeted trans activism.

Before Herrera Beutler's election in 2010, Democrats had owned the seat for 46 of the previous 50 years. She appeared to be what the GOP needed: a woman of color with purplish politics in an increasingly suburban district. But she riled the GOP's base by voting to impeach Donald Trump in the ex-president's second trial.

A reporter for *The Chronicle* in Centralia summarized the stances of three local congressional challengers at a Conservative Ladies of Washington forum: Heidi St. John said transitioning and trans people were "from the pit of hell" and told the crowd she doesn't respond to emails from publicists who list their pronouns. Joe Kent contended that the "transgender issue" is "all about control" and breaking up families. Wadi Yakhour mocked the "LGBTQ BLT sandwich community" and said they're "building a genetically modified army, almost."

Kent went on to best Herrera Beutler in the primary and knocked her out of the general election and office. Kent was narrowly defeated in November by newcomer Marie Gluesenkamp Perez, returning the seat to Democrats.

Performative attacks on trans people and their allies migrated across the country's pixels, algorithms and statehouses in 2022. The Associated Press called it a classic "wedge issue" that motivates a political base—and could be used to establish conservative credentials.

In Pennsylvania's 2022 high-stakes Republican primary for a U.S. Senate seat, candidate Dr. Mehmet Oz was attacked by a rival's campaign ad for once hosting an episode about trans children on his TV show.

In Missouri's Senate race, an ad by GOP contender Vicky Hartzler targeted trans athletes. Twitter also suspended Hartzler's personal account for violating its rules against hateful conduct with a transphobic tweet.

In a spat with another member of Congress whose daughter is trans, Marjorie Taylor Green stuck a "Trust the Science" poster outside her office. Greene was stripped of committee duties for promoting unproven conspiracies. *Twitter*

Even the walls of Congress were weaponized. Marjorie Taylor Greene put up a sign in 2021 outside the office of Democratic Congresswoman Marie Newman, whose daughter is trans. It said: "There are TWO genders: MALE & FEMALE. Trust The Science!" Greene, a Republican from Georgia, had already been stripped of her committee assignments in the House over statements and social media posts supporting false conspiracies.

Anti-trans animus even became a rallying point around Vladimir Putin. The Kremlin had sought for a decade to win over allies on the American right, in part by denouncing gay rights, said Andrew S. Weiss, a Russia expert at the Carnegie Endowment for International Peace. On the eve of Russia's invasion of Ukraine in February 2022, Steve Bannon, a former adviser to Trump, commended Russia for its opposition to transgender rights. Bannon praised Putin as "anti-woke."

BOTZER'S PARENTS MET in Hawaii during World War II. William Botzer, from Mossyrock in southwest Washington, served in the Navy. Judith Clapp from Kansas City ran a camouflage factory and worked for the Red Cross. Marsha can't swear for its accuracy, but she heard that before her father sailed off to the Battle of Leyte Gulf, he arranged to have flowers sent to her mother every day for a month. After the war, the couple came to Seattle. They settled on Queen Anne Hill and William Botzer practiced law.

Marsha got the impression her parents wanted, maybe craved, peace and quiet. "It wasn't, 'I won't talk about it,' " Marsha recalls. "It was—and this is my guess—they had seen enough tension, pain and struggle that they were hoping it was over." Add the ultra-conformist 1950s and Seattle's stoicism, and Marsha remembers growing up in what felt like a small, quiet town.

Until 1962, when down the hill from the Botzer home arose The Space Needle and exotic exhibits of the World's Fair at Seattle Center. It left a mark. "I had never seen that much difference before," she says. That summer she'd offer to escort vis-

Botzer likens the Seattle of her youth to a small, quiet town—until the marvels of the 1962 World's Fair landed just down the hill from her famliy's home. *Washington State Archives*

itors her parents knew around the fair if they'd pay for her ticket.

Otherwise, Botzer kept pretty much to herself at Queen Anne High. She played some sports, but like her later foray into construction work she suspects she was probably trying on stereotypes "to be the male the world kept telling me I was supposed to be." One English class tickled her curious mind. The teacher, whose name escapes her, "went all over the place." Freud, Nietzsche, Darwin and more. The class fed Botzer's desire to understand more, discover more about one's sense of self.

Mostly, she came home and read books. She felt something she couldn't put into words. "Nothing was very clear then. Nothing at all," she recalls. "And there were no sources of information. So not only could I put no name on the feelings, I could not find anything if I had."

This was long before smart phones—even before "Little Big Man" depicted a Native American two-spirit person on the big screen, and Renee Richards, a trans professional tennis player, was outed in 1976 by Tucker Carlson's father. Botzer did not know that a U.S. Army veteran from the Bronx made headlines in 1955 after transitioning to "blonde beauty" Christine Jorgensen.

The most Botzer would allow in her own feelings was "seeing my mom with a number of her friends, women, getting together for maybe coffee or something, and wondering vaguely why I'm not like they are."

That's a difficult thing for a young person to feel. "So I quickly put it away," she says.

At the University of Washington, she was drawn to the free speech, civil rights and anti-war movements. She read *Helix*, the underground newspaper. She listened to noncommercial KRAB-FM. She knew she was expected to head for a profession through college. But with the identity struggles roiling her insides, she couldn't focus on studies and dropped out of the UW. Hired on as a helper with a Washington Natural Gas maintenance crew, she busted concrete and dug up streets to install meters and fix transmission lines. Very physical work, and almost a relief.

In Plumbers and Pipefitters Local 32 she discovered the labor movement. It provided an entry point, a vision for how you might change things. She learned about commitment when her local went on strike, about taking great risks for others, about breadwinners willing to go without a paycheck for something bigger.

Seattle's KRAB hosted one of the earliest American gay and lesbian radio shows in 1971, "Make No Mistake about It, It's a Faggot and a Dyke." *Jack Straw Cultural Center*

THE WORLD WAS CRACKLING with kinetic molecules of generational, cultural and political upheaval. Botzer vacationed in England to see a friend from the UW. It was the Swinging London of 1967: Chartreuse mini-skirts, paisley jackets, flouncy sleeves, flowing scarves, floppy hats. Change hung over Carnaby Street like a purple cape on a long-haired man. On to Paris, where Botzer glimpsed some of the unrest that would grip France the next year.

Back in the U.S.A., Botzer bought a VW van, painted it psychedelic colors and drove to San Francisco. But by then the acid tests and hippie vibes had been dimmed by harder drugs. "And things were getting messy."

While rich with lessons, none of the adventures provided the hoped-for answers to her questions about gender and identity.

Botzer saved money, cleared out her bank account, quit work, and headed back to Paris in 1968. Students and workers had joined in protests that nearly toppled the French government. "Now, I can't claim to have any part in it," Botzer says. But she saw students and workers clasping hands. "And back home that wasn't the case." Hardhats were more likely to hammer hippies than hug them. Paris gave her great hope.

Like many young seekers, she hitchhiked around Europe. There was a culture on the road. Whether sleeping on trains, or in hostels, people were exchanging perspectives, possibilities, toting Vonnegut books in their backpacks, sharing newfound wisdom and dreams. Taboos were shattered. Life wasn't a prescribed path. Botzer heard young Germans singing the civil-rights anthem "We Shall Overcome." How odd and wonderful. Crossing Spain, she slept outside and read Ken Kesey's *Sometimes a Great Notion*. While staying with a Spanish family, she dropped a bottle of wine while packing, smashing it on her hosts' floor. The Spaniards laughed, told her not to worry, and sent her off with one of their bottles.

From city to city, there was a pattern. Go to a popular square. Meet other young people. Talk, sing, eat, drink, learn. Late in the summer she made her way to Venice and headed for Piazza San Marco, and its vast plaza surrounded by ancient buildings such as St. Mark's Basilica. She knew nothing about the square's reputation as "the drawing room of Europe."

On the road in Europe, Botzer would go to a city, find a popular square, meet other young people, laugh and learn. In the summer of 1968 she headed for Venice's vast Piazza San Marco and came away feeling, "I'm not alone." *Wikipedia Commons*

"I don't want to put too glowy a thing on it," she says. "But for the most part, it was possible then, maybe for just that brief moment, to travel about, and come into a city, and know there'd be a group of hippie-type folks in a square or gathering place, who would just welcome you to sit down. And there'd be music. I never had a violent incident. Never. And then you'd get into conversations. And by that time, I was just so hooked on learning other people's stories, and just hearing what their culture was like."

In the hippies' corner of the square, Botzer heard someone say something about a cousin who made a gender change. It hit hard. She spent nights thinking, "I'm not alone. Maybe there's hope."

After a jaunt to Formentera, a Mediterranean hippie haven, and with her money dwindling, she returned to Seattle with the idea she needed to do something about her pain and frustration. She went back to the union hall, where cigarette smoke floated to the ceiling and drifted downward around her Local 32 brothers. She went back to carving through pavement with a 90-pound jackhammer.

In Seattle, freedom still floated on the "macrobiotic" kilowatts beamed by KRAB-FM. "Notes from the Underground" was a Sunday night show hosted by budding novelist Tom Robbins. "Make No Mistake About It, It's a Faggot and a Dyke," one of the earliest American gay and lesbian radio shows, aired on KRAB in 1971. It was hosted by Paul Barwick and Shan Ottey, who went on to play prominent roles in the LGBTQ community.

One night in her work truck, Botzer heard someone on KRAB mention transsexuals. (The term "transsexual" was later considered outdated, in the same way "homosexual" was replaced by "gay" and "lesbian.")

"I just about drove into a ditch," she says.

BOTZER BEGAN CALLING doctors because it was the only path she could imagine. But doctors would say they didn't know anything about gender issues, they couldn't help, or just hang up. She saw 13 therapists who told her she was gay or a transvestite. She spent the early 1970s trying not to sink into hopelessness. She stayed in construction for a total of 17 years, making decent money, but "treading water."

She would still have those 3 o'clock in the morning shivers when she'd tell herself: "I cannot go on like this, not having an answer to this feeling that my body doesn't match who I am."

One day, while in the Seattle Public Library, she saw a book with "Ingersoll" on its cover. She thought it was about the company that made compressors used in construction work. Instead, she found Robert Ingersoll's quote about happiness. She interpreted it as a sermon about freedom. She came to think, "when we free ourselves anything can happen." She came across the Seattle Counseling Service. Founded in 1969, SCS has touted itself as "the oldest LGBTQ-focused community mental health agency in the world." But the service was more oriented to "LGB" than "T" back then.

That led to another of Botzer's great life-lessons: "If it doesn't exist, we can make it." In 1977 she created Ingersoll Gender Center. She began building relationships with therapists and doctors. In a crude form of pre-internet outreach, Botzer would sneak business cards into Seattle Public Library books that had anything to do with sex and gender. It was her way of indicating that Ingersoll, and help, was just a call away.

The center's main mission was to always be there for support. It started hosting regular meetings every Wednesday and incorporated as a nonprofit in 1984.

Several years earlier, Botzer had heard about Dr. Stanley Biber, a Korean War U.S. Army M*A*S*H surgeon who opened a practice in Trinidad, a Col-

Botzer's interest in philosophy led her to Robert G. Ingersoll, namesake of the Gender Center. *Library of Congress*

orado mining town about 200 miles south of Denver. In 1969, Biber started performing genital reassignment surgeries in Trinidad—and gaining attention, more than he ever had as a M*A*S*H legend who once operated on 37 consecutive soldiers before passing out from exhaustion. "Going to Trinidad" became a euphemism for transitioning. He welcomed both male and female patients.

While extremists called him "Satan's physician" and Trinidad the "anteroom to Hell," Biber, a former rabbinical student, did not judge his patients. "By the time they get to me, they've already completed their gender identity change," he said. "I simply add the accoutrements of anatomy."

In 1981, Botzer was feeling ready. She took her savings and went to Trinidad. Many of the townspeople were conservative. But they tended to respect Biber, an Iowa native who revered John Wayne and ranching. He had delivered their babies, sutured their appendectomies and set their broken bones. His office wasn't secluded, but above a bank at the downtown corner of Commercial and Main.

He gathered clergy and local officials and told them the visitors coming to their town needed help. And he could relieve their pain which was the right thing do. As patients streamed in, they turned out to be good for business, and acceptance grew, wrote journalist Martin J. Smith in his 2021 book, *Going to Trinidad*. Smith's book includes Botzer, "a foundational figure in the Seattle LGBTQ community," as well as Dr. Marci Bowers, who became Biber's protégé. Bowers was the first trans woman to perform such surgeries. Botzer had introduced Bowers to Biber when Bowers practiced in Seattle.

Dr. Stanley Biber helped turn Trinidad, an old mining town along the Santa Fe Trail, into the country's gender-change capital. Botzer published a study about the satisfaction of his patients. *The Legacy Project*

Botzer guided more than 100 people through Trinidad, as Biber wound up performing over 6,000 surgeries. Fortunate that she hadn't lost her job or family, she offered herself up as a trans ambassador for a long, sympathetic 1986 story in *The Seattle Times.* "One reason I'm public about this is because there is so much pain out there," she said. Her mother said she was proud of her only child, adding, "She brings these people over to the house and you can tell they want love. They need their families."

And she started building alliances. Most of her co-workers in construction were supportive. "I will forever praise those union members around me," she says. They said she was a good worker, and they liked her. So, well, they were OK with her change.

"One way to educate is to live a good life," she says. "Get into the world. Take your message of health and happiness to everyone you meet."

That became her mission.

SHOULD TRANS PEOPLE have their own movement separate from the lesbian and gay communities? Some suggested that, but not Botzer. Folding her fingers tightly, she said, "I want to see us like that. In my mind we all progress together."

She joined as many affinity groups as possible. "Sometimes it would take years to win over the understanding of an organization. So that meant I had to do the work, take a committee assignment for a couple of years and then when they saw 'no problem here,' I could start to say, 'Could we involve some other folks with some other gender issues?' It took so much energy and so much time."

She became an early member of Hands Off Washington, a statewide coalition formed to thwart anti-gay ballot initiatives being carried over the state line by an Oregon group. With chapters across Washington, HOW and its "decline to sign" campaign played a part in keeping Initiatives 608 and 610 from gathering enough signatures to qualify for the ballot.

Emboldened, HOW pushed its own Initiative 677 to the ballot in 1997. It would protect people against discrimination because of sexual orientation in jobs, housing and public accommodations. It had high-profile support from Governor Gary Locke. But it was crushed at the polls, losing even in King County.

Undeterred, Botzer helped author a 1999 amendment that added gender identity to her hometown's non-discrimination law.

Seattle became only the third major U.S. city to pass legislation that protected trans people from discrimination.

In 2004, she was a founding member of Equal Rights Washington, a successor to Hands Off Washington. The very name of the group suggested a shift in LGBTQ civil-rights strategy. It was no longer about warding off evangelicals trying to ford the Columbia River. It was focused in-state, on basic rights. Botzer's new group had a hand in finally pushing an anti-discrimination law across the finish line in Olympia, after decades of frustration.

And it protected gender identity as well as sexual orientation.

By the early 21st century, Washington lawmakers like many Americans were becoming more aware of the distinctions between gender, genitals and gender

Botzer helped pressure Walmart to adopt anti-discrimination protections for gays and lesbians in the workplace. Displaying Walmart's announcement, she said, "I look forward to continuing our discussion and eagerly anticipate the day when they will also include gender identity in their non-discrimination policies." *Associated Press*

identity. Martin Smith, the *Going to Trinidad* author, summarizes them neatly, if generally: Genitals—long synonymous with gender—are biological, the product of genes, hormones and flesh. Even then, genitalia are not strictly binary. A small percentage of people called intersex have sexual anatomy that is not what we think of as standard-issue. (Some things are smaller in men and larger in women, for instance.) That doesn't come as a great surprise to scientists. Every human embryo starts with female substructure. Men and women both produce estrogen and testosterone. Biology, across species, strives for diversity.

Gender identity, on the other hand, is the interplay of flesh, hormones, socialization and "something vastly more important—the brain."

To assign gender by glancing between a baby's legs, Smith writes, is a blunt instrument, like extrapolating from a single speedometer that a vehicle is a green, rusted 1952 International Harvester half-ton pickup truck. Gender identity is more than body parts, but "innumerable acts we perform." It's more like a language we use to communicate ourselves to others, and understand ourselves.

Which leads to another lesson, albeit simplistic: sexual orientation is who you go to bed with; gender identity is who you go to bed as.

BOTZER'S PROFILE GREW. After growing close to Biber, he gave her and an academic colleague access to anonymized but numerically coded records of his trans patients. While maintaining patient confidentiality, she used it to follow-up on the histories of 200 patients. Her study found 93 percent satisfaction with Biber's surgeries. She presented it at a conference of the World Professional Association of Transgender Health. She later served on the association's board of directors and helped craft its 2012 international standards of care.

She became the first trans co-chair of the National Gay and Lesbian Task Force in 2005. It was the most trans-inclusive of the national groups, Botzer says, and later changed its name to the National LGBTQ Task Force

One of the task force's first directors was Charlie Brydon, a Seattle businessman, and the gay community's most visible early leader in the state. Brydon made inroads and allies at City Hall, particularly with Mayor Wes Uhlman, in the 1970s. Before then, no elected official had dared to meet publicly with an LGBT group.

In 2008, Botzer became one of the five co-chairs of the Obama Pride Campaign. She gave a spirited speech in front of the U.S. Capitol for the National Equality March the next year. She concluded with a signature riff: "All allies, all loving partners, all identities, safe. All. Not singular," she said, her index finger aloft. "But together," her hand closed and raised.

The rewards kept coming. In 2010, her hands helped hoist the pride flag atop the Space Needle for the first time. Then she went to China for a program sponsored by the Los Angeles Gay and Lesbian Center. She jumped at the chance to help what she believed to be the world's largest LGBTQ population. "My job was to work with emerging trans organizations, which are now all shut down or locked up, it's really sad," she says.

Botzer, National Gay and Lesbian Task Force co-chair, revisited a place that expanded her horizons in 1962, to raise the Pride flag on the Space Needle in 2010. *Marsha Botzer*

At the time of her visit, a Chinese city might have a bar or a space where LGBT folks could gather, and one or two organizations. "But they couldn't advertise it, and they couldn't put a flag out, or a name on the building or anything like that."

China's government clamped down hard, though, as authoritarianism seemed to be marching around the world. In 2021, it censored an LGBTQ group's online accounts and called for broadcasters to ban "sissy men" from television. "China's LGBTQ community is fading from rainbow to gray," read a CNN headline.

Israel was another story altogether. Botzer and then Seattle Mayor Ed Murray visited Tel Aviv in 2015 for a conference organized by Israel's pioneering LGBTQ group, Aguda, and a San Francisco organization, A Wider Bridge. Murray gave the keynote speech. But before he did, activists in Seattle argued he should boycott the conference. It was an example of "pink-washing," they said, or painting over problems in Israel—specifically, the treatment of Palestinians—by representing Israel as gay-friendly.

Like Murray, Botzer trooped to Palestine. "I was there because there were human beings feeling the exact same thoughts about gender and identity in Isra-

Botzer was at the Capitol with Ty Stober, co-chair of Equal Rights Washington, when Gov. Gregoire signed the marriage equality bill. "Today I am even more proud to call Washington my home," she said. *National Gay and Lesbian Task Force*

el and Palestine and everywhere else." Identity is what they discussed, she says, and nothing that could be colored as pink-washing.

WHEN ASKED IF she would join in advocating a marriage equality law in 2012, Botzer paused for a moment. In some ways, marriage was an oppressive institution, she observed. In Washington state, a husband could legally rape his wife until 1983. And it wasn't until 2013 that marriage was completely eliminated as a defense against sexual assault charges.

While marriage wasn't at the top of her wish list, team play was. The lesbian, bisexual and trans communities have been intertwined, in part, because research suggests a majority of trans people are also LGBQ. If state leaders of the community were rallying around marriage, then she was in. She became a coordinator in Washington United for Marriage, the group fronting the 2012 campaign in the Evergreen State.

She smiled for photos at the statehouse when Governor Chris Gregoire signed a marriage equality bill in February. "Today I am even more proud to call Washington my home," she gushed in a posting by the National Gay and Lesbian Task Force.

Botzer married her longtime lesbian partner a few years later.

AFTER THE PASSAGE of marriage equality, and a presumption the biggest battle had been won, it seemed a tipping point had been reached. Whether Barack Obama was a Jedi knight or weather vane on LGBTQ issues, he was more supportive of the community than any president in U.S. history.

While Congress and the Supreme Court did their parts—such as passing a federal hate crime law protecting LGBTQ people and ending federal and state bans on same-sex marriage—Obama filled in gaps. He signed executive orders prohibiting federal contractors from discriminating against LGBTQ people. He lifted the military's rules prohibiting trans people from openly serving. He was the first president to mention trans people in a State of the Union speech.

"That was quite a big deal," Botzer says. "So, yeah, we didn't get everything we wanted, for sure. But it was still worth all the fight."

Trans men and women became more visible. And in what some see as a cultural breakthrough akin to Ellen DeGeneres coming out on TV, Amy Schneider streamed and beamed into millions of middle-American homes as a mega champ on *Jeopardy!* with a winning streak spanning from November 2021 into the new year. The Ohio native in pearls was "just an appealingly wonky, nerdy know-it-all kicking butt on a game show, who seemed like a really nice person," said Susan Stryker, author of *Transgender History*.

But more visibility incited hostility. Of course, it wasn't all won, particularly for trans people. Conservatives targeted them as a small and vulnerable population they could score points off.

The opposition has grown more sophisticated, Botzer says. Instead of vile epithets and spittle, trans people now face book-length arguments supported by right-wing think tanks, such as the Heritage Foundation, a Washington, D.C., mainstay.

Schneider's success unfolded against the worst year on record in terms of anti-LGBTQ legislation in many parts of the country. By early 2022, a flood of nearly 200 state bills sought to restrict or erode LGBTQ rights, mainly for trans youth. They fell into three chief categories: banning gender-affirming medical care for teens; blocking classroom discussions, curriculum and library books about LGBTQ issues, and barring trans youth from competing in sports.

After her run as *Jeopardy!* champ, Amy Schneider (right) was grand marshal at San Francisco's Pride parade, threw out the first pitch at a Giants game, and married her girlfriend, Genevieve Davis (left). *Amy Schneider*

Critics said the crusade was political opportunism and transphobia in the guise of "protecting children"—a catchphrase and strategy used decades earlier to motivate homophobic voters.

Utah Governor Spencer Cox stood up against a bill that would ban all trans girls from competing in school sports. Cox, a Republican in a deeply conservative state, vetoed the bill. He cited five statistics: 75,000 Utah kids participated in high school sports; 4 of them were trans; only 1 was playing girls' sports; 86 percent of trans youth nationally reported suicidality; 56 percent have attempted suicide.

Decades ago, Botzer put Ingersoll Center business cards inside Seattle library books that had to do with sex and gender as a form of outreach. She became co-chair of the Washington LGBTQ Commission after it was created in 2019. *Washington State LGBTQ Commission*

Utah lawmakers overrode his veto and their bill became law.

While Botzer feels positive about her home state of Washington's protections and advances, she knows there's always a need for vigilance. And she is not the retiring type. She was part of newly elected Seattle Mayor Bruce Harrell's transition team. She is co-leader of the state 15-member LGBTQ Commission. Because the pandemic led commissioners to meet remotely, she said the group still felt new, two years after its creation.

"All these advances, the positive laws and policies, the healthcare access wins, the support for individuals and families, all these were hard won and required years of work. This process is the real and often unseen heart of all the change we have made. This work is what I cherish the most. It is done by many, together, and it is what brings a better life for everyone."

For most of its existence, Ingersoll solely relied on volunteers. It now has paid staff members, and a support-group meeting streak that survived the pandemic and is approaching 2,600 consecutive weeks.

After thousands of hours in meetings, decades in founding and supporting organizations, untold conflicts and joys, Botzer still says there is no better way to spend your heartbeats than by helping others.

"I love good people. I want to meet more of them and work with them. Together. Not singly. Together. That gives me such joy when we create something together. Whatever it is. Those moments are everything."

Bob Young

JEFF HEDGEPETH & JOHN MEDLIN

THEY COULDN'T WAIT.

Jeff Hedgepeth and John Medlin didn't want to wait any longer to make the most traditional of commitments. And they wouldn't wait for Americans to legalize marriage equality as a capstone to their 27-year "engagement." In 2003, Hedgepeth and Medlin drove three hours north and seized the opportunity to get married in Canada. They made the front page of the *Seattle Post-Intelligencer*. They were one of the first U.S. same-sex couples to take advantage of British Columbia's trailblazing stance on marriage equality—which would influence the U.S. in time. Their noon ceremony in Vancouver's Stanley Park was witnessed by their good friends, Brad and Dennis. It was pure coincidence, Hedgepeth says, that the two couples wore summery white shirts and trousers. Three of the four had shaved heads. "It looked like John had been captured by bald space aliens," he jokes.

In Seattle, John worked in Special Collections for the University of Washington Libraries; Jeff was an administrator at the UW Business School until he left in 2000 for the Pride Foundation. As Pride's grants coordinator, Jeff often acted as an ambassador—a recurring role for him—in the five states where he doled out funds to LGBTQ groups. Much of the money was available because of a record-bequest from one of Microsoft's first employees, Ric Weiland, and it fed the grassroots on the path to Washington marriage equality in 2012.

Jeff and John seem a case of opposites attracting. Jeff is a New York City native, African American and an extrovert who often rode with the painted, naked bicyclists in Seattle's quirky Solstice Parade. John hails from Georgia. He grew up in whites-only public schools, segregated by state law. In a sly drawl, he identifies as a "practicing introvert."

A week before the couple celebrated 46 years together, their devotion was

Facing page: Jeff Hedgepeth and John Medlin, with Fudge, back at the Vancouver Hotel where they stayed for their historic 2003 wedding. *Jeff Hedgepeth*

Marriages like Jeff and John's panicked U.S. conservatives. The next year GOP strategist Karl Rove orchestrated state constitutional bans on same-sex marriage in 11 states. *MOHAI, Seattle Post-Intelligencer Collection*

obvious as they sat on the patio of their Seattle high-rise, where Jeff expertly tends to the community garden and befriends blue jays. John keeps a watchful eye on Fudge, their dachshund-terrier mix—20 muscular pounds of squirrel-obsession.

Jeff says care and respect are key to the couple's longevity. He's not a church-goer; but John is. So, Jeff fashions cuts from his garden for Sunday floral arrangements in John's church. He feels "very much a part of that community because they have welcomed me."

"And they leave him alone," John deadpans. "They don't nag him, 'Why don't you ever come to church?'"

In the give-and-take that sustains couples, Jeff notes that he used to run marathons and John "hates running." But John would soldier on for Jeff's marathons and wait at assigned corners to take the sweaty clothing Jeff wanted to shed. "When the soggy T-shirt fell in my face, I knew my duty was over," John says.

He once went above and beyond. He stood near the finish line and handed Jeff a cigarette and a plastic martini glass filled with paper olives.

HEDGEPETH AND MEDLIN met just after America celebrated its 200th birthday in 1976, and just before Jeff's 24th birthday. It was seven years after the Stonewall riots in Greenwich Village birthed the gay liberation movement. Both Jeff and John lived in Manhattan's Upper West Side. On a Sunday at the start of August they both went to nearby Central Park, and an area popular for sunbath-

Jeff's mother was a trained beautician but his father was opposed to her working outside the house. *Jeff Hedgepeth*

ing and gay meetups called The Ramble. John was "just plain" struck by Jeff's looks. But he couldn't catch his eye. Finally, the introvert walked over and asked to borrow a section of Jeff's *New York Times*. Over the crossword puzzle, a life together started.

Jeffrey Donald Hedgepeth was born in New York's Brooklyn Jewish Hospital. "And yes, I am cut," he says, laughing. He was raised in what he calls a "slum" building in a "Jewish-Italian-Caribbean-Southern Black-Puerto Rican neighborhood." When he was 10, a fire gutted the building and his family moved to a nicer apartment nearby. His parents' roots were in North Carolina. His father worked in New York's garment district and seemed, in his son's recollection, well-liked at his job. His mom was a beautician who later worked as a teacher's assistant and school-bus driver when they moved back to North Carolina in 1974.

Many of his Brooklyn school friends were Jewish and he recalls his mother telling him to be extra careful at their homes because they had "really expensive lamps and if you break one, we'll never be able to afford a replacement."

Hedgepeth saw the country's stark divide growing up. When a school year ended in Brooklyn—where his grades would propel him to advanced classes—he spent summers at his grandparents' farm in North Carolina, close to where the coastal sandy soil meets the Piedmont red clay. He learned to fish, pick cotton and tobacco,

Jeff visited his grandparents' farm near Rocky Mount, North Carolina every summer. He learned how to fish and wring a chicken's neck for dinner. *Jeff Hedgepeth*

make lye soap, and wring a chicken's neck for dinner. He also learned that Southern whites treated Black people differently.

Jim Crow laws were in his face. Blacks were not allowed to drink from white

John's childhood with his parents was like a "domestic sitcom" written by Tennessee Williams. *John Medlin*

fountains, or use the same restrooms as whites.

John McRae Medlin was born in Rome, Georgia, about an hour's drive northwest of Atlanta nowadays. It was a two-hour car trip back when his father made the daily commute to his job at as a state teacher certification specialist. His mother was a housewife, occasionally a secretary. When John was seven, the family moved to Atlanta. He doesn't recall seeing or hearing racial hostility when young, only being told to be nice to "colored people."

"I just grew up, I guess, thinking Black people were some kind of lesser category of people we had very little to do with."

Life in Atlanta was sort of like a sitcom, he says, "although my parents' marriage was not that happy. More like a domestic sitcom by Tennessee Williams."

MEDLIN SAYS he first felt an inkling he was gay at 13 or 14. While other boys would get excited if a girl's skirt blew up in the breeze, "it just occurred to me that I kind of feel that way when some football player takes his shirt off." His public school of 2,500 students was friendly, he says, and he doesn't recall any bullying. But he became an introvert around that time. He didn't want people to find out he was gay and "the best way was just to be quiet."

In New York, meanwhile, Hedgepeth who had been a sickly child with asthma, grew into a healthy teen "with a vengeance," jumping into sports and adventure, including sexual discoveries.

He also showed flashes of activism at Wingate High School. When the school prohibited girls from wearing pants, Hedgepeth and a few

Jeff played a "hippie" in his senior-class production. Other alumni of Brooklyn's Wingate High School include: U.S. Senator Barbara Boxer, Studio 54 owner Steve Rubell, and pioneering female rapper MC Lyte. *Jeff Hedgepeth*

SCRIBBLER
"Georgia's Finest High School Newspaper"
North Fulton High School
Atlanta, Georgia

SCRIBBLER STAFF, from left to right: Barbara Smith, Danny Raubani, Buddy Ballenger, Dianne Raymo, Peggy Melcher, Winston Blumberg, John Medlin, Carey Barnes, Linda Southerland, Carter Smith, Dana Palmer, Miss Connell, and Donna Demeree.

Although an introvert, John (center) was the editor of his high-school yearbook. He later edited a business magazine, *Administrative Management. John Medlin*

boys donned skirts in a demonstration of solidarity.

When the Class of '69 put on a production for parents called "Sing," they chose a musical with a heavy message. (*Hair* was nearing the end of its four-year Broadway run.) On one side of the stage were hippies, including Jeff, and all they wanted was love. On the other side were businessmen who just wanted money.

"And bringing them all together was a hooker, because she got them both," he recalls. "The whole production was about this!"

Graduating near the top of his class, Hedgepeth was accepted at Harvard and other Ivy League universities. He let his younger brother, then six years old, pick the winner out of a hat. He chose Princeton. He majored in political science and joined the Gay Alliance of Princeton. He wrote his senior thesis on repression of homosexuality.

He wasn't sure what to do upon graduating in 1973. He wasn't really aware of the possibilities, but had to work. He was accepted in a corporate training program at Sears, Roebuck,

Jeff's Princeton thesis on repression of homosexuality was hardly ground-breaking research, but he was proud he was bold enough to write about it. *Bayard Rustin Center for Social Justice*

the nation's largest retailer. But wearing a suit and tie to scale a corporate ladder "wasn't the true me."

Medlin, after high school, went to the University of North Carolina, where he majored in English. He and two of his friends "were doing a lot of gay stuff without admitting we were gay—even to each other," he recalls. Students on the second floor of his dorm, Joyner, tended to stay there for all their undergraduate years at UNC, making it a family-like place. "And the other guys in the dorm seemed to think we were just sort of clownish and silly."

John and his friends went to a bar, the Tempo Room, in Chapel Hill which was known for being half-and-half. "You went to the bar, but you always knew which half of the bar you preferred—the straight or the queer side," he says.

After college, he lived in New York City with one of his best college friends. John became an associate editor at a business magazine, *Administrative Management.*

The mix of gays and straights in Chapel Hill's Tempo Room provided a space for curious or uncertain people to "experience a gay environment without necessarily claiming a gay identity." *Digital North Carolina*

Then his father died, and John went back to Atlanta to stay with his grandfather. He got a master's degree in education and a teaching certificate. He was hired by a local school, which he soon realized was a "seg academy," a private school intended to skirt racial integration laws. He left to work for an adult literacy program.

One of his most memorable students was Jack, a towering Black welder who wanted to learn to read for his church. Jack and his wife had seven children, and Jack's job, along with his family duties, and need to sleep made it hard for him to study. But he persevered. And he eventually did his reading at church. Slight, white Medlin attended, alongside Jack's wife and kids. "And the congregation of people sort of stared at me because we looked so different. I just said, 'Actually we're twins.'"

MEDLIN HEADED back to New York. After meeting Hedgepeth, the two reveled in the camp and louche spirit of the late 1970s, hauling friends to see an off-Broadway version of "Women Behind Bars," starring Divine, the cult drag queen. But the city that never sleeps was losing its sparkle, if not puking on its shoes. The treasury of America's greatest metropolis teetered on bankruptcy; it was as much a spiritual crisis as a fiscal one.

The whole city seemed to be wobbling on a skyscraper ledge. The subways were dirty and untrustworthy. "You'd go to the post office to get a package and if they couldn't find it, they'd come back and yell at you," Hedgepeth recalls.

He and John were ready for a new adventure. They made a scouting trip to

Jeff and John made their first trip to Key West on Air Sunshine, which delivered on its name. Stepping on to the tarmac, they could smell frangipani blossoms in the warm breeze. *Airhistory.net*

Key West. They stepped off an Air Sunshine flight ("The Florida Keys' Own Airline") directly on to the tarmac. "And we could smell frangipani blossoms," Jeff says, "and in New York it was so cold and nasty."

They eased right in to Key West's lifestyle. Jeff got a job at the county assessor's office converting paper archives to computer records. The manager doing the hiring was impressed by his Princeton degree. He got John hired on to the same project. Locals were astonished. They told the couple they had rarely, if ever, seen out-of-towners have such good fortune with civil service jobs, which tended to be held by longtime Cuban residents. Jeff and John quickly found themselves in the midst of Cuban culture, embraced by grannies at work who took them to restaurants, and gave them recipes for *ropa vieja*.

They bought a little house. But it wasn't long before they were staring at the prospects for sustainable living in Key West: open a business catering to tourists—which they didn't want to do—or be artists, which they lacked the talent for.

Key West had its charms. And they occasionally saw Tennessee Williams in a supermarket. But they were bored. And Jeff was wary of becoming a lifer there, like some former New York friends. "I'd go for a walk in the morning and it would be 11 o'clock and they'd be mixing Martinis. And I was, 'God, we've got to get out of here.'"

THEY SET OUT to see America in what John calls the "Better Homes and Gardens" version of a van. Jeff had built a sleeping pad and places to store coolers and a hibachi, on which he grilled duck and other dinner treats. After getting drenched by "freakish" summer rain in Seattle, they drove south. While crossing the Columbia River, the sun came out. "And everything felt good," Jeff says. "We got great hotels. People were wonderful." They settled in Northeast Portland's Hollywood neighborhood, and then at the base of the West Hills. John taught adult basic education. Jeff studied a passion, landscaping (his gardening talents would later be spotlighted in *The*

After Key West, John and Jeff spent the 1980s living in Portland, which they found a bit uncultured for their tastes. *Jeff Hedgepeth*

Seattle Times and a national publication), before landing at Lewis & Clark College as an assistant director for career planning. He stayed for 10 years, becoming the assistant dean of students.

But Portland in the 1980s was hardly a billboard for big-city culture. Jeff and John missed a good symphony and diversity. "I'm not a person who needs to be surrounded by Black people," Jeff says of Portland. "But we'd go downtown some days and we'd sit in a restaurant and look out the window and just wait to count the number of people of color we saw go by."

They had great friends, and were involved in the Rose City's LGBTQ community, through pride marches, and organizations such as Brother to Brother, the Gay Games, and Front Runners, a walking and running group. "And it seems we were always volunteering for something," Jeff says. "At work, I was one of the faculty advisers for the queer student group."

But they found themselves traveling to Seattle and Vancouver, B.C., for amenities Portland was then lacking. "Vancouver was always attractive to us," John says.

THEY RELOCATED to Seattle in 1990 and found more cosmopolitan culture, cuisine and gardening centers. They were quickly immersed in the community, joining a gay reading group, volunteering at theaters, and more. Jeff pitched in on the campaign for Cal Anderson, the state's first openly gay legislator. John worked the next 17 years for UW Libraries. Jeff spent a decade at the UW, most of it as associate director of the undergraduate program at the School of Business Administration. He also ran a program geared at attracting and graduating students from disadvantaged backgrounds.

Jeff, then 48, took a leap from the comfortable college environment for a job at Pride Foundation. The Seattle-based philanthropic nonprofit supported the LGBTQ community with grants, scholarships, and leadership programs. Founded amid the AIDs crisis in 1985, Pride had originally focused on grants in Seattle with a smattering in Portland and Anchorage. By the time Jeff arrived, assistance and networks had expanded to Alaska, Idaho, Montana, Oregon and Washington, funding both urban and rural groups. Regional outreach coordinator, Kevan Gardner, was based in Spokane.

"I land in this job," Jeff says, "and lo and behold, I start traveling to all these places running local grant reviews and supporting Kevan in his organizing work."

He had gotten involved with Pride through donor events. "I was just impressed by the breadth of what they were doing. I was completely impressed by

Audrey Haberman," he says of the foundation's former executive director.

Soon, he made national news. Walmart, then the nation's largest private employer, expanded its anti-discrimination policy to protect gay and lesbian employees. It was July 2, 2003. The Walmart news was broken by the Pride Foundation, which had invested in the company for two years so it could challenge its workplace policy as shareholders. As investors, Pride had already successfully pressured General Electric and McDonald's to offer protections for gays and lesbians.

Hedgepeth went to the office on the day of the Walmart news, sensing it would be hectic and likely historic. "We did our best to field the telephone calls and answer questions from media all over the country," he says. "It was wild."

AP photographer Elaine Thompson stopped by and snapped a picture of Hedgepeth, his Pride colleague Sara Elward, and board member Marsha Botzer. The trio were memorialized coast-to-coast in an image of Botzer displaying Walmart's letter. It even appeared in Medlin's hometown newspaper, the *Rome News-Tribune*.

Hedgepeth played a small role in Pride's "shareholder activism push." It was led by board members Botzer and Ric Weiland and Executive Director Audrey Haberman, he says.

Audrey Haberman, center, together with Marsha Botzer and Ric Weiland, were leaders of the Pride Foundation's "shareholder activism" that pressured major corporations to adopt discrimination protections for gay and lesbian employees. *Philanthropy NW*

When Paul Allen and Bill Gates started Microsoft in New Mexico, Ric Weiland, center, joined them as the company's general manager. He drove a red Corvette around Albuquerque with the license plate, "Yes I am." *Lakeside School*

Weiland helped pioneer the strategy in the LGTBQ community. Employee number-two at Microsoft, he was high school chums with Bill Gates and Paul Allen. When the duo started Microsoft a few years later in New Mexico, Weiland joined them as the company's general manager.

Haberman recalled how Weiland challenged a corporate giant in 1999. Weiland, "who was not a big public speaker," traveled to General Electric's corporate headquarters and stood up in front of some 2,000 people gathered for a shareholders' meeting. "He ex-

plained how adding sexual orientation to the company's anti-discrimination policy would help GE retain employees."

Weiland contrasted the values of GE and Microsoft. "From the beginning
there was no secret about my sexual orientation, because Bill Gates and Paul Allen
had known me for a number of years already," he said. "Luckily for me, I knew
what they were interested in was the quality of my work, not whether I dated
someone of the same sex."

WEILAND WENT ON to make what was then the single largest donation to the
LGBTQ community—a $65 million bequest after his death in 2006. Of that, $19
million went to the Pride Foundation, increasing its endowment from $3 million
to $22 million. It was a transformative boost for the nonprofit. It helped stretch
Pride's work in five states, seeding and nurturing local groups and leaders. Weiland gave to 10 other LGBTQ groups, includ-
ing Lambda Legal, a leader in courtroom
battles for marriage equality. A Lambda executive called Weiland the most consequential donor in the organization's history.

Known as "Grumpy Santa" and "The governor of Capitol Hill," George Bakan ran the
Seattle Gay News from 1982 until he died at
his desk in 2020. He was one of the most influential gay people in Seattle's history. *Flickr.
com/sea turtle*

"Ric was just a wonderful person. I still
mourn him every time I drive by his old
house," Hedgepeth says. Weiland's gift lifted the very idea of LGBTQ philanthropy.
"Ric's imprimatur was a beacon to others that
these organizations were top notch. So much
publicity enhanced the concept of LGBTQ
philanthropy in general."

In Hedgepeth's recollection, his work
coordinating grants was not directly related
to marriage equality. George Bakan, the famously blunt *Seattle Gay News* editor,
used to yell about the foundation sprinkling money around to PFLAG chapters
and lesbian drum corps "so they can order cookies." But when it was time for the
marriage campaign, Hedgepeth realized Pride had helped build networks that
came into play. "We knew who to go to in the community, who to talk to, to phone
bank."

LONG BEFORE that, Hedgepeth and Medlin had married in Canada. They were
on the leading edge of an emerging population that saw merit in a June 2003 ruling

by Ontario's highest court. It said same-sex couples were discriminated against by "traditional" laws. The British Columbia provincial government followed suit in July. On the 27th anniversary of their meeting in Central Park, Hedgepeth and Medlin planned to marry at noon in Vancouver.

Mike Frederickson, a close friend and former director of the National Lesbian and Gay Journalists Association, thought their wedding was newsworthy. He asked if he could recommend it to Seattle media. The *Seattle Post-Intelligencer* sent reporter Mike Lewis and photographer Gilbert Arias to cover the ceremony. Jeff and John figured their wedding story would be stuck somewhere inside the next day's edition of the *P-I*. They were wrong. It was on the front page above the fold. Friends could see their photo dominating newspaper boxes around Seattle. In keeping with the good vibes that seemed to follow the couple, they didn't hear any negative feedback.

They had a big party at their house the next week. The Very Reverend Robert Taylor, the openly gay dean of St. Mark's Episcopal Cathedral, blessed their rings. They were happy to see Ric Weiland among their guests.

At the time of their ceremony, it was unclear to Canadian officials how many Americans had made a similar trip. But it was apparent that U.S. leaders lagged behind their counterparts to the north. "I believe marriage is between a man and a woman," President George W. Bush insisted at a news conference the week that Hedgepeth and Medlin were married. Bush's political guru, Karl Rove, would launch an offensive in 2004, supporting constitutional bans on same-sex marriage in 11 states that year.

Canada had set off a panic among conservatives. Some believed when gay couples married in Canada and returned to the U.S. their legal unions would have to be accepted. Legal analysis wasn't so clear, but the U.S. Supreme Court's leading conservative jurist, Antonin Scalia, perceived a threat. "The court today pretends … that we need not fear judicial imposition of homosexual marriage, as has recently occurred in Canada," Scalia wrote. "Do not believe it."

New York activists organized the "Civil Marriage Trail," an overnight bus caravan that brought couples to Toronto for ceremonies. "After hundreds of couples had married in Canada," wrote journalist Sasha Issen-

Edie Windsor, left, won a 2013 U.S. Supreme Court case that overturned the Defense of Marriage Act. Sally Jewell, then U.S. Secretary of the Interior, posed with Windsor outside the Stonewall Inn, the first LGBTQ national monument. *Department of Interior*

berg, "the New York State attorney-general at the time, Eliot Spitzer, issued an opinion declaring that the state would recognize same-sex marriages from other jurisdictions even though New York did not allow gay and lesbian people to marry there. Among the beneficiaries of the new policy were Manhattanites Edith "Edie" Windsor and Thea Spyer, an elderly couple who married in Toronto in 2007 under the auspices of the Civil Marriage Trail."

Although New York considered Windsor and Spyer married, the federal government did not. Spyer died in 2009 and left her estate to her wife. But the IRS denied Windsor the spousal tax exemption that heterosexual couples enjoyed. Windsor "was hit with a $350,000 estate-tax bill that would never have been levied, as she liked to say, 'if Thea was Theo.' "

Windsor paid the IRS and sued the United States. The U.S. Supreme Court ruled in 2013 that her tax bill amounted to unconstitutional discrimination. The opinion struck down part of the Defense of Marriage Act and required the federal government to treat all couples equally without regard to sexual orientation, if their marriage was recognized in the states where they lived. Windsor's case set the stage for the nation's highest court to legalize same-sex marriage two years later.

MEANWHILE, LAWMAKERS in Washington state passed domestic partnership laws, from 2007 through 2009, that conferred many legal benefits of marriage

John and Jeff were at the Capitol in 2012 to cheer Gov. Gregoire's signing of a marriage-equality law. *The Seattle Times* quoted Jeff saying, "I definitely see us as a 'Till Death Do Us Part' couple." *Jeff Hedgepeth*

to same-sex couples. Until then, despite their Canadian ceremony, Hedgepeth and Medlin didn't have the same rights as married heterosexuals, such as hospital visitations and care decisions in emergencies. Jeff and John were early to register as partners.

They were at the Capitol on February 13, 2012 to witness the next triumphant advance. The state's lawmakers had passed a bill approving marriage equality. An overflow crowd packed into the bill-signing room and spilled into the hallway to see Governor Chris

Gregoire make it official. John and Jeff squeezed in to hear the chants of "Thank you! Thank you!" when Gregoire entered the room. Jeff was quoted in *The Seattle*

Times saying, "I definitely see us as a 'Till Death Do Us Part' couple."

Despite the celebration, Jeff and John knew Christian conservatives would likely file an initiative to overturn the law. And they did so within hours of Gregoire's bill-signing. With the marriage movement gaining momentum, LGBTQ activists had already begun using sophisticated research to craft new strategies, messages, and fundraising. Jeff was in meetings where activists planned the all-important pivot from talking about hospital visits and burial plots to campaigning on love and commitment. The debate was shifted from the head to the heart.

Jeff and John didn't see a need to get hitched again after Washington legalized marriage equality in 2012. They had so many weddings of friends to attend that Jeff sharpened his "Rainbow Cake" baking. *Jeff Hedgepeth*

The new tactics helped defeat a statewide ballot measure by Christian conservatives. Hedgepeth and Medlin saw no need to get remarried in Washington when it legalized equality in 2012. "If you met a heterosexual couple married in B.C.," Hedgepeth says, "would you expect them to get married again if they moved to Washington?"

They had plenty of weddings to attend. Their friends were married at Buddhist weddings, country club weddings, drag-queen dominated weddings, and more. They were also happy to get on a contact list to witness, and take pictures, for other couples who came from out-of-state to take advantage of Washington's law.

FOR ALL the joy that 2012 brought the LGBTQ community, Hedgepeth was struggling. Haberman, the Pride executive who helped make his time at the foundation "magical," left for another job in philanthropy. He didn't jell as well with new leaders. What's more, "my father was dying a really horrible, scary dementia death," he says, and he was shuttling across the country and on the phone constantly trying to help his family.

The tail end of the year was rewarding "because suddenly there was marriage, and all the work we had done had come to fruition, and we had been through this long campaign."

But he felt exhausted. Burned out. "My father died about a week and a half before election day. So, I ran home for the funeral." The reverend for the service in North Carolina saw in Thurman Hedgepeth's biography that he had a son in Seattle with a husband. He took the opportunity to launch an "anti-homosexual 101 through 501" screed. Jeff was tempted to drop a New York City tirade on the guy. "But I just stared a hole into that man's head until he couldn't look at me."

He hurried back to Seattle for election day. "And I just never recovered," he says. In early 2013, John told him, "I'd rather be a little more poor than for you to come home in a body bag."

Jeff chokes up at the memory.

"And that's what my relationship with this man is. We support each other. Sometimes— the really hard times—you say, 'Oh my god, I've got this person in my life who's amazing.' "

He decided to take a step back for his

Jeff on his role as a gay-ambassador: "I do have an open personality. I don't threaten people. And I'm curious about people." *Jeff Hedgepeth*

health. He left Pride. He mainly joined John in retirement. He took a short post with the Gay City Health Project, helping introduce Obamacare to the LGBTQ community in King County. He also did some seasonal work at his favorite garden center, and for the last five years, has been a freshman application reviewer for the UW.

Jeff sees his legacy as that of an ambassador, going back to Princeton, and how he'd visit nearby high schools to talk about sexual orientation. "This whole ambassadorial thing really kind of revved up," he says, when he was at Pride Foundation, which did not believe it could accomplish all its goals in a big city. "I often found myself out in rural Idaho talking to people that were not expecting a Black gay man to come to Idaho to talk about queer rights."

The opposites began merging over time. Jeff used to listen to only rock music; John was all-classical. Jeff came to love opera. John developed a taste for classic rock. They both love watching football. *Jeff Hedgepeth*

Jeff and John also put themselves out there at events such as the 50th reunion of John's all-white high school class. They were the only openly gay people there. And Jeff was the only Black person except for servers and bartenders at the

Even if they'd be poorer, John wanted Jeff to retire from Pride Foundation for his health. "And that's what my relationship with his man is," Jeff says, choking up. "We support each other." *Jeff Hedgepeth*

event. Although a recluse in high school, John had been the editor of the student newspaper, and had produced a 50th anniversary yearbook. "He was the most popular guy there," Jeff says, giving the couple ample opportunity to spread their good-vibe diplomacy.

"Even at the gym," Jeff says, "I think about the 60-year-old straight white guys that would stand around naked and talk to me about marriage and my husband. I think it's because I do have an open personality. I don't threaten people. And I'm curious about people.

"If there's some way that who I am, the real me, can be out there and help somebody else get used to being around the real me, then that's kind of what my goal is in life."

THROUGH THE years, the opposites began merging. Musically, John used to be all classical; Jeff, all rock and roll. Jeff came to like opera as much as John. John developed a taste for classic rock. They both love football.

For their 46th anniversary on August 1st, 2022, they planned an evening with old friends at a spendy Capitol Hill restaurant. They didn't like the table they got. They left and went across the street to a gay bar. "We had a blast sitting outside yakking, drinking and eating burgers and fried food," Jeff says. "The night couldn't have been better."

Two days later they celebrated his 70th birthday. They went to the very up-scale Canlis "for an astoundingly wonderful and expensive dinner," Jeff says. "A very young man was seated mid-meal alone next to us. We started a conversation. He asked me if John and I were more than friends. I said for way longer than he had been alive."

It turned out it was also the young man's birthday, his 26th, and his boyfriend had to work. He had decided to treat himself anyway.

"We wished him and his boyfriend a happy, long life together," Hedgepeth says. "He seemed pleased to meet two old, married geezers."

Bob Young

LAURIE JINKINS

STILL DISMANTLING BARRIERS

On a dank December day in 1954, the Democrats clinging to control of the Washington House of Representatives by the slenderest of margins, 50-49, assembled in a hotel ballroom to choose a new Speaker. "After three hours of wrangling, recessing and side-caucusing," they narrowly decided on John L. O'Brien, an ambitious accountant from South Seattle. The runner-up was Julia Butler Hansen, a force of nature from tiny Cathlamet along the Columbia. Some who were there said she lost by one vote on the first ballot. One thing's for sure: In 65 years, no woman had ever come so close. "Hopelessly disgusted with small-minded, conniving men," the future congresswoman wondered "just how long" it would take for a woman to win the gavel.

Another 65 years.

All four contenders for Speaker of the House in 2019 were women. Laurie Jinkins' victory, after only nine years in the Legislature, was a double first. The Tacoma Democrat is also a lesbian, "out and proud" to be a trailblazer.

Jinkins' dad, a large-animal veterinarian in Wisconsin for 35 years, liked to say, "Experience is always the best teacher, but sometimes the cost of tuition is high." In other words, No pain, no gain.

Dr. Jinkins' bright, tenacious daughter has been on the front lines of the see-saw battle for equal rights since the 1980s when she arrived in Tacoma to attend law school. The failure of a municipal nondiscrimination initiative in 1990 was a galling setback. When a vocal anti-gay movement metastasized from Oregon, Jinkins became a leader of Hands Off Washington, the first statewide LGBTQ organization. In 1994, it repelled two anti-gay ballot initiatives. Three years later, however, nearly 60 percent of the electorate rejected an initiative to prohibit discrimination against homosexuals. In 2006, the state's anti-discrimination law was finally amended to include "sexual orientation"—with a setback that summer

Facing page: Washington's first female Speaker of the House wields the gavel. *Legislative Support Services*

when the Washington Supreme Court narrowly upheld a ban on gay marriage. The Legislature responded by approving same-sex domestic partnerships. And, in 2012, marriage equality. "Success is measured in increments," Jinkins says. "And we're still dismantling barriers."

Now, as one of the most influential politicians in the Northwest, Laurie Jinkins knows she may face the fights of her life in the months and years to come. It may be necessary to erect barriers to protect rights codified by Washington voters. When the conservative majority on the United States Supreme Court overturned *Roe v. Wade*, which established abortion as a constitutional right, Justice Clarence Thomas declared that the court's landmark rulings on same-sex marriage, the right to engage in private sexual acts, and obtain contraceptives were also "demonstrably erroneous decisions."

"What Justice Thomas is saying is that he wants to control people's decisions about their own bodies," Jinkins says, "whether it's transgender people, other LGBTQ people, married or unmarried people who want to use contraceptives. It's all about controlling other people. The way they're doing it is by trying to say the Constitution should never be viewed as anything different than when it was written" 235 years ago.

Jinkins and Governor Jay Inslee, a fellow Democrat, note that Washington's abortion rights law, enacted by referendum in 1970, is unambiguous: "The state may not deny or interfere with a pregnant individual's right to choose to have an abortion prior to viability of the fetus, or to protect the pregnant individual's life or health."* As another layer of state's rights protection, Inslee and Jinkins want to enshrine that right in the state constitution through a constitutional amendment. But that would require two-thirds majorities in both chambers of the Legislature and ratification by the voters. At this writing, Democrats have a 58-40 majority in the House and a 29-20 majority in the Senate. Proponents would need 66 votes in the House, 33 in the Senate, to advance a constitutional amendment.

Written by Justice Samuel Alito, the Supreme Court's majority opinion overturning *Roe v. Wade* repeatedly emphasizes that the decision to abandon Roe poses no threat to other precedents hinging on a right to privacy. "Nothing in this opinion should be understood to cast doubt on precedents that do not concern abortion," Alito wrote. The court's three liberals warned, however, that "no one should be confident that this majority is done with its work."

Girded for battle, Jinkins told a pro-choice rally in Seattle that women in our neighboring state of Idaho and thousands of others from around the nation will

---

* Fifty-six percent of the electorate favored Referendum 20 in 1970. A revised abortion rights initiative was narrowly approved in 1991.

PRO-CHOICE RALLY AND PRESS CONFERENCE 5/3/22
REP. LAURIE JINKINS (D)

Jinkins at a pro-choice rally and press conference in Seattle in 2022 after the U.S. Supreme Court overturned *Roe v. Wade. TVW*

be fleeing states where abortion rights are being curtailed. And despite Washington's legacy as the first state to legalize abortion by popular vote, she said thousands of Washington women still lack access to abortion services.

No one could recall ever seeing her more forceful, more passionate. Jinkins jabbed the air with her right fist, declaring: "And as we have been for so long in this state, we'll be a beacon of light and of help, and of hope and of action for the women of this country." Then, paraphrasing an anthem by rocker Tom Petty, she vowed: "We won't back down! We won't get turned around. You can back us up to the gates of hell and we will not back down!"

The year ended with a landmark victory. On December 13, 2022, when President Biden signed into law legislation recognizing same-sex and interracial marriages, Jinkins was jubilant. Advancing marriage equality was one of her key goals when she decided to run for the Legislature in 2010. Two years later, that dream was achieved.

The legislative mandate signed into law by Governor Chris Gregoire was challenged at the ballot box by opponents of same-sex-marriage. On November 6, 2012, same-sex marriage was affirmed by nearly 54 percent of the electorate. Jinkins and other gay and lesbian rights activists worry nevertheless about a new, apparently rising tide of homophobia—and the fact that only 10 of the state's 39 counties backed marriage equality. King County's overwhelming support, 67 percent of 953,600 votes cast there, was decisive.

GIVEN LAURIE JINKINS' roots in rural Wisconsin, her rise as a national gay rights leader might seem improbable. But the oldest of Jack and Donna Jinkins' five lively kids—three daughters and two sons—was exceptional from early childhood. Born in 1964, Laurie was unfazed by risk-taking and immersed in current events, beginning in grade school. When she shared the news she had been elected Speaker, one of her sisters texted, "You always were the speaker of our house!!" Those two exclamation points speak volumes.

Jinkins as a 9-year-old member of the 4-H Club in Wisconsin. Her dad was a veterinarian. *Laurie Jinkins*

When people talk about Jinkins' dad and what he meant to the community, Lake Wobegon comes instantly to mind. If Garrison Keillor had met "Doc Jinkins" he might have had him ministering to the cows of his mythical hamlet—maybe as a Lutheran rather than a Methodist, but there'd be no mistaking the resemblance. Montfort, Wisconsin, and Lake Wobegon, Minnesota, "where all the women are strong, all the men are good-looking, and all the children are above average," could be interlocking pieces of the jigsaw puzzle of America's rural Midwest. Except Montfort is a real place, with about 700 humans and thousands of cows.

Montfort was so small that every kid—tall or short, clumsy or athletic, musical or tone-deaf—had to participate in everything. Otherwise, Laurie Jinkins says, there would be no teams, no class play or band. "So I got comfortable with trying things I didn't know if I could do, or didn't care about that much. And comfortable, too, with not being the best. Just being a team member. That was how I learned about community. Even if it wasn't the most important thing to you, if you wanted somebody to be able to do something that was important to them, you needed to help." In middle school, the girls on the softball team competed against their mothers because there were no other teams nearby. "It took us two years before we were able to beat our moms. But we stayed together through high school and ended up becoming a top-tier team." By then, she was one of the starters. "I was on every sports team. I was in the band, too, even though I never learned how to read music. They gave me a trombone, and I made sure to sit next to the best trombone player and do whatever she did. I did everything in high school: I partied hard. But I was a good student; I was a jock; I did drama stuff and forensics. I was president of my high school class for three years." There were 84 students in the Class of 1982 at Iowa-Grant High School.

Pat Raimer, a Village of Montfort trustee, is three years younger than Jinkins. He went to high school with her brother Chuck. Montfort is a tad bigger today than when they were growing up, Raimer says. Corporate farms are taking over. But Chuck Jinkins still operates Hardwood Farm, the spread his dad founded, and Montfort is still surrounded by "cornfields, cows and trout streams." Madison, the state capital is about 60 miles away. Montfort is now less sheltered, less close-knit than when Laurie and her sibs were growing up with a classic stay-at-home mom. Though Jinkins notes that she and a high-school girlfriend—both closeted—wore each other's class rings and had a noisy breakup in the gymnasium "in front of everybody," she couldn't believe no one suspected she was gay. If so, it might have raised a murmur or a few clucking tongues. Today, Raimer says, there are gay folks around town, and the attitude is "*Que sera, sera*—there's a lot of other things to worry about!"

"Montfort was a great place to grow up," Jinkins remembers. "But as I got to my teenage years, when it became clear to me that I was a lesbian, it got harder to be in such a small town."

Showing dairy cattle as a 9-year-old member of the 4-H Club did nothing to inspire an interest in becoming a veterinarian, perhaps as her dad's partner. "I thought about becoming a police officer; I thought about joining the military, which was a quick way to get out of a small town. But I was diagnosed as being a juvenile diabetic when I was 12. And that ended any thought of military service." Today, trim and fit at 58, Jinkins is in good health, thanks to advances in the treatment of diabetes and her enthusiasm for hiking. "But in my childhood days, treatment meant that you took one insulin injection a day and tested your urine. And you survived until your early 50s, with complications. That influenced how I thought about my life. Things were always a little bit urgent. I felt a need to get things done because I didn't think I'd have that long."

Jinkins was at the University of Wisconsin-Madison studying for a bachelor's degree in business administration when she came out as a lesbian. After receiving a master's degree in public health administration, she enrolled at the University of Puget Sound's Law School in the fall of 1987. Laura Wulf, her future wife, was a classmate. It was practically love at first sight. "I decided I would always live an out life," Jinkins remembers. "I felt like secrets had really kind of nearly destroyed me." Tacoma was a fresh start in a new place 2,000 miles from home.

The unfinished business was coming out to the folks back home. "I did a bunch of research before writing the letter," she remembers, laughing at herself. "That's very much me—to get books on how to come out to your parents! Laura and I were having a party at our house when my parents called. My dad talked to me for an hour about why insurance companies fail and all sorts of other things, and never mentioned the letter. I had never talked to my dad for more than 10 or 15 minutes on the phone. It was very clear to me that he was trying to say things were OK. He just did not want to discuss it. But my mom did say, 'We got your letter and things are fine.' Later, she said she never had any idea I was a lesbian."

After his retirement in 2002, Jack and Donna Jinkins built their dream house a few miles east in Dodgeville. Dr. Jinkins still drove back to Montfort several days a week to play cards with old friends at a gas station, arriving extra early "in anticipation of winning up to 28 cents in any given day," friends remember. He died at home at the age of 77 in 2020, nine months after Laurie became Speaker of the House. Asked about her relationship with her father, Jinkins had to pause for nearly a minute to clear the catch in her throat. "My mom told me, 'Oh my gosh, Laurie, I would have to tell him to stop bragging about you. Everywhere he went he would talk about you and what you had done.' Also, he would respond to my e-news and give me feedback. He was a Republican, but he bragged about having voted for Obama. My mom and her family were big FDR Democrats."

THE NEXT BIG QUESTION is "Why Tacoma?" When Jinkins decided to pursue a career in law, she realized that if she applied for and was accepted at her alma mater's law school, "I'd probably never leave Wisconsin. I decided to push myself to go somewhere else. It was scary—and exciting."

A college friend had traveled all over the country. "If you could live anywhere in America, where would it be?" Jinkins asked. "Puget Sound," her friend said without hesitation.

The photos "looked amazing"—sailboats on the Sound, book-ended by the Cascades and Olympics; cities with museums, cafes and energized people—including gays and lesbians. She applied to several Northwest law schools. "The admissions director at UPS was the nicest to me, so that's where I decided to go." She hitched a U-Haul trailer to her Ford Escort and headed west. "From my first week in Tacoma, with Mount Rainier looming majestically as I walked to the law school downtown, I knew I'd made the right decision."

By her third year at the University of Puget Sound, Jinkins was an active member of the school's Coalition for Diversity. She helped organize a sit-in and boycott of classes as part of a nationwide protest over the dearth of minorities and women on law school faculties. Of the 19 tenured faculty at the UPS Law School, only two were women—and one of those was a librarian, not a professor. Yet nearly half of the school's 825 students were women. Minority enrollment was 10 to 15 percent, but there were no people of color on the faculty, Jinkins noted. "In fact, this law school has a miserable record of converting women and minorities from tenure-track to actual tenure," Jinkins told reporters. "There are too many white males in the legal profession and in teaching. What we're really asking for is to end racism, sexism, classism and heterosexism at all law schools." That's a lot of "isms," but Jinkins was "young and eager to make a difference."

Jinkins on the day they raised the Pride Flag over the Tacoma Dome. *Laurie Jinkins*

Tacoma had an activist gay community and a progressive City Council. In the spring of 1989, it voted 7-2 to make it illegal to discriminate against LGBT people in housing, employment, public accommodations and business transactions. Opponents gathered enough signatures to place the issue on the general election ballot that November. Jinkins joined the Committee to Protect Tacoma Human Rights, a coalition of gays, feminists and trade union members. They organized a "Ban the bigots" rally when Lon Mabon, Oregon's militant gay rights opponent, arrived in town to stoke what he described as "a civil war of values."

More than 80 conservative church pastors and lay leaders from around Pierce County urged voters to overturn the civil rights ordinance. In response, several ministers from Tacoma's "mainline" congregations decried the tenor of the opposition, particularly the characterization of gay men as child molesters.

"We lost that election by 825 votes," Jinkins remembers ruefully. "I wasn't deeply involved in that campaign because I was immersed in law school. But the next year, after I graduated, I had more time. We convinced ourselves that the vote was so close because people were confused. A 'yes' vote would repeal the ordinance; a 'no' would uphold it. So we did a pro-active initiative, gathered signatures and put it back on the ballot in 1990. We thought, 'If we're clear with people and get it back on the ballot then we'll be good.' But we went from bad to worse: More than 70 percent of the voters opposed our anti-discrimination measure. That was really hard; really shocking. It was a devastating loss. I learned the importance of regrouping."

Jinkins, only 27, was soon elected chairwoman of the Tacoma Hate Crimes Task Force. When she spotlighted the harassment of 10 Black students at Puyallup High School as the tip of an iceberg, Tacoma's *Morning News Tribune* featured the city's "determined, quotable" new activist in a major Q&A. "There seems to be a great deal of complacency among people when it comes to hate crimes," columnist Art Popham observed. White supremacist and anti-gay movements were targeting the Northwest at a time when economic stresses and concerns about immigration were sowing division. "What price do we pay for people not being diligent?" he asked. Jinkins, in words that seem disquietingly prescient of America 30 years on, said: "I think we can see that the price we pay is having a very much less tolerant society. We're showing we're a much more divided nation than a united nation. And we really need to examine that. I think it goes to the core of everything this country is and aspires to be. And we need to be very careful to examine how tolerant or intolerant we are becoming in society. ...We need to make sure that we draw lines around people and include everyone instead of drawing lines between us."

Jinkins and her wife, Laura Wulf, pause for a selfie at a sporting event. *Laurie Jinkins*

AFTER PASSING the bar exam, Jinkins and her partner, Laura Wulf, joined the Washington Attorney General's Office. In lieu of marriage, the pair made a commitment to each other on February 6, 1989. Deputy Attorney General Mary Fairhurst, a future Washington Supreme Court justice, recruited both. The attorney general, Republican Ken Eikenberry, had the final say. The morning of Jinkins' interview, the *News Tribune* featured a story quoting her criticism of the mayor for not calling a meeting of the Hate Crimes Task Force. "We were getting calls from people saying they were coming to kill us," Jinkins remembers.

"The attorney general and I were having a nice conversation, when he opened a manila folder with my name on it. I saw the article from the paper and thought to myself, 'You're probably not getting this job!' *And I wanted it*. But Ken looked up and said, 'This is awful stuff! Are you OK?' I said I was. And he said, 'I'd like for you to work for me in this office.' I always have given Ken Eikenberry great credit for that. He had evolved from old-guard Republican thinking. He gave me my first fulltime job after law school, and I felt like I could be out. He knew I was a lesbian—an activist, no less—and he hired me. He got more doctrinaire when he ran for governor [in 1992], but he had a good heart."

In 1993, a new threat to the advancement of gay civil rights "oozed across the Columbia River to plant seeds of intolerance and hatred," as Charlie Brydon, a legendary LGBTQ activist from Seattle, put it.

Though 56 percent of Oregon's voters in 1992 had rejected Measure 9, which would have amended Oregon's constitution to declare homosexuality "abnormal, wrong, unnatural, and perverse," the Oregon Citizens Alliance led by Lon Mabon sprouted a Washington branch. Laurie Jinkins, her new friends, Anne Levinson, Jan Bianchi and Mona Mendoza, together with Charlie Brydon, Don Moreland, George Bakan and hundreds of other gay rights activists, mobilized to head off the OCA's advance. Washington Citizens for Fairness launched its campaign with a catchy name suggested by Levinson: "Hands Off Washington." The idea, Levinson explains, "was to say, 'Look, here are these outsiders trying to come into our state, telling you that you need to discriminate against your fellow Washingtonians. And we're not going to put up with that, right?' "

Levinson, an astute lawyer, had worked in the Seattle Mayor's Office alongside Cal Anderson, who in 1987 became the state's first openly gay legislator. Levinson remembers Jinkins as a political prodigy. As Hands Off Washington was ramping up, Jinkins taught her the importance of forming chapters because "you can't have people from Seattle telling everybody" what to do. "What works in Tacoma, or Spokane, or Humptulips" might not work elsewhere, Levinson says. "You've got to let the local people decide." Likely that was Jinkins remembering what was good for Madison probably wouldn't go over so well in Montfort.

Washington Citizens for Fairness had a nimble board of directors, with Jinkins representing Tacoma and its dedicated corps of gay rights supporters. Every chapter was given considerable leeway. "We did overarching things like logos, materials, talking points, and overall strategy," Levinson says. "We'd have statewide meetings by phone conference and some in person. But then we said, 'Whatever works best for your local community is what we want you to do.' "

Fast forward to the 2009 campaign to preserve Washington's new "every-

Laurie Jinkins with other marriage equality advocates in 2012 after Gov. Gregoire signed the same-sex marriage bill into law. From left: Margie Witt, Laurie Johnson, Jane Abbott Lightly, Pete-e Petersen, Rep. Jamie Pedersen, Rep. Jim Moeller, Jinkins, Diane Divelbess, Grethe Cammermeyer, Lynn Grotsky, Lisa Brodoff and Anne Levinson. *Laurie Jinkins*

thing but marriage" law. Levinson remembers having frequent debates with a member of the Knights of Columbus, a Catholic men's fraternity. "He would say things like 'You're responsible for the end of society as we know it.'" She and Jinkins contemplated wearing T-shirts that proudly proclaimed, 'I'm responsible for the end of society!' "

Jinkins laughs at that mischievous memory, quickly adding that "Hands Off was the most profound political experience" of her life so far. "My experience promoting LGBTQ rights defines everything else I do. I see analogies to every other thing I work on. My very best friends are still people like Anne Levinson and Mona Mendoza, who now lives in Hawaii. They became my mentors, together with Jan Bianchi, our state chairwoman, Charlie Brydon and George Bakan, the longtime editor of *Seattle Gay News*—sadly, all three now deceased. And let me tell you, we were all very different people! *Quite different people.* But that was a great experience to be around a table where you knew everyone was fighting for the same goals, yet with very different perspectives about how to get there. Mona was then the commissioner of the Spokane Human Rights Commission. She and I knew we needed people from outside of King County, so that was the genesis of what I told Anne when we talked strategy." Mendoza, an award-winning educator who described herself as a "feminist-Chicana-lesbian-activist," was "the first person who taught me about the interconnectedness of oppression," Jinkins says.

"She taught me why it was important to think about other racial communities. She really pressed me to see the truth. That was before email was big, so she and I wrote all these letters back and forth."

Hands Off Washington became an energized grass-roots coalition. "I think we were the first advocacy group that polled communities of color and BIPOC groups so we could get really reliable data," Jinkins says. "We raised enough money so we could drill down deep and determine what the Black community thought; what the Asian community thought."

In 1994, platoons of Hands Off "Bigot Busters" trailed their opponents and talked people out of signing petitions for two anti-gay initiatives. Neither gained enough signatures to qualify for the fall ballot. Hands Off was even more resourceful and resolute a year later, Jinkins remembers, thwarting two more anti-gay initiative campaigns. One aimed to counter state and local anti-discrimination ordinances and bar schools from teaching that homosexuality is an acceptable "lifestyle"; the other sought to ban adoption by gays and lesbians. "We have won this battle," if not the war, Jinkins told reporters. "The people of this state have seen the ugly face of discrimination and rejected it. …While we have a long way to go, we have come so very far. Washington is a warmer, safer place to be."

She was too optimistic.

Gay rights opponents vowed to take their case directly to the state Legislature—and to the halls of Congress in the other Washington. Battle lines were being drawn all over America. When Hawaii's Supreme Court ruled in 1993 that denying same-sex couples the right to marry violated equal-protection laws of the state's constitution, it kindled a national debate over gay marriage. The Republicans who controlled the U.S. House and Senate passed the Defense of Marriage Act in 1996. "Boxed in by his political opponents," Bill Clinton, the first president to champion gay rights, signed it into law. Washington Senator Patty Murray and a lot of other Democrats who also voted "yea" would soon strive to make amends.

In the middle of the DOMA debate, Cal Anderson died of non-Hodgkin's lymphoma, a complication of AIDS. Relentless and shrewd in his determination to pass a gay civil rights bill, Anderson also was no one-trick pony. He fought for low-income housing and gun control, forging alliances across the political aisle, Jinkins and others remember. That said, there was no denying that when a talented, collegial gay person joined the Legislature it "provided an example that we're not monsters," as Anderson put it.

Anderson was succeeded by his protégé, Ed Murray. The Legislature's second openly gay lawmaker strove to advance civil rights legislation while also making his mark as an all-around lawmaker, rising to Senate minority leader. Jinkins says she and Murray had "an incredibly complicated relationship," bound up in decisions over strategy.

WASHINGTON'S NEW GOVERNOR, Gary Locke vetoed a same-sex marriage ban passed by the Republican-controlled 1997 Legislature. Having thwarted attempts to advance anti-gay initiatives, Hands Off Washington believed the momentum was theirs.

Jinkins was president of Hands Off Washington when it spearheaded the drive to put an anti-discrimination initiative on the General Election ballot in 1997. A Hands Off survey of gays and lesbians in the Tacoma area found that more than two-thirds had experienced job discrimination. Initiative 677 emphasized, however, that the proposed law would not require employers to provide domestic partnership benefits, quotas or preferential treatment. Further, religious organizations and employers with less than eight employees would be exempt. Opponents said the initiative would force employers to adopt workplace rules "honoring and legitimizing homosexuality"—and "they still want your kids."

Murray strongly counseled Hands Off's leadership that the initiative was ill-timed. Cal Anderson had felt the same way about a counter-initiative strategy, according to Wayne Ehlers, a Speaker of the House in the 1980s. Ehlers had lobbied for Hands Off Washington and the Privacy Fund, the Seattle-based gay and lesbian political action committee Murray helped found. "Ed worried that if the initiative failed it would set back his legislative efforts to pass a gay civil rights bill," Ehlers says. "Carrying on for Cal, he felt he was getting closer. But if the initiative went down badly, which we predicted, we said politicians would be wary of supporting legislation their constituents had rejected at the polls."

"Our polling gave us optimism," Jinkins remembers. "It was in the low 80s that people thought it was wrong to fire someone for being gay. In fact, most thought it was already illegal. So our job was to inform people that it was still legal, and they should go with their values. It's also true that one of our problems was that the LGBT community really did not agree on whether we should do a pro-active initiative. By that time, Hands Off Washington was dominated by people who did not live in Seattle. King County already had anti-discrimination protections. So fund-raising suffered. I remember very distinctly feeling like I was Martin Luther King in the Birmingham Jail and having moderate ministers tell me that I was pushing too hard. And I was like, 'How dare you sit there when you have these rights and protections and lecture me that I should wait!?' So we got into a situation where our community was conflicted. I think we probably wouldn't have won anyway, but I just didn't realize how bad it was. The divisiveness the approach raised in my community is something I will always regret and hope never to repeat. That was a really good hard lesson."

I-677 was rejected by 59.66 percent of the voters.

"That year was like a 'tsunami of no,' " Jinkins says, shaking her head at the memory. "The NRA invested more than $2 million to fight a trigger-lock initiative. There was a medical marijuana initiative on that ballot. And another empowering dental hygienists. Every initiative lost.

"It became very clear nationally and locally that what changes people's minds forever on these topics is knowing someone personally who is LGBTQ. It becomes really evident that for queer people the most personal thing we will ever do becomes the most political thing we will ever do, which is coming out. And being out."

The ballot box whupping was followed by the Legislature's override of Governor Locke's second veto of the Defense of Marriage Act. Several Democrats helped ensure success of the override, fearing another gay rights initiative could energize conservative voters in swing districts. Jinkins was among those who now worried that back-to-back debacles at the ballot box could set back the movement for a decade. Friends and colleagues say her resilience is her strong suit. She has a shirt silk-screened with "Gotta give 'em hope," a Harvey Milk quote. "That's always what I go back to. I'm not good at all at either celebrating victory or staying in despair. I'm always about the next step. It has helped me in many roles in having that as my approach to the world."

When Jinkins laughs, which is often, it seems contagious. She is amused when someone, comfortable in her midst, remarks offhandedly that gay people now seem so, well, normal. "At the State Department of Health I worked with a guy and his wife at the very beginning of conversations about marriage equality," she remembers. "One day he came into my office and said, 'Listen, Laurie, the real issue people have about gay people is really about gay men having sex. People really don't like that. But here's what people don't get: Once you get married, people quit having sex! So everyone should be in favor of gay men getting married because then they wouldn't have to worry about men having sex anymore.' And I go, 'Well, Bob, I'm not married but I'd like to be, and I'm not sure what this says about your marriage!' I would always tease his wife that that was his argument for gay marriage."

FOR JINKINS, the next major political engagement was in 2001-2002 when the City of Tacoma adopted an anti-discrimination ordinance protecting LGBTQ people. Tacoma United for Fairness—"TUFF" for short— squared off with backers of Help Us Take Back Tacoma Again!, the group advocating repeal of the ordinances.

"We ran that campaign with national partners who were really aligned and dedicated to helping us," Jinkins recalls. "People were seeing that if they came out they were more accepted. National media was starting to cover more LGBTQ people. Ellen DeGeneres had come out in 1997 on national TV. All of those things played together.

"One of my more profound political experiences before I came to the Legislature was really Tacoma United for Fairness—in part because I'd been involved in the 1990 campaign that ended in disaster at the polls. So over a 12-year period I got to be part of remaking history. There's nothing like experiencing all that pain—remembering it and seeing the damage it did to people, and then to be able to coalesce people around the same issue 12 years later and remake our community and remake history. Tacoma in 2002 retained its anti-discrimination ordinance by a larger margin [59 percent] than any city in the history of the United States had ever done before."

The impediments LGBTQ people faced in the workplace and in denial of an array of legal rights came home in a profoundly personal way in 2001 with the arrival of Wulf Jinkins, a son for Laurie and Laura. Civil rights and same-sex domestic partnerships were still years away. "He's my biological son," Jinkins explains. "Laura gave birth to him and we had to adopt him to make it clear who his legal parents are."

Wulf Jinkins, Laurie and Laura's son, liked to sit in the governor's chair. *Laurie Jinkins*

Jinkins volunteered for Chris Gregoire's first campaign for attorney general, writing a briefing paper on the death penalty. She was active in every subsequent Gregoire campaign, including the historic 2004 governor's race. "The first time I ever testified on a bill in Olympia was alongside Chris when she pressed really hard for sexual orientation to be added to existing malicious harassment 'hate crime' laws," Jinkins says. "Then, when I was an assistant secretary at the Department Health, I disagreed with some of her policy decisions in my work area. My good friend Lyle Quasim, the agency's former secretary, told me, 'Listen, Laurie, there's three kinds of jobs in the world: there's sales, there's development, and there's when you do both. You've been doing both. Now the governor is telling you she's in development, and you're in sales. If you can't sell the things she's developed then you need to go. That was good advice. I was in my mid-30s. I learned to move on and not burn bridges."

Jinkins and Gregoire remain friends to this day.

"It's important to emphasize that Chris Gregoire touched every part of the advancement of the LGBTQ community," Jinkins says. "And when we got to the doorstep of marriage equality, I told her it was going to be an important part of her legacy, 'and I guarantee you you'll be so proud.' "

From the outside looking in, Jinkins had learned that "the Legislature transforms by increments. But we wouldn't transform at all if we didn't have people outside of us pushing for change and to protect rights."

She was adamant that Ed Murray's gay civil rights bill, stymied by the state Senate, was the crucial precursor to marriage equality. Jamie Pedersen, a gay lawyer poised to run for the Legislature, was working to advance same-sex marriage. "Every time we'd meet, I'd say, 'If you pass marriage equality you could get married, but then get fired from your job for getting married. We need anti-discrimination first.' So we had our own internal conflicts. But Jamie is a good friend who has taught me an incredible amount. He is an Eagle Scout from beginning to end."

THE BREAKTHROUGH for the gay civil rights bill came as the Legislature got under way in 2006. Senator Bill Finkbeiner of Kirkland, the former GOP minority leader, reversed his stand from the year before and crossed the aisle to vote with the Democrats.

That summer, the Washington Supreme Court's 5-4 decision to uphold the state Defense of Marriage Act revealed the justices were deeply conflicted. In a stinging dissent, Justice Bobbe Bridge, a former lobbyist for the Privacy Fund, blasted "the Legislature's blatant animosity toward gays and lesbians" and predicted the majority's ruling would be viewed by history as "a mistake born of bigotry and flawed legal reasoning."

Only a few more increments remained.

After co-chairing the victorious 2009 campaign for "everything but marriage"—when Washington became the first state in the nation to ratify domestic partnerships for same-sex couples—Jinkins talked herself into running for the

Legislature:

"I was 46, and hadn't been involved in party politics for a long time. I was very clear in the years preceding that I didn't want to be in a policy position because I'd done that in the executive branch. I understood that I'd have to care about things that didn't necessarily interest me. When you're an advocate you get to choose what you advocate for. But circumstances changed. I thought I had convinced my friend Dennis Flannigan not to retire from the Legislature. A few days later, he announced he would not seek re-election. So that shows how highly persuasive I can be! I really wasn't thinking of running at all. I had a great job as deputy director of the Tacoma-Pierce County Health Department, but I wasn't developing any new skills. I was using my old skills. I was getting asked to serve on boards I had served on 20 years earlier.

"The biggest thing, however, was that it was clear that the crucial debate over marriage equality was approaching. There'd never been an out lesbian serving in the Legislature. And I thought, 'I'll be damned if the lesbian community is not going to be represented.' That was never anything I ever said publicly, but every morning when I woke up, especially on mornings when it was raining, I'd think, 'I don't want to doorbell today!' Then I'd say to myself, 'Laurie, do you want to be the first out lesbian serving in the Legislature or don't you?' Then it was, 'OK, I guess I'll go out doorbelling!'

"I was excited about what I could do in terms of budgets, health care, education and all sorts of other important things. I was also a public-school mom and a longtime community college trustee. But for personal motivation, the thing that got me up every day was representing the lesbian community. That's the thing that kept me fundraising. I frequently tell candidates, 'You've got to find your 'why,' and the 'why' doesn't have to be something you tell everyone else. It's the thing that makes you do everything you need to do to win."

With Sam Reed in 2011. The secretary of state invited all the freshman legislators to his office to present them with cards certifying their election. *Laurie Jinkins*

In the fall of 2010, after a hard-fought campaign, she defeated Tacoma City Councilman Jake Fey, a fellow Democrat, for a

House seat from the 27th Legislative District.

Two years later, after Senator Mary Margaret Haugen, a centrist Democrat from Camano Island, announced she would cast the crucial 25th vote for gay marriage, Ed Murray and Jamie Pedersen's bill passed the Senate. A jubilant Gregoire signed it on the eve of Valentine's Day, 2012. Representative Jinkins was part of the cheering crowd. A Bremerton man shouting "Do not betray Christ!" was the lone protester.

Opponents secured enough signatures for a referendum.

Jinkins says the unsung heroes of the campaign to uphold marriage equality are the volunteers who staffed the phone-banks to get out the vote. "The average phone call lasted 18 minutes, largely because we were careful to ask questions in a neutral way," she says. "We'd say, 'Tell me what marriage means to you.' We wanted to engage people in real conversations. I was out in the community motivating people, recruiting, so I didn't get to make many calls. But many of the phone-bank people I talked with at our offices on Pacific Avenue in Tacoma were in tears because people they were talking to were crying, too. People disclosed incredibly intimate things about what their marriage meant to them—that they'd been divorced; why it happened; what it means to love and be loved. It was a very non-judgmental process. Frequently we never even brought up the referendum, or asked them how they were going to vote. Our job as phone bankers was to just get people thinking about what marriage meant to them—and to get people out of their stuck-spot. Because we knew if we could get them out of their stuck-spot they were moving our way. There were thousands of people all over Washington who were doing that. That's what made the difference."

That November, more than 53 percent of the voters endorsed gay marriage. The law took effect on Dec. 9. Jinkins and Wulf were married by their friend and mentor, Chief Justice Fairhurst, in front of 400 friends at Tacoma Union Station on July 20, 2013.

JINKINS' PROGRESSIVE legislative agenda included a capital gains tax to require the state's "wealthiest few to pay their fair share," paid family leave, and the nation's first program to help offset the staggering cost of long-term care.

She demonstrated early on that civility was one of her core values, praising J.T. Wilcox, the Republican floor leader, for his even-handedness. Serving on Appropriations and the Health Care and Wellness Committee, Jinkins became chairwoman of the Civil Rights and Judiciary Committee, heavily involved in mental health reforms.

When Frank Chopp, the state's longest-serving Speaker of the House, announced he would step down after the 2019 session, Jinkins felt she was ready. "As I got better and better at being a committee chair, I started to see myself as able to pull different levers and help make things happen," she says. "But I had not sat at the leadership table at all in a caucus where women were the majority—31 of 57 seats.* Our caucus had already decided that the next Speaker would be a woman."

With Speaker Frank Chopp. *Laurie Jinkins*

Jinkins was the senior member of the four women in the race. The others were June Robinson of Everett, Gael Tarleton of Seattle and Monica Stonier of Vancouver. "I don't know how it would have been had there been men in the mix," Jinkins says. "But all four of us were committed to showing that our caucus could have a competitive speaker's race, and that it would be OK whoever won. We're all friends. A few days before the vote, we all got calls from different members of the communications team asking what kind of press release we wanted to have on each of our candidacies. I called the other three and said, 'Can't we just agree on one press release, and a joint statement on whoever wins—congratulating the winner, and saying we stand with her?'

"None of us knew who was going to win. I thought I was a good vote-counter and that I had a good shot, but the extraordinary thing about the four women who ran for speaker is that it was going to be the same statement no matter who won. I respect each of them deeply. I don't know if I would have asked that had there been men in the race. I don't know if it would have worked."

Why did Jinkins win? "If you serve the caucus well you'll do well if you decide you want to try to become speaker," she says. "I chaired the highest-volume com-

---

* When Julia Butler Hansen ran for Speaker of the House in 1955, there were nine women in the entire Legislature, four Democrats and five Republicans—all in the House. In 2023, there are 36 female Democrats and 10 female Republicans in the House, and 14 female Democrats and six female Republicans in the State Senate, for a total of 66 female legislators.

mittee in the Legislature, so I really focused on moving other people's bills. It was an easy thing to do because I enjoyed it. The second thing was that I talked to people about what they wanted in a speaker. I was pretty clear that I wasn't Frank, and that there were other things that I wasn't. I probably talked to a third of the caucus before I decided to run. It helped me decide whether I wanted to run. But it also helped me shape the kind of speaker I wanted to be. In the end, I

Chief Justice Mary Fairhurst administers the oath of office to Speaker of the House Laurie Jinkins as Jinkins' spouse, Laura Wulf, and their son, Wulf Jinkins, look on in 2020. *Legislative Support Services*

won and those of us running also accomplished another goal: we had a competitive race and we all still work together very well."

Jinkins soon found herself dealing with the deadliest public-health crisis in more than a century; mask-mandate protests; moves to expel a Spokane Republican accused of "domestic terrorism," and a controversy over how the House releases investigative reports reviewing allegations of misconduct or inappropriate behavior by lawmakers. As news organizations pushed public-records requests, Jinkins said, "I may be equally or maybe more frustrated than you are." Admitting she had made "a huge mistake" in 2018 when she supported leadership's move to dilute the Public Records Act's impact on legislators, Jinkins said, "This place has a lot more inertia than I was actually prepared for. I want transparency and I also want complainants to be protected."

A year later, in the wake of the insurrection at the U.S. Capitol, Trump supporters converged on the Capitol Campus in Olympia and broke through security at the Governor's Mansion.

The 2022 Legislature got under way almost fully virtual, and adjourned 60 days later with more than half its members on the floor, albeit masked and mostly socially distant. Nevertheless, Jinkins says the lawmakers approved a $64 billion supplemental budget that includes investments in statewide transportation projects, K-12 education, pandemic recovery, and affordable housing, with $800 mil-

A congratulatory cake for the new speaker. *Laurie Jinkins*

lion in reserves. In response to the death of a fraternity pledge at Pullman, it also unanimously passed an anti-hazing bill that mirrors Jinkins' anti-bullying efforts decades earlier.

"There is virtually no one serving in the House who knows a speaker other than Frank Chopp, so everything I do is compared to him. He sets the standard, good and bad," Jinkins says. "And my guess is that he changed a lot over the 20 years he was speaker. I see myself learning and changing during my three years in this role. I now understand things he did that I didn't understand before. I sometimes find myself saying, 'I'm turning into Frank Chopp.' Especially when I stop to think, 'Oh, now I understand why he did this. It's not a bad idea after all.' There are lots of things he did that I'm going to keep, like establishing a Committee on Committees to appoint committee chairs and members. And, there are things that are changing, especially because we need to bring the way we work into the 21st century.

"But most of the time I'm just me, trying to put in practice all the things I've learned since I first came out and became an activist. I strive to keep learning. The minute I set foot in the House of Representatives, I knew it was my home. I knew there was no other place I ever wanted to serve. I've only ever run for one office. I just run for it over and over again until I get it perfect!" Jinkins says, laughing.

"There's no end to learning. The great thing about history is to evolve and learn—and always be learning. Never stop learning because it teaches you how to move the world forward."

You also learn that success is mostly measured in increments.

John C. Hughes

JAMIE PEDERSEN

OUTLAWS TO IN-LAWS:
"MY LIFE'S WORK FOR 17 YEARS"

Jamie Pedersen was a Puyallup kid who scooped fries at McDonald's before he went east to college. After graduating from Yale Law School, he took a well-worn path to Washington, D.C., to clerk for a federal judge. It was August 1994 and the humidity would lick your face and seep through your shirt in a walk from the Metro station to Judiciary Square.

In high school, Pedersen was the kind of boy moms liked to invite over for dinner. He was polite and neat. His parents were teachers. Then, he told his girl-friend he thought he might be gay. Her mom said if she talked to Pedersen, she'd get AIDS. He didn't come out to his parents until the day he graduated from law school.

Waiting in his new courthouse mail box was the case of Joseph Steffan, who had admitted he was gay just before his graduation from the U.S. Naval Academy. Steffan was an excellent midshipman. But the Navy immediately discharged him. In Pedersen's first week on the job, he was thrown into arguments with two other clerks and U.S. Court of Appeals Judge Stephen Williams about an early legal test for gay rights. Was saying you were gay protected free speech? Was implied conduct—sex with another man—enough to end the career of a promising Navy officer?

Shortly after Judge Williams sided with the Navy in his decision, Pedersen had a dinner with destiny. At a Dupont Circle restaurant, he met Evan Wolfson, a young lawyer and early evangelist for same-sex marriage. At the time, most activists saw marriage as a distant dream or a shimmering mirage. But Wolfson argued it was the issue, the one battle that mattered most. The LGBT community should go all-in, he urged. And from legal marriage, civil rights they had long been denied, would flow.

Across the restaurant table, Pedersen and Wolfson spent hours debating fine

Facing page: Jamie and Eric Pedersen with their sons, Leif, Erik, Trygve and Anders. *Jamie Pedersen*

points of law. Pedersen came away converted. "Marriage equality became my life's work for the next 17 years," he says.

He climbed fast. At 31, he became co-chair of the board at Lambda Legal, a national gay rights organization at the vanguard of landmark victories. Still, his journey would mirror the see-sawing struggle for gay rights. When he first got involved, a conservative backlash had swamped the movement. In 1996, the U.S. Congress adopted, in a wildly lopsided vote, the Defense of Marriage Act, or DOMA. Its purpose was to ban and squash the very idea of same-sex marriage. Bill Clinton, struggling to save his presidency from his own philandering, signed it into law.

"It was a low point," Pedersen recalls. More disappointment awaited, as new gains were often punctured by letdowns. Gay marriage and Lambda Legal, with Pedersen as co-counsel, won a breakthrough case in King County Superior Court in 2004—only to see the state Supreme Court sink hope two years later by reversing that ruling.

Encouraged by Ed Murray, the state's pre-eminent political advocate for gay rights, Pedersen was elected in 2006 to the state Legislature, representing central Seattle. He and Murray set out on an incremental strategy, with Murray running bills in the Senate, and Pedersen shepherding legislation in the House. They got three domestic partnership laws approved, and then their capstone, a marriage-equality statute signed by Governor Chris Gregoire.

Their strategy snowballed to justice in 2012, when conservatives tried to stop marriage equality at the ballot box. Using family values rhetoric, which had worked so well for their opponents, LGBTQ advocates concentrated their message in a single word. Love.

On election night, 2012, voters in Washington and two other states, approved—for the first time in U.S. history—marriage equality. On a sunny June day three years later, the U.S. Supreme Court followed, welcoming the entire country to the other side of the rainbow. It was a stunningly swift turnaround. No one—not even those who thought marriage equality was inevitable—had expected such a historic triumph.

And Pedersen's work wasn't done.

NEARING GRADUATION from Puyallup High School in 1986, ("We are Vikings, strong and free, '86 was meant to be.") Jamie Pedersen was still unsure about his sexual orientation. But he knew one thing for sure. He didn't want to go to a college where jocks were as revered as in Puyallup.

Puyallup High Debate Club in 1986. Jamie Pedersen is in the bottom row, second from right. Coach Craig Beetham is top right, with a mustache. *Puyallup High School*

It's not that the Pedersen family wasn't into athletics. His dad was a longtime junior-high coach. His sister lettered in sports throughout high school. And the family spent many wintry Tuesday and Friday nights inside warm gyms watching high-school hoops.

Jamie's competitive energy went into debating. Puyallup's debate team thrived under teacher Craig Beetham, who later became a successful Tacoma lawyer. Pedersen won awards for extemporaneous speaking.

But the Puyallup environment was not so welcoming for a student like Pedersen, who, given the option between taking shop or home economics, chose sewing, cooking and home ec. His female debate partner dared to date a girl. "She got outed," he says, "and the blowback was so furious and severe that she attempted suicide and ended up moving away for like a year."

Although he grew up in an idyllic setting, with a raspberry farm next door, he had been bullied. "I had a group of kids when I was in 8th grade at Edgemont Junior High School who would just harass the crap out of me. They would kind of lie in wait and call me 'faggot,' " he recalls.

When it came time for college, he aimed high, and applied only to out-of-state schools. Stanford sent him a booklet featuring football on its cover. No way, he thought. Yale sent a "lovely" brochure. He read it cover-to-cover. Yale didn't have fraternities; it impressed him as super-academic and public-service focused. "I was like, wow."

Jamie's great-grandparents, Elbert and Olianna Pedersen, lived in Pacific County, at the start of the 20th
century. *Jamie Pedersen*

At Yale, he was still torn by
his attraction to men and his belief
it was sinful. His high-school girl-
friend had sent him "three pages
of handwritten Bible verses about
how I was going to hell," he recalls.
A friend studying divinity was ap-
palled by his views. "And she made
it her personal project to take me to
lunch several times and explain to
me what modern biblical scholarship
had to say about gay and lesbian people," he says. Another friend, who
was gay, took him to see "My Beauti-
ful Laundrette" and other acclaimed films with gay central characters.

Still, he mostly dodged the question of his sexuality, while pursuing interests
such as singing with the celebrated Yale Russian Chorus. It wasn't until his first
year of law school that he dated a guy, an undergraduate, and came out. And it
wasn't until two years later that he told his parents. "I had tried a few times and
it didn't work out," he says. "They are, now, super-supportive and have been for
many years, but they did not take it very well at the time. Like not angry or whatever, but my mom cried, and I think mostly they were just really worried about
me."

HE CAME BACK to Seattle to work in corporate law at Preston, Gates and Ellis.
Evan Wolfson, the marriage-equality crusader, connected him to the Legal Marriage Alliance. Pedersen took on a project to identify all Washington laws that
treated couples differently depending on whether they were married or not. There
were hundreds of examples to catalog: Did you know rare sea-urchin fishing licenses could only be passed on to legal spouses if the license-holder died?

The research was done, in part, because Wolfson had won a case in Hawaii,
opening a legal door to same-sex marriage. It was 1996 and progress seemed possible. A terrible disease had played a part. "AIDS shattered the silence of gay people's lives," Wolfson said, and helped show that homosexuals "are rounded people
who love others, fight for loved ones, who grieve losses, and are harmed by exclusion or denial."

But conservatives responded with fervor. They launched the Defense of Marriage offensive, which was not about offering massages or candlelit dinners to stressed couples. Its purpose was to stop gay activists in their tracks. Instead, it stimulated a marriage-equality movement that few activists previously had any appetite for.

The next year brought more grim news. Washington still did not have a state law prohibiting discrimination on the basis of sexual orientation in employment and housing, despite the best efforts of Cal Anderson, who became the state's first openly gay legislator in 1987. A Vietnam War vet, Anderson had won medals as the lead court reporter on the My Lai massacre investigation. He was a genial and skilled lawmaker, respected by peers. But he did not pass gay rights before his 1995 death from AIDS.

President Clinton signed the Defense of Marriage Act in 1996, banning federal recognition of same-sex marriage. The only member of Washington's congressional delegation to oppose it was Jim McDermott. *Washington State Archives*

Frustrated activists over-reached by taking the issue to the electorate. Their anti-discrimination Initiative 677 landed on the 1997 ballot alongside a gun-control measure, "which turned out the gun people in droves," Pedersen says. I-677 won just 40 percent of the statewide vote. It even lost in King County, home to Seattle's vibrant LGBTQ community.

"Not only were we not getting marriage," Pedersen says, "but the voters had overwhelmingly rejected the civil rights bill, and the Republicans were in control. It was just a sad, sad state of affairs."

THE PENDULUM started to swing back. Steve Davis, an attorney at the firm that hired Pedersen, was on the board of directors at Lambda Legal, a national group pushing civil rights boundaries. Davis recruited Pedersen for the Lambda board. But a committee rejected his nomination. At 29, they thought he was too young and wouldn't be able to drum up donations. Davis urged persistence. Pedersen helped raise a record amount for a Lambda event in Seattle. His name was resubmitted for the board and accepted in October 1998. He soon became its co-leader.

In 2003, some states still had sodomy statutes that criminalized activities between homosexuals, including consenting adults, in the privacy of their bedrooms. Simply put, those laws made it illegal for gay people to have oral and anal sex. (Washington had repealed its sodomy law in 1975 in a bill signed by Republican Governor Dan Evans.)

Lambda brought a case to the U.S. Supreme Court involving a Texas couple. Responding to a noise complaint, Houston police entered John Lawrence's apartment. They found Lawrence and another adult, Tyron Garner, having sex. The two men were charged with a misdemeanor. Lambda lawyers appealed. Pedersen attended the oral arguments in Washington, D.C., sitting in the front row of the regal courtroom, where in 1986 five of the nine justices upheld a Georgia law, saying there was no Constitutional right to homosexual sodomy.

Lawrence v. Texas was decided by the nation's highest court on June 26, 2003. Justices in a rearranged court dropped a bombshell. Their 6-3 decision overturned the court's 1986 ruling. This time they found sodomy laws a breach of privacy rights guaranteed by the 14th Amendment's due process clause. Two newer justices— Stephen Breyer and David Souter made the difference—along with Sandra O'Connor who changed her view. Blast waves spread far and wide.

When Pedersen was term-limited off the Lambda Legal board, he helped create a new fundraising arm, Lambda's National Leadership Council, and led it for more than a decade. *Jamie Pedersen*

"It really became the foundation on which all the subsequent victories at the Supreme Court were built," Pedersen says.

Months later, the Supreme Judicial Court of Massachusetts held that excluding same-sex couples from marriage was discriminatory. The cause was revived. Pedersen and his future husband Eric Cochran, a high school teacher and assistant principal, had planned to get married in Massachusetts and honeymoon in Provincetown. But they scrapped that idea and waited for the chance to legally marry in Washington, where Pedersen's family had been rooted since the 1880s.

ADVOCATES FOLLOWED with a bold move. In March, 2004, Lambda Legal and the Northwest Women's Law Center filed a lawsuit, *Andersen v. Sims*, arguing that Washington's ban on same-sex marriage was illegal. The plaintiffs were eight couples, who included a firefighter, a cop, a nurse, and a teacher.

In August, King County Superior Court Judge William Downing agreed with advocates: the state's gay-marriage ban was unconstitutional.

King County Superior Court Judge William Downing found the state ban on same-sex marriages unconstitutional, setting the stage for a state Supreme Court ruling on marriage equality. *William Downing*

Pedersen is not a litigator and didn't argue the case. But he took depositions of plaintiffs, organized legal support through friends-of-the-court briefs, and was listed as co-counsel for Lambda. After *Andersen* wound its way through the appeals process and landed in the state Supreme Court's lap, advocates sat back anxiously. And waited—for 16 long months after oral arguments.

The ruling finally came in July 2006. In a 5-4 decision, the lead opinion by Barbara Madsen found a "rational basis" for upholding the state's ban on same-sex marriage.

In a decision some scoffed at and others found "muddled," Madsen wrote: "Limiting marriage to opposite-sex couples furthers procreation, essential to the survival of the human race, and furthers the well-being of children by encouraging families where children are reared in homes headed by the children's biological parents."

In a stinging dissent, Justice Mary Fairhurst said her colleagues in the majority relied on discriminatory speculation and circular reasoning. Critics pilloried the idea that marriage was dependent on procreation. Should licenses be withheld from women past menopause and people who were infertile? And, just how did denying marriage to gays encourage procreation? "It was a dreadful, dreadful decision," Pedersen says.

WHAT NEXT? Pedersen was term-limited off the Lambda board. His marriage-equality case had made it all the way to Olympia's Temple of Justice, where it did not persuade the highest arbiters of state law.

What was left to do? He and Eric were remodeling their 1909 Victorian house, and preparing to have kids. He had become a partner in

Justice Mary Fairhurst, while dissenting on the Supreme Court's 5-4 decision to ban same-sex marriage, called it discriminatory. *Washington Courts*

the law firm. Was corporate law his future?

Then Ed Murray called. Murray had been carrying the banner for gay rights and fighting for a beachhead in the Legislature. Like his mentor Cal Anderson, Murray tried year after year to pass a civil rights law for the LGBTQ community. It usually died in the Senate. But in early 2006, it finally passed—when King County Republican Bill Finkbeiner, who voted against it the previous year, switched his vote.

Murray was convinced the state Senate needed someone with his tenacity. Murray decided to abandon his House seat for a run at the higher chamber. He encouraged Pedersen to seek his seat. "I had zero, zero, zero political experience at that point," Pedersen recalls.

He consulted with law-firm colleagues and his partner, Eric. He filed his candidacy. Murray, known for his temper, exploded. He hadn't yet formally announced his own campaign for Senate, and now Pedersen had scooped him. "He literally yelled at me and was angry, angry, angry, and then didn't talk to me for at least six months after that," Pedersen says. It was the start of a stormy but productive relationship.

Soon, Pedersen incurred the wrath of Dan Savage, outspoken gay editor of Seattle's influential newspaper, *The Stranger*. Savage heard that Pedersen volunteers had said he was the only candidate vying for Murray's House seat who supported marriage equality. That wasn't true about the crowded field of liberal contenders—although Pedersen was the only gay candidate.

Savage lambasted Pedersen as a "drip" and worse.

"Welcome to politics," Pedersen says.

Murray had said he wasn't going to endorse anyone for his House seat. But he called the Supreme Court's ruling that summer a "political earthquake in the gay and lesbian community."

He said the movement needed another community leader in Olympia. He endorsed Pedersen, noting his work on marriage equality. Pedersen barely edged five rivals in the Democratic primary for the uber-liberal 43rd Legislative District, which guaranteed a November triumph.

He and Murray began planning. "One thing we were completely aligned on was doing an incremental approach," Pedersen says.

Murray believed, and Pedersen agreed, that having lost on marriage equality in the court, the best path forward was "attacking it little piece by little piece." And so, he went back to his project on state statutes, which eventually identified 425 rights and obligations that depended on marital status.

A tragedy in Seattle would give their piecemeal strategy a heartbreaking push.

GALE FORCE winds and fierce rain swept through Western Washington on December 16, 2006. Trees and power lines fell. Torrents overran drainage systems. In all, 14 people would die from the effects of the tempest, called the Hanukkah Eve Wind Storm.

Kate Fleming shared a home in Seattle's Madison Valley with her longtime partner, Charlene Strong. Fleming "touched thousands of

Charlene Strong rushed to the hospital after a flood in Seattle trapped her longtime partner, Kate Fleming, in her basement. At the hospital, Strong was told she couldn't see Kate until a relative approved. *Charlene Strong*

lives" as the narrator of some 250 audiobooks. When a flash flood hit her house, Fleming raced to her basement recording studio to salvage equipment. She was trapped below, and submerged.

A rescue crew pulled her out, unconscious, some 15 minutes later, and sped to the hospital. Her partner Strong ran to the emergency room but was stopped by a social worker, who said the state could not recognize same-sex partners in such situations.

Strong needed permission from Fleming's family to be near her, and make decisions for her care. Strong frantically dialed Fleming's sister in Virginia, until she got the necessary blessing.

Fleming died hours later with Strong by her side. Fleming's death certificate said she was not married. The funeral director wouldn't let Strong make arrangements, such as cremation.

Strong became a compelling voice for legal domestic partnerships, the first plank in the Murray-Pedersen blueprint. Their 2007 bill—sponsored by Murray in the Senate and Pedersen in the House—would provide domestic partners with hospital-visitation rights, the ability to authorize autopsies and organ donations, and inheritance rights.

One of the bill's critics, Representative Judy Warnick, a Republican from Moses Lake, said it would cause economic and social "chaos." Nevertheless, it passed and was signed into law by Governor Chris Gregoire with Strong at her side.

The state produced wallet cards for legal partners. "That came out of Charlene's experience too," Pedersen says, so domestic partners could show they were entitled to hospital visits. For years after that, he recalls, people would come up to him in the grocery store and pull out their cards with teary gratitude.

After the first domestic partnership law went unchallenged by ballot measure, Pedersen and others wanted to push for a marriage equality law in the upcoming 2008 session. But Gregoire balked, in a tense conversation with gay and lesbian lawmakers. Perhaps the governor's instincts (and self-interest in re-election) were beneficial. Californians voted that fall to ban same-sex marriage via Proposition 8—by a 700,000-vote margin—a foreboding sign in a liberal state.

Pedersen cataloged hundreds of instances where married people received benefits others did not in state law—down to sea-urchin fishing licenses, which could be passed on to a spouse when the license-holder died; if they were unmarried, the license reverted to the state. *Jamie Pedersen*

Murray and Pedersen instead produced another incremental bill, adding domestic partners to laws about probate and trusts, community property, and guardianship. "The overriding theme for this package is the financial security of domestic partners and their families," said Pedersen, recognized by the media as a political leader in the LGBTQ movement.

Pedersen, now chairman of the House Judiciary Committee, and Murray continued their step-by-step march. In 2009, they filled any remaining gaps in the domestic partnership statute with an "everything but marriage" law.

This time, opponents overreacted. That fall, they sought to repeal the law—which they said would lead to marriage—by popular vote with Referendum 71. But public opinion had begun to shift, nudged by popular TV shows such as "Ellen" and "Will and Grace," and mainstream movie stars such as Tom Hanks, Hilary Swank and Denzel Washington.

This time, electoral support for the LGBTQ movement reached 53 percent statewide. It was the first time in history that voters, as opposed to courts or lawmakers, had approved such rights for same-sex couples.

A HOLDING PATTERN followed in 2010, with the rise of Tea Party and GOP gains in the Legislature. The next year, however, New York legalized gay marriage, which advocates saw as game-changing. Same-sex marriage was legal in six states and the District of Columbia.

Near the year's end, the moderate editorial board of *The Seattle Times* gave marriage equality a full-throated, let's-do-this endorsement. The encouraging shove had come from the Blethen family's fifth generation of owners. Like many younger people, the Blethen "fifth edition" couldn't fathom why people who found love shouldn't be allowed to wed.

Going into 2012, advocates in Olympia were poised to push full marriage-equality legislation. At the start of the year, Gregoire, a Catholic, vowed to support it, marking a public shift in her own journey. In her 2004 campaign for governor, she said the state wasn't "ready" for it. But eight years later, polls showed national support climbing to 48 percent, and a bit higher in the Evergreen State. Her conversion was urged by her daughters, she said, who considered gay rights the civil-rights issue of the 21st century.

An Eagle Scout since 1984, Pedersen marched with his son Leif in the 2017 Seattle Pride Parade. *Jamie Pedersen*

"I don't think she took that much converting once she had won [re-election in 2008] and was in her last term," Pedersen says, noting "she became beloved in the LGBTQ community because of all the progress we made on her watch."

A marriage bill was introduced at Gregoire's request. Pedersen rounded up the necessary support in the House, with longtime Speaker Frank Chopp becoming the bill's 50th and decisive sponsor in the lower chamber.

A tougher battle awaited in the 49-member Senate, where advocates counted 24 solid "yes" votes and 21 unmovable opponents. "We had four 'maybes' and we had a one-by-one campaign to figure out every way we could to surround those four senators gently," Pedersen says. Persuasion, in one case, extended to a pair of barber's scissors. State Senator Andy Hill, a moderate Republican, got his hair cut by a guy who sang with Pedersen in the Seattle Men's Chorus. When Hill sat in his chair, the stylist tried to sound him out and soften him up.

In a hearing on Senate Bill 6239, Murray testified first, followed by his longtime partner, Michael Shiosaki, who talked about his parents' 56-year marriage. "That commitment I see in the relationship Ed and I share," Shiosaki said, talking about how he and Murray leaned on one another during illnesses and deaths in their families. But unlike his parents, they couldn't marry.

Jamie and Eric's triplets, Leif, Erik and Anders, at Bridal Veil Falls above, were at the Capitol for Gov. Gregoire's signing of the marriage-equality law in 2012. *Jamie Pedersen*

Also testifying were a gay Iraq War veteran, a gay state trooper, a straight home-economics teacher with a gay daughter, and a 16-year-old who said he hoped to marry a man he loved someday.

Still, advocates couldn't get to 25 votes, until Mary Margaret Haugen, a Catholic who had previously opposed same-sex marriage, came around. Gregoire signed the bill in a festive atmosphere. Lawmakers snapped proud "selfies" at the event. News photographers filled frames with Pedersen's four blond toddlers who attended. He and Eric had conceived the boys, including triplets, through egg donors and surrogates.

Everyone knew that a challenge, in the form of another citizen initiative, loomed. And they knew the track record at the ballot box was worse than dismal.

THE QUESTION of same-sex marriage had been put to a vote in states 31 times, and was rejected 31 times. But lessons had come out of the devastating California loss, in particular.

Evan Wolfson had created a new organization, Freedom to Marry. Researchers there, along with California strategist Amy Simon, were conducting intensive focus groups, sifting through polling data, and studying with renewed resolve.

Too often in the past, LGBTQ advocates had played scattershot defense against conservatives' inaccurate claims by assuming the posture of "bigot busters." Simon flipped the script. Research showed that voters unsure, torn, or leaning against gay marriage were not bigots. When asked what marriage meant to them, they said love and commitment. And when asked why gay people wanted to marry, "most commonly, respondents said they simply didn't know."

In previous debates, advocates for gay rights had focused on fairness in the workplace and the military, or around privacy. Researchers found the most potent message, instead, was that committed same-sex couples were doing the same things as married hetero couples. They needed to talk about that.

A first step for advocates was to stop referring to "same-sex marriage" and "gay marriage" and call it "marriage equality." They were seeking the same thing other couples had, not something separate. And campaigns underway in four states that year— Maine, Maryland, Minnesota and Washington— needed "ruthless discipline" to stay on that message.

Meanwhile, Wolfson's Freedom to Marry had made inroads at the White House. Neither Barack Obama nor Joe Biden had advocated gay marriage in their 2008 presidential campaigns, although LGBTQ support had become a pillar of the Democratic Party. Obama cited respect for traditional values in explaining his stance.

In 1983, Evan Wolfson, a Harvard Law student, wrote a dissertation about how gay people could win marriage rights. Then he made the cause his crusade. Keys to the marriage movement's success—14th Amendment legal theories and messaging focused on love—were in his dissertation. *Freedom to Marry*

In May 2012, the president had a different message. He said he thought about his own staffers in committed relationships, raising kids. He considered troops willing to defend America, but unable to marry loved ones. He mentioned his faith's emphasis on the Golden Rule. "I think same-sex couples should be able to get married," he told ABC News anchor Robin Roberts. Biden said the same on "Meet the Press."

Wolfson was behind Obama's carefully chosen words. There was the president, talking to Roberts, an African American journalist. He didn't mention discrimination or civil rights. He talked about love and commitment. The debate was being shifted from the head to the heart.

Centering the debate on "love" was already underway in Washington. An unscripted tour de force came in a four-minute speech by state Representative Maureen Walsh. A Republican from Walla Walla, Walsh was moved to talk about her marriage to her husband, who died six years earlier, and about her lesbian daughter.

With her hand-on-hip candor, Walsh talked about not missing sex with her husband so much, but longing for the love they shared. "How can I deny anyone the right to have that incredible bond with another individual in life? It seems almost cruel."

Later, about her daughter, she said, "By God, someday I want to throw a wedding for that kid." Walsh was the second sponsor on Pedersen's marriage-equality legislation. She would be one of just two Republicans in the House to vote for it. Her speech went viral on the internet. And she followed Betty White on stage at a Los Angeles gay-rights event.

An email to Jeff Bezos from Seattleite Jennifer Cast would give the cause a bigger megaphone. Cast had been one of the first Amazon employees and an executive under Bezos. Now she was a volunteer on the Washington United for Marriage campaign and raising four kids with her partner.

"To be very frank," Cast wrote, "we need help from wealthy straight people who care about us and who want to help us win." She asked Bezos to contribute $100,000 or $200,000 to the campaign on Referendum 74.

She didn't know how Bezos might respond; she had "never, ever" broached the issue with him. Two days later she got a brief reply.

"Jen," his e-mail said, "this is right for so many reasons. We're in for $2.5 million. Jeff & MacKenzie."

The early money mattered. The campaign hired professionals steeped in political science, not amateurs intuiting what strategies might work best. Six-figure donations from the likes of Bill and Melinda Gates not only paid for consultants and door-to-door canvassers, the fundraising edge was parlayed to tactical advantage. It bought TV ad time at earlier, lower rates than opponents would later pay in the campaign homestretch. That meant more eyeballs on ads featuring the disarming Maureen Walsh and other straight supporters.

Polling showed that voters favored marriage equality, albeit by a thin margin.

ON ELECTION NIGHT, Pedersen and others gathered at the Westin Hotel in Seattle. By 10 p.m., with more than half of the statewide ballots counted, it became a victory party. Marriage equality was winning with 52 percent. It ended up at 53.7 percent.

Throngs spilled into the streets of Seattle's Capitol Hill, the epicenter of Pedersen's district. "It's something that's going to go down in history as one of the biggest moments for civil rights in this generation," said one of the revelers, Kort Haven, 26.

Less than three years later, the U.S. Supreme Court legalized same-sex marriage in the *Obergefell v. Hodges* case. Writing for the 5-4 majority, Justice Anthony Kennedy twice cited the work of Washington historian Stephanie Coontz. A longtime faculty member at The Evergreen State College, Coontz's 2005 book, *Marriage: A History*, made her an authority.

As with many Americans, bubbling beneath the conversions by Governor

Gregoire and President Obama, was a change, over two-plus centuries, in the essence of marriage. Coontz wrote that matrimony had evolved from a property contract, in which husband was the master, to a gender-neutral bond of love. (Her book was subtitled *How Love Conquered Marriage*.) Once strict roles of a breadwinning father and submissive mother had largely dissolved, and women were fully in the workforce, and contraception was legalized, the rationale that marriage should be reserved for procreation seemed strange. And marriage equality appeared inevitable; yet still shimmering on a horizon.

When the U.S. Supreme Court legalized same-sex marriage in 2015, it cited Stephanie Coontz, a Washington historian. Marriage had evolved from a property contract to a gender-neutral bond of love, Coontz wrote, making marriage equality inevitable. *The Evergreen State College*

Coontz was surprised at how quickly it arrived. "It's one of the fastest changes that we've seen as historians," she said. Others called it the swiftest such shift.

How did it happen? In Washington state, the incremental strategy and domestic partnerships "did not lead to the failure of civilization," Pedersen says, as doomsayers predicted. Popular media—from the Oscar-winning movie "Philadelphia" to the surprise TV hit, "Queer Eye for the Straight Guy"—smoothed the way. Demographics and younger voters helped too.

Pedersen and Coontz agreed on perhaps the most important factor. More and more LGBTQ people had come out, in a soft parade. Therein was a key distinction with the civil rights struggles for racial equality. Gay people could choose when to reveal their sexual orientation. They could be known as family members, friends, co-workers and teammates, without prejudice, before coming out.

"Compared to almost every other civil rights movement, LGBTQ have a gigantic advantage, which is that we pop up randomly in families everywhere," Pedersen says.

HE REACHED a summit, at 44, when Washington joined Maine, Maryland and six other states in marriage equality. He had left the law firm of Preston, Gates and Ellis (which merged into K&L Gates in 2007). He became general counsel and executive vice-president at Seattle-based McKinstry, which specializes in energy-efficient building construction. He and Eric were legally wed on the ninth

"My life's work for 17 years," culminated in Jamie and Eric's 2013 wedding ceremony, with Anne Levinson, Evan Wolfson, Joe McDermott, Jamie, Eric and Leif Pedersen, Mary Fairhurst, Ed Murray, Michael Shiosaki, Karen Poirier and Laurie Jinkins. *Jamie Pedersen*

anniversary of when they had tied the knot at their local church, a block from Seattle's Cal Anderson Park. They had four young boys who made every family stroll an adventure.

What to do now?

Plenty, it turned out. Murray left the Legislature in 2013 to become Seattle's 53rd mayor. Pedersen was elected to Murray's Senate seat. Christian conservatives knew marriage equality was a lost cause. But, like the LGBTQ lobby, they were a powerful constituency, with battle-tested, ready troops. What would they fight over next?

The defection of two Democrats, Rodney Tom and Tim Sheldon, gave the Republicans control of the state Senate at the end of 2012 with a "majority coalition." That created a different set of battlegrounds, Pedersen says. "So, then we fought about transgender access to bathrooms for two years." There were also debates about conversion therapy and parentage, including surrogacy, and gender-markers on public records.

More recently, Pedersen has pushed for mandated infertility treatment in health care. "And that's a big economic privilege issue," he says, "because you get someone who has a high income and they can pay for a surrogate or can pay for [in vitro fertilization]. And then people who have an equally burning desire to be parents but don't have the financial resources to pay for that are unable to have biological children."

While challenges remained, America had transitioned. In 2004, 60 percent opposed same-sex marriage. Fifteen years later, the numbers flipped; 60 percent supported it. Laurie Jinkins, who had been in the LGBTQ civil-rights trenches for a couple decades, was elected the first female Speaker of the House in 2020. Pedersen became Senate Majority Floor Leader in 2022. And Tim Sheldon, the conservative Democrat who aligned with Republicans in the Senate, announced his retirement that year. Sheldon said he regretted voting against marriage equality and other bills aimed at advancing LGBTQ civil rights. "I think I've been educated a lot by my daughter and my wife," Sheldon said.

Looking back, Pedersen thought about his former paralegal, the matronly Dorothy Nelson. She had likened marriage equality to the fall of the Berlin Wall. One day, the obstacles loomed; the next, the sky was clear.

And who was hurt? As Evan Wolfson liked to say: there's no shortage of marriage licenses.

Bob Young

ANNE LEVINSON

"THE WOMAN BEHIND THE CURTAIN
OF MARRIAGE EQUALITY"

When the religious right set out to repeal Washington's "everything but marriage" domestic partnership law in 2009, Christian conservatives were on a roll. They had dealt a severe blow to LGBTQ civil rights in California the previous year. Using potent fear-mongering ads, conservatives had persuaded voters to amend their state constitution to ban same-sex marriage. What happened next in the Evergreen State would ripple across the country. Would progress be set back again in 2009? Or would Washingtonians become the first voters in United States history to endorse legal family recognition for gays and lesbians?

Community leaders turned to Anne Levinson. A former judge, Levinson had been in the civil rights trenches for a couple decades. She was one of the first "out" officials in the state when she was chief of staff and chief problem-solver for Seattle's first African-American mayor, Norm Rice.

Her 2009 challenge was fraught. Evangelicals were collecting signatures to put Referendum 71 on the November ballot, arguing in churches and on street corners that domestic partnerships were a stepping stone to same-sex marriage. Given the results in California and other states, LGBTQ advocates did not want to risk making the vote in Washington a litmus test for marriage. Levinson would need to motivate allies and voters with a cause—domestic partnerships—that at first glance appeared a dry mix of pension and medical-leave rights, a medley of uninspiring benefits.

While she liked to stay out of the limelight, Levinson was battle tested. In 1990, she led a fight against the repeal of funeral-and-sick leave for Seattle city employees with domestic partners. A few years later, she helped create and name "Hands Off Washington," a statewide group that aimed to halt Oregon an-

Facing page: Anne Levinson, a former judge, pronounced Jane Abbott Lighty and Pete-e Petersen married at Seattle's Benaroya Hall on Dec. 9, 2012. *Anne Levinson*

ti-LGBTQ extremists sweeping across the border. And when initiative-hawker Tim Eyman tried to steer the anti-gay bandwagon in 2006, she was asked to stop him.

She was described as a "very gentle person with a spine of steel," "warm and approachable but excruciatingly precise," and a taskmaster "diligent to a fault." Levinson briefly detoured from LGBTQ civil rights after dispatching Eyman. In stealthy negotiations, she engineered a deal with the Oklahoma oil-and-gas tycoons who had bought the Supersonics and Storm professional basketball teams. While Clay Bennett and his crewcut gang hauled the Sonics off to the thunderous plains, Levinson managed to keep Sue Bird, Lauren Jackson and the Storm in Seattle under ownership of local women.

That long-shot bid featured her signature skills. And they were first learned when the "little jock" took up the cause of saving women's sports at the University of Kansas. Without the aid of a legal or political guru, she figured out how to build coalitions, attract publicity, and find common ground with potential allies—rather than dwell on their differences. She filed one of the first discrimination complaints on behalf of women athletes under the federal Title IX law. Although it took years, she prevailed.

All of her savvy would be required in struggles for Washington's paramount LGBTQ causes: domestic partnerships via Referendum 71, and its 2012 sequel, Referendum 74, where she was "the woman behind the curtain of marriage equality" in our state.

LEVINSON WON a scholarship, although it's tempting to put quotation marks around the term, to play field hockey at the University of Kansas. At 5 feet 3 inches, Levinson lettered in three high-school sports and was a prolific scorer in field hockey, although left-handed in a sport that only allows right-handed sticks. She was drawn to Kansas for several reasons, including that scholarship. It turned out to be the team's only one—$1,000, in toto, she recalls—and it would pass to her when she was a sophomore and the incumbent recipient had graduated.

After her freshman year, however, the university announced it was going to end funding for all women's sports except basketball.

She began figuring out how to stop the gutting. To draw attention to the cause, she enlisted women athletes to run a 30-mile, baton-passing relay from the KU campus in Lawrence to the state Capitol in Topeka. On the Capitol steps, the women removed a petition from the baton and handed it to the governor and female legislators. The feat garnered front-page attention in the *Kansas City Times*.

Levinson sees a link between Title IX opponents and 2022 attacks on trans athletes: "It's just another way for intolerant folks to try and marginalize, diminish, ostracize people who are different from them for a wholly imagined set of harms." *Newspapers.com*

Within hours, state legislators voted to restore some funding to the university.

What's more, the baton brigade caught the eye of Elizabeth "Betty" Banks, a KU professor of art history.

Banks encouraged Levinson to file a Title IX complaint, which was something the student-athlete knew nothing about. Banks told her to research it. Title IX had been adopted as federal law in 1972 to ban gender discrimination in any educational institution receiving federal funds. It took three slow-walking years for the Department of Health, Education and Welfare to craft rules for implementing the new law.

Levinson found funding disparities in every aspect of men's and women's sports at KU: scholarships, facilities, coaches' salaries and more. She filed a complaint in 1978. The federal Office of Civil Rights chose her claim to be among the first eight cases it would investigate for their broad implications.

Critics, including editorial writers at the student newspaper, said Title IX would effectively end men's sports by draining money away for women. Undeterred, investigators found discrimination and told KU to comply or lose up to $27 million in federal funding.

The university eventually came up with a multi-year plan to improve women's athletics. It was too late to benefit Levinson and her classmates, but it laid a foundation for all women student-athletes who followed.

ANNE LEVINSON was born in Topeka in 1958. Her parents were both New

Yorkers, whose grandparents were born in Eastern Europe. When Levinson's father was a boy, he immersed himself in reading as a way of escaping his family's poverty in their small town.

Harry Levinson found his way to Kansas State Teachers College. He served in the Army during World War II and "often tried to teach illiterate Army friends how to read," said his lengthy obituary in *The New York Times*. After the war, he married Roberta Freiman, and with his bride, he came back to Kansas to earn his doctorate in clinical psychology. He later worked at Topeka's Menninger Foundation, which became the country's largest training center for psychiatric professionals.

When Anne was 10, Harvard Business School hired her father, a renowned thinker on mental health and work. The Levinson family moved to a Boston suburb, Winchester, seven miles from Harvard Square. Neighboring cities included Woburn and Medford, or "Woo-bun" and "Meh-fah" in the local dialect.

Young Anne was definitely not in Kansas anymore. "I had a different accent. I had different clothes. I was not a big city girl."

She asked to try out for the boys' baseball team in junior high because girls didn't have a team. "I wasn't intentionally being a rabble-rouser but just wanting to play," she recalls. "The coach let me bat once and that was it."

A "late bloomer" on other fronts, she says she "got pure joy out of the athletics and the opportunity to do something fun with a group of people." She played point guard in basketball, where her chief strength was scoping out the court and dishing the ball to teammates in scoring position. She was a dashing forward in field hockey. "It was my preferred sport because it was fast-paced and strategic. It was like ice hockey without hitting each other."

Levinson shooting on goal in field hockey.
Anne Levinson

She didn't realize it at the time, but her parents—who later divorced—had exposed her to the Jewish tradition of *tikkun olam*, or mending the world. "NPR was always on the car radio," she recalls. Her parents often had dinner guests who were engaged in political or community activism. That seeped in. And *tikkun olam* "must have stuck, because that clearly has been in my DNA since I've grown up."

HER TITLE IX advocacy aroused her interest in studying law. Despite her father's connections at Harvard, she didn't see it as her community. She was drawn to Northeastern University. Founded in a YMCA at the turn of the 20th century, Northeastern was a Boston college for working people. NU's uber-urban "campus" was closer to diverse neighborhoods such as Roxbury than it was to rowing shells gliding on the Charles River. Its subterranean classrooms shook when old trolleys screeched and rattled down the middle of Huntington Avenue, the school's lifeline.

When the first same-sex marriage licenses were issued in Boston, sharpshooters on the roof of City Hall protected attorney Mary Bonauto, who Barney Frank called "our Thurgood Marshall." *Freedomtomarry.org*

NU Law School was known for producing public-interest attorneys. It admitted women 28 years before Harvard. Levinson's contemporaries at the school included Urvashi Vaid, later National Gay and Lesbian Task Force leader, and Mary Bonauto, who won a 2003 breakthrough case for same-sex marriage in Massachusetts. ("Our Thurgood Marshall," gay Congressman Barney Frank called Bonauto.)

Students were required to alternate course work with externships overseen by attorneys. One of Levinson's "co-ops," as Northeastern calls them, took her to Colorado to clerk for Justice Jean Dubofsky, the first woman and youngest person to sit on that state's Supreme Court. After later stepping down from the high court, Dubofsky was the lead attorney in a 1996 LGBTQ victory, *Romer v. Evans*, at the U.S. Supreme Court.

For her last co-op, Levinson jumped at an opportunity in the Seattle City Attorney's Office, working on anti-discrimination law. She didn't even glimpse Lake Washington through the persistent drizzle, but she saw "what a progressive and welcoming city Seattle was for women and for LGBTQ folks and that sealed the deal for me." She moved out in the spring of 1983, and passed the bar exam that summer. Soon she journeyed to Iowa for foot-soldier duty in the presidential campaign of U.S. Senator Alan Cranston, a California Democrat, who wanted to abolish nuclear weapons.

CALLED A "bald craggy-looking, none-too-charismatic man," Cranston won just 7 percent in Iowa's first-in-the-country sweepstakes. Levinson and other campaigners were cut loose without so much as bus fare out of Cedar Rapids. White House incumbent Ronald Reagan went on to pummel Walter Mondale in a November landslide.

Her idealism still intact, Levinson volunteered for the re-election campaign of Seattle Mayor Charley Royer. She recalls piling into a colleague's station wagon and making cassette recordings of many debates between Royer and his challenger Norm Rice, a City Council stalwart. Royer won and hired her at City Hall.

In the mayor's office she worked alongside Cal Anderson, who was Royer's scheduler. Anderson had come out to his parents while he was in the U.S. Army during the Vietnam War. In his groundbreaking 1987 campaign for state representative, Anderson "didn't run as an LGBT candidate, but as a candidate who happened to be gay," Levinson says.

Seattle was trailblazing in its mid-1970s adoption of laws that prohibited discrimination against gays in housing and employment. Anderson urged forming a group that would press legislators to adopt a statewide law like Seattle's. Since 1949, Washington had a law forbidding discrimination on the grounds of race, religion and gender, but it was silent on sexual orientation and gender identity. Advocates had been trying to change that since 1977 to no avail.

Anderson, Levinson, Charlie Brydon and a handful of others, created a political action committee, the Privacy Fund. "We called it that out of fear that if we used the l-word or the g-word we wouldn't get support," Levinson says. Bobbe Bridge, later a state Supreme Court justice, was hired as the organization's lobbyist.

Levinson became one of the state's first public officials to come out. "There wasn't a dance party," she says. "I just let it be known and started working on these things in a very visible way.

"And it was clear we needed to be visible, we needed to be out—that it was going to be harder for people to hate us if they knew us. And it would certainly make it harder for other people to watch or sit to the side and not support us."

TO LEVINSON'S SURPRISE, when Norm Rice was elected mayor in 1989, he reached out to hire her. As Royer's liaison on public safety—the powder keg of mayoral politics—she had often shuttled down a City Hall back stairway from the mayor's office to negotiate with Rice, the City Council's leader on policing issues. "I was not expecting him to think of me in a positive way after all of those battles," she recalls.

She ended up staying for both of Rice's terms, serving as his legal counsel,

Levinson calmed activists from AIDS Coalition to Unleash Power who occupied the mayor's office in 1990. The AIDS crisis created a "real community," she says, with "gay men and lesbians working in the trenches side by side." *MOHAI, Seattle Post-Intelligencer Collection*

chief of staff, deputy mayor and arm-twister.

"City policy, simply put, works like this: Rice has an idea. Levinson figures out how to get it done," said a story in *The Seattle Times* headlined, "Anne of the thousand details."

Their accomplishments ranged from developing some of the country's first transitional housing run by the homeless to recruiting the city's first professional women's basketball team, the Seattle Reign.

Levinson worked with such focus that Rice said "others might think she's impersonal."

On the LGBTQ front, the City Council had taken a progressive step in 1989 by creating domestic partnerships for city employees. Straight and gay workers could use their sick leave to care for a live-in partner, or attend the funeral of a partner—a benefit equal to what married employees enjoyed.

Christian conservatives, aided by retired state Supreme Court Justice William Goodloe, filed an initiative challenging the policy as a threat to traditional families.

In 1990, Levinson, a self-described "workaholic," spent evenings and weekends campaigning for Rice's innovative $69 million Families and Education tax levy, which she had helped craft, and against Initiative 35.

I-35 sought to repeal the leave benefits that applied to 4 percent of the city's workforce. To oppose it, Levinson assembled a coalition of the city's business establishment, labor unions, LGBTQ community, and religious leaders.

The Seattle Times editorial page—later a cheerleader for marriage equality—argued for overturning the benefits. *The Times* cited their cost as prohibitive.

Seattle voters disagreed; 58 percent voted to keep the benefits. Levinson detected a pattern: Gay-rights opponents seemed to think they were victimized by granting equality to others.

A NEW THREAT arose from the south in the early 1990s. Christian conservatives in the Oregon Citizens Alliance had overturned anti-discrimination protections for gay employees in state government. With hellfire rhetoric, the OCA followed up with Measure 9 in 1992. It would have amended Oregon's constitution to declare homosexuality "perverse," on par with pedophilia, and ineligible for any "special rights."

In what was considered the most divisive campaign in Oregon history, Measure 9 was rejected by 57 percent of the voters.

Extremists united LGBTQ advocates and allies, says Levinson, who once thanked opponents, "because your cruelty, and your over-reaching, and your lack of humanity, and compassion, it helped us." *Western Washington University*

Undaunted, OCA leader Lon Mabon came to Seattle in 1993, declared "there is a war going on" and revealed plans to create a Washington branch.

LGBT leaders in Washington anticipated such a move. In a pre-emptive strike, Seattle activist Charlie Brydon had locked up the name Washington Citizens Alliance before Mabon could get it. "We just bought it so they couldn't use it," Levinson says. She expected bruising combat against Mabon. She suggested branding their campaign "Hands Off Washington."

"The idea was to say, 'Look, here are these outsiders trying to come into our state, telling you that you need to discriminate against your fellow Washingtonians. And we're not going to put up with that, right?'"

Levinson wanted to make sure allies were visible. A "Hands Off" logo could be plastered on bumpers, coffee mugs, t-shirts, and more. "We gave them to businesses. We had them in churches. People were able to show their support for us,

24 hours a day," she says, "and in a very affordable way."

Mabon and his allies proposed initiatives 608 and 610 in 1994. Together, those would ban anti-discrimination laws protecting gays, prohibit schools from positively depicting homosexuality, and stop LGBT couples from adopting, fostering or having custody of kids.

Levinson organized a press conference in Clark County for business and civic leaders—near Oregon and far from Seattle—to register their opposition to Mabon. She asked Seattle Police Chief Norm Stamper to march in the Pride Parade, in uniform, with Mayor Rice, followed by Fire Department

Deputy Mayor Levinson, far right, walks behind Mayor Norm Rice (waving) in the 1993 Seattle Pride Parade. Norm Stamper would be the city's first police chief to march in the parade the next year. *Seattle Municipal Archives*

trucks. It was the first time Seattle police participated in the parade. Hands Off Washington fought to keep the measures from getting to voters with a "decline to sign" movement and TV ads before their opponents even qualified for the ballot.

Christian conservatives failed to gather enough signatures for their initiatives. They blamed the "Gay Klux Klan."

The Seattle Times named Levinson one of the "power gay leaders" in the state, and added, "Her record as an effective, behind-the-scenes facilitator is unsurpassed in local government."

"THIS IS THE FIRST selfish thing I've done in seven years," Levinson said in late 1996, stepping away from City Hall. At 38, she said it was "time to get a life." Rice, nicknamed "Mayor Nice," said, "I've been known to burn a lot of people out."

If that was Levinson's condition, it didn't stick. Governor Gary Locke appointed her the following year to head the state's regulation of energy and telecommunications industries. In his announcement, Locke lined up praise for Levinson from business executives, leading Latino activist Roberto Maestas and her old friend, Bobbe Bridge, then a King County Superior Court judge. "She is always unflappable, fair and has a good sense of humor," Bridge said. Levinson's stint as a utilities' regulator would prove instrumental when she later negotiated a deal to keep the WNBA's Storm from being taken to Oklahoma with the Sonics.

But Levinson held the post in Locke's cabinet less than two years before Seattle Mayor Paul Schell tapped her for another challenge. She took a pay cut to become Honorable Judge Levinson of the Seattle Municipal Court.

She didn't settle into a robed career, however. Instead, like Justice Dubofsky in Colorado, Levinson found herself itching to get back to advocacy. "I really missed community activism and as a judge you are foreclosed from all of that. And I really hadn't given that a lot of thought when I said 'yes' to being a judge."

She even felt guilty about sitting on the bench with all that was going on. Vermont had approved civil unions for same-sex couples and the Supreme Judicial Court of Massachusetts legalized marriage equality.

Seeing a grave threat, Christian conservatives mobilized on offense. Karl Rove, chief strategist for President George W. Bush, saw a chance to boost Bush's sagging support among evangelical voters. Rove orchestrated campaigns in 11 states to constitutionally ban same-sex marriage in 2004. All of them succeeded.

Nevertheless, optimism gripped Washington's LGBTQ community 15 months later. After trying for 29 years in Olympia, advocates finally thought they might have the votes in the Legislature to add sexual orientation and gender identity to the state's anti-discrimination law.

The previous year's drive fell one vote short in the state Senate. When senators took up the bill on Friday, January 27, "activity in the Capitol all but halted." Galleries overlooking the Senate were packed. Debate was long and emotional. State Senator Ed Murray, the leading gay rights advocate in the Legislature, watched in the wings alongside his longtime partner Michael Shiosaki.

Senator Bill Finkbeiner, a King County Republican, rose to speak against discrimination. "We don't choose who we love. The heart chooses who we love," he said, changing his position to cast the decisive vote in a 25-23 tally.

A celebration was held that night in the lobby of Seattle's Paramount Theatre. Its marquee said: "Now Playing – A Victory for Equality." After a slide show and speeches, Louisa Jenkins, an auto mechanic, stood among the crowd rocking her infant to Pat Benatar's "Love Is a Battlefield."

George Bakan, publisher of *Seattle Gay News*, expected the long-sought vic-

Seattle Gay News publisher George Bakan predicted a "dogfight" after state lawmakers passed an anti-discrimination law in 2006, celebrated by a marquee, and conservatives vowed to overturn it. *Anne Levinson*

tory to be challenged by the right in what would be the "dogfight of the year."

What Bakan hadn't anticipated was who would be leading the other side's pack.

BEFORE GOVERNOR Chris Gregoire even signed the new law, Tim Eyman announced he would try to repeal it at the ballot. The watch salesman known for anti-tax initiatives was veering into another lane.

Levinson took on the challenge of leading a team against Eyman. Washington Won't Discriminate was created in the model of the "Hands Off" campaign, with chapters around the state, familiar faces talking to newspaper editorial boards, and known allies to enlist for "decline to sign" canvassing.

Levinson had learned from earlier battles. "Each time they attacked us, it helped us in the long run because we were better prepared, more strategic, the public was more educated. And we had stronger coalitions."

Editorial boards condemned Eyman's misleading "high-octane" rhetoric about quotas and preferential treatment for gays. The *Tacoma News Tribune* called his ploy "reprehensible." Others, from *The Walla Walla Union-Bulletin* to the *Yakima Herald-Republic*, joined in the berating.

Washington's highest court delivered a crushing blow to marriage equality in 2006. On the brighter side, Tim Eyman failed in his effort to repeal the state's anti-discrimination law. *Anne Levinson*

Eyman and his Christian cohorts needed 112,400 valid signatures to qualify for a statewide referendum—which meant a ballot choice to "approve" or "reject" the existing law. With that effort lagging, Eyman trumpeted "Referendum Sunday," calling for voters in 5,400 churches to cancel "preferential treatment" for LGBT people.

With the deadline for submitting signatures closing in, Eyman appeared at the Secretary of State's Office in a Darth Vader costume, toting a plastic light saber instead of petitions.

Eyman said he was waiting for more to come in from Spokane and he'd be back the next day. But when the last signatures trickled in before the 5 p.m. final bell, Eyman looked at the thin stack and muttered, "Jesus." The remark "only highlighted the bizarre marriage of convenience that has existed between Eyman and the religious right over the last few months," wrote journalist Eli Sanders.

Gary Randall, president of the Faith & Freedom Network, was so frustrated that he "maneuvered out of a television-camera shot that seemed to have both him and Eyman in it, later scolding the camerawoman for picturing the two of them together."

The dogfight that *Seattle Gay News* had envisioned ended with a whimper from backbiting foes. Voters had made up their minds: "They declined to sign," said *The Seattle Times*.

Washington became the 17th state with laws protecting sexual orientation and the seventh to protect transgender people.

GIDDINESS ABOUT Eyman's over-reaching was soon shattered. In Olympia's Temple of Justice, the state Supreme Court ruled, 5-4, that there was a "rational basis" for the Legislature's ban on same-sex marriage.

Not long after the Court's "terrible" 2006 decision, Levinson felt pulled to another cause. The Seattle Sonics and Storm were sold to a group of Oklahoma investors led by Clay Bennett, who were soon vilified in Washington. With all the focus on the NBA franchise, it looked like no one was trying to keep the women's team in Seattle.

A Storm fan, Levinson began poking around in early 2007 and kept hearing "it couldn't be done." She was told Bennett was fed up with how he and his partners had been demonized and sued by local officials. And he wasn't interested in talking to anyone in Washington.

Bennett and his partners were also Republicans. Some had contributed to anti-LGBTQ causes and candidates. "Couldn't have been more different than me and the work I had done," she says.

She turned the prism. In Oklaho-ma, Bennett and his partners were civ-

Levinson invited legendary Latino activist Roberto Maestas to join her courtside for a 2010 WNBA Finals game. "Anne holds a special place in my heart for doing something so kind and special for Roberto," said his widow, Estela Ortega. An avid fan, he died weeks later. *Anne Levinson*

ic leaders. They raised money for the state fair, and for a memorial to 168 lives lost in an Oklahoma City bombing by right-wing extremists. Bennett's crew had a history of other good deeds. At home they were local heroes, not plundering vandals.

But how to open a back channel to Bennett?

Levinson had a connection. Jim Roth was a regulator on Oklahoma's utilities commission. He was also openly gay and she knew him from their mutual work for the Victory Fund, a national LGBTQ political group. She asked Roth if he'd be willing to vouch to Bennett that she was fair and honest, and not one of the folks making his life miserable.

Roth said he'd give it a shot.

Based on Roth's reference, Bennett agreed to talk. Beforehand, Levinson scoured his past, looking for common ground. That was something she learned in her Title IX quest. She had found male allies who didn't care much about women's sports but were troubled by glaring unfairness. And in finding those commonalities, she learned that some differences with others didn't make them bad or mean-spirited. Bennett had grown up in the Midwest, like her, and had gone to a state school, OU, while she was at KU. He was private and not self-promoting. He was raised by a Jewish mother. He and his wife owned a book store. He had a record of civic duty.

"He knew I was a lesbian. He knew I was a liberal Democrat," she says. But

Levinson, hailed as "the calm that saved the Storm," and co-owners Dawn Trudeau, Ginny Gilder, and Lisa Brummel. *The Seattle Times*

once they got talking, "we laughed about our differences and what we had in common."

Operating in secrecy, she approached three local women who were Storm fans with the financial resources she lacked. She asked if they'd be willing to buy the team if she could find a way to save it. She was blunt. She put her chance of success at about 5 percent. They agreed to go for it.

For a face-to-face meeting with Bennett, she suggested a neutral site: Portland. They could negotiate at a hotel, and take a break to wander the stacks at nearby Powell's Books.

Levinson worked solo on probably the most difficult transaction of her career. She had to untangle the business affairs of the Storm, which were intertwined with the Sonics, but very much subordinate to the NBA team. She had to find a new practice facility and offices for the Storm. She also needed to strike an arena deal with the city of Seattle because the Storm's lease was set to expire in 2007.

And that feat looked more like a half-court heave than a dunk. Jilted Seattleites had passed Initiative 91 which mandated that the city could not subsidize deals with team owners; it had to receive market value. She hurdled those obstacles and more: helping Oklahoma get its own WNBA franchise and haggling down the Storm's $10 million purchase-price.

The Storm's new owners were unveiled in January 2008. Levinson was part of the quartet, along with Lisa Brummel, Ginny Gilder and Dawn Trudeau, accomplished businesswomen who had put up the money to buy the team. Levinson became the group's initial chairperson, similar to Bennett's position among his Oklahoma partners.

"We knew the right thing to do for Seattle was to work with Anne's group to see if we could make this happen," Bennett said at the time.

Levinson was hailed as "the calm that saved the Storm." She and Governor Gregoire were named grand marshals for the 2008 Seattle Pride Parade.

AFTER WAVING, royally, from the back of a parade convertible, Grand Marshal Levinson was soon handed the keys to saving the marriage movement in Washington.

After the state Supreme Court's crushing decision in 2006, advocates turned to another strategy. Led by Ed Murray and Rep. Jamie Pedersen, they pursued a legislative approach to secure domestic partnership rights. Pedersen, a Seattle Democrat, identified hundreds of instances in state law where marital status affected basic

After waving royally, from the back of a parade convertible, Grand Marshal Levinson was handed the keys in 2009 to saving the marriage movement in Washington. *Anne Levinson*

rights, such as hospital visitations, community property, and inheritance rights. Those rights were organized into three buckets. Murray and Pedersen began sponsoring bills over three consecutive years that conferred a triad of benefits to domestic partners.

Gregoire signed the last of the domestic partnership bills, called "everything but marriage," in May 2009, and opponents announced they would try to repeal it in November via Referendum 71.

The struggle for marriage rights had taken a devastating turn in 2008. In California, an alliance of Mormon, Catholic and Protestant clergy, aided by a keen strategist, had reported raising so many campaign contributions in early October that the Secretary of State's website crashed. They made education their battleground. In mailings and ads, the Proposition 8 campaign warned that children would be indoctrinated by a pro-gay curriculum if their measure was not approved.

"Mom, guess what I learned in school today?" a little girl said in one spot. "I learned how a prince married a prince." A voice-over said: "Teaching about gay marriage will happen unless we pass Proposition 8."

Research showed the message swayed voters who had "live and let live" beliefs—as long as those did not have serious implications for society.

Barack Obama won California by 3.2 million votes that year. Like Governor Chris Gregoire he wasn't ready to support marriage equality yet. At the same time, the Golden State banned same-sex marriage by a 600,000-vote margin.

With the forecast choppy at best in Washington, Levinson led a new statewide coalition, Washington Families Standing Together trying to accomplish what no one had—a statewide vote to legally recognize LGBTQ families. (Only courts and legislatures had approved civil unions and same-sex marriage in states such as Vermont and Massachusetts.)

"If you look at the national landscape," Levinson says, "for people working in the movement, there was a huge concern that if we lost this, it would set back things everywhere, not just in Washington state."

Building on 2006, she quickly brought together business, labor, faith and other groups in Washington. Levinson's team organized volunteers to oversee signature verification by the Secretary of State's Office in Olympia every day during the summer. They filed a challenge, claiming opponents' technical errors kept them from having enough valid signatures to qualify R71 for the ballot.

Conservatives said disclosing names of people who signed their initiative petitions would lead to harassment. Secretary of State Sam Reed and Attorney General Rob McKenna took the case to the U.S. Supreme Court, arguing the names should be public. The high court agreed, 8-1. *Washington Secretary of State*

But a Thurston County judge decided against them. Opponents cleared the threshold by 1,400 signatures. Levinson scrambled on the election front with just two months to go. "The numbers were not with us, and if we didn't do everything just right, we were going to lose."

DESPITE HER DISCOMFORT with the spotlight, Levinson faced off against opponents before editorial boards and on the airwaves. Her discipline was needed. "One of the reasons people wanted me out front was because I had an ability to stay calm and respectful. Or, to keep in mind that we're not trying to win the debate. I wanted folks to look at me and say, 'Oh that could be my niece, or daughter, or neighbor. Look at how they're attacking her, that's just not right.' "

Similar thinking applied when Levinson wanted to produce homegrown TV ads. Some in her camp pushed to feature young faces. If they don't like us, tough, they'd argue.

"And I would say, 'Sorry guys, but the polling shows that women just do better for folks still concerned about LGBTQ stuff. And older women do even better, because people don't like the idea that two older women who are living together can't look out for each other in health care.' "

She organized a TV commercial featuring two retirees (and grand dames of the movement), Jane Abbott Lighty and Pete-e Petersen in their West Seattle backyard. "And I had them talk about how they lived their lives together and Pete-e had been an Air Force nurse. And all they wanted to do was make sure if one of them needed something the other could be there. They could have medical care."

In an "off-year" election without national or state races, 2009 turnout would be lower. And it would tilt towards older voters, who tended to lean conservative. That was another reason to showcase Jane and Pete-e.

The big church money that propelled Prop. 8's $40 million campaign in California never materialized in Washington. The election-drive for domestic partners raised $2.2 million compared to $500,000 reported by opponents.

Referendum 71 was approved with 53 percent. Levinson and the coalition had cleared a runway for flight in 2012.

AFTER NEW YORK LEGALIZED marriage equality in 2011, the movement regained altitude. In 2012, marriage equality would be on the ballot in Washington, along with Maine, Maryland and Minnesota.

The California debacle had been thoroughly examined under a new lens. Advocates began to deeply explore the question of why voters, especially those in the "muddled middle," weren't keen on same-sex marriage. This led advocates toward "deep canvassing" that would be deployed in Washington. In a radical

Levinson recommended the marriage-equality campaign make Jennifer Cast (left, with her partner and their twins) its chief fundraiser. One of Amazon's first employees, Cast received a $2.5 million contribution from Jeff and MacKenzie Bezos. *Freedom to Marry*

departure from conventional politics, field workers would stay at the door-steps of "micro-targeted" voters to talk at length about their feelings and questions. Oregon researchers Thalia Zepatos and Lisa Grove showed that many Americans were on a journey to understanding same-sex marriage. And having "the conversation" with gay relatives, neighbors or their supporters was often pivotal.

Levinson, by then, had a new job, one of the toughest in Seattle. Mayor Mike McGinn appointed her the civilian expert to review how the police department handled misconduct complaints—at a time when the city's officers had come under a federal order to remedy their pattern of using excessive force against minorities.

The marriage equality campaign would be run by a full-time professional manager, Zach Silk. Levinson would advise and head the legal team. She turned over her 2009 playbook to Silk and recommended he put Jennifer Cast on the point for fundraising. One of Amazon's first employees, Cast would prove crucial. She solicited Jeff Bezos for a contribution that summer, saying, frankly, she and her family needed people like him to step up. Bezos and his wife, MacKenzie, donated $2.5 million, by far the largest check the campaign received. (Opponents would raise $2.8 million in all, and were outspent five-to-one.)

With the homestretch approaching, Levinson—confined to her couch after a biking accident—had a brainstorm. If we win, she realized, state and national attention will be focused on us. Given their different dates for implementing new marriage laws, Washington would hold weddings before other victorious 2012 states. Building on newfound public support, how could those first weddings advance the cause?

"It is, I think, fair to say that were it not for Washington's decades-long success we wouldn't be where we are in the country," says Zach Silk, the R74 campaign manager. *Zach Silk*

Levinson wanted to deliver on the campaign's promises of love and devotion. "But I was realizing at the same time that we still had a really significant public education, media education strategy that was needed," she recalls. "Remember, this was all still considered pretty radical, a pretty dramatic change. But also, we had clerk's offices—the people who deal with marriage licenses—we had secretaries of state, we had religious institutions, we had all of these different entities who were like, 'what is going to happen with 'X?' And we had all of these couples who wanted to know, 'If it does pass can I get married right away? Oh, there's a waiting period? Oh, you have to apply—how does that work?"

Levinson wanted to showcase the first legal marriages for the media. Above is the lobby of Benaroya Hall just after Levinson officiated the wedding of Jane Abbott Lighty and Pete-e Petersen. *Anne Levinson*

Levinson had question-and-answer guides prepared for county clerks and other officials. She put together volunteer "SWAT" teams in each county where she had asked diverse couples, known in their communities, to participate in the first registrations and marriages in different parts of the state. Volunteers would also help reporters and photojournalists prepare. And in places where the media might not attend, volunteers would capture video, audio and photos to distribute on social media.

After marriage equality won 54 percent in Washington, Levinson set out to direct scenes with a wide frame and deep focus.

"We would overwhelm them with images and stories and interviews and background that reinforced everything we'd been saying for so many years. This was it. These were people's lives. And because they voted the way we asked them to, everybody's lives were now changed for the better."

Consonant with the campaign's central message, she wanted to depict marriage equality as shoring up an institution of stability, not taking anything away.

Her storyboard featured long-term couples. In the state's largest media market that would translate into a midnight show on December 6—the first chance for licensing—at the King County Courthouse. Matriarchs Jane Abbott Lighty and Pete-e Petersen would be the first recipients. In Thurston County, the first license went to Lisa Brodoff and Lynn Grotsky, who had been together 32 years. The *BBC*, *The Christian Science Monitor* and *USA Today* covered the ceremonies.

As a judge, Mary Yu was prohibited from politicking. So Yu officiated adoptions by LGBTQ couples, such as Emily and Sarah Cofer, the first same-sex couple married in Seattle—by Yu. *Barb Kinney*

Licensing was a rehearsal for marriages that would be consummated after the state's three-day waiting period, at the stroke of December 9th. Levinson had been talking with King County Superior Court Judge Mary Yu, who wanted to officiate the first marriages at 12:01 a.m. Plans were set in motion for Yu's courtroom, and others around the state.

Sarah and Emily Cofer, two public-school teachers, were the first in line for Judge Yu. Just out of the camera shot, Levinson held their 9-month-old daughter during the ceremony.

Yu's crew officiated until 7 am. Then a second shift would start at Seattle City Hall a few hours later. Volunteer judges were stationed around the spacious lobby, far enough apart, so that each couple would appear in their own shots, giving the ceremonies a personal feel. Then, couples would exit down the half-block sloping staircase outside City Hall, where friends, family and supporters could shower them with flowers and applause. It was the chef's kiss of photo ops.

Seattle journalist Dominic Holden, later, national LGBTQ reporter for *Buzz-Feed*, called Levinson, "The woman behind the curtain of marriage equality this year."

RUNNING ON ADRENALINE, Levinson readied for a grand finale. Later that day, the beloved Seattle Men's Chorus would perform its annual holiday show at a sold-out Benaroya Hall. The concert drew audiences young and old, gay and straight, and for many it was a family tradition.

Dennis Coleman, the chorus director and conductor, had been thinking about the important message it would send if the chorus could host one of the state's first same-sex marriages. He asked the Men's Chorus and Women's Chorus to each select a couple. Maestro Levinson would officiate.

The event unfolded this way: Just before intermission of the Men's Chorus performance, conductor Coleman asked the audience to remain seated. Stashed backstage, the Women's Chorus came out and stood with the Men's Chorus.

Levinson was introduced. A trellis was wheeled out. Levinson supplied a little history before Jane Abbott and Pete-e Petersen, both aglow, exchanged vows and rings. The crowd whooped and whistled when Levinson said "by the authority *now vested* in me by the state of Washington."

They stood, clapped, hugged and cried when the wedded couples came off the stage and walked down an aisle to the lobby. The audience joined them there in celebrating the intermission with 3,000 wedding cupcakes.

On the first day of marriages, Conductor Dennis Coleman suggested the Seattle Men's Chorus host a ceremony during a sold-out holiday show at Benaroya Hall. *Anne Levinson*

Public opinion had shifted. It was not going back.

In 2013, the U.S. Supreme Court struck down the federal Defense of Marriage Act in the case of *U.S. vs. Windsor*. Edie Windsor and Thea Spyer had lived together as a couple since 1968. Their marriage in Canada was recognized by New York. After Spyer died in 2009, Windsor sought a spousal exemption to federal taxes on her inheritance of Spyer's estate.

In a 5-4 decision on June 26, 2013, the high court ruled that the federal Defense of Marriage Act deprived gay people of equal liberty protected by the Fifth Amendment.

Two years later, to the day, the Supreme Court issued a decision in the case of *Obergefell v. Hodges*.

Ohio residents James Obergefell and his ailing partner, John Arthur, were married in Maryland, so that when Arthur died from Lou Gehrig's disease, Obergefell would be his surviving spouse. In another 5-4 decision, Justice Anthony Kennedy again wrote for the majority. Under the due process and equal protection clauses of the 14th Amendment, Kennedy declared that same-sex couples were entitled to marry.

Zach Silk, the manager of Washington's campaign for marriage equality, says the long-time dedication of Levinson and others created an infrastructure for success. Referendum 71 was "extraordinarily" important as a trial run for how to organize against attacks on relationship recognition. And he credits much of his 2012 success—and its larger impact—to Levinson's playbook.

"It is, I think, fair to say that were it not for Washington's decades-long success we wouldn't be where we are in the country."

Gregoire considered Levinson an adviser, albeit an exacting one, at times, pushing the governor to do "everything humanly possible" for the cause. "She's not going to sugarcoat anything. OK? She's going to be very straightforward and honest. And challenging. But that's just Anne."

When dealing with an issue as significant as marriage equality, Gregoire says, "having that personality is gold."

A POLICY OMNIVORE, Levinson likes to tackle interlocking and seemingly intractable issues. After marriage equality, she focused on matters such as child welfare (co-chairing a governor's blue-ribbon panel), domestic violence and firearms (advocating "extreme risk protection orders"), and daylighting "dark money" in Washington's political system (pushing reforms as leader of the state's Public Disclosure Commission). One reporter called her a "polymath of politics, business, and law."

"Anne is one of the great civic leaders in Washington state, in any number of domains," says Silk, the R74 campaign manager.

While some activists seek publicity or "status amplification," he says, Levinson is very aware that hunting the spotlight often doesn't get the work done—and can impede it. Because of her work ethic, people are eager to "welcome her" to their cause.

"She's got her fingerprints on a lot of very consequential things that make Washington a civic innovator, just really an innovative state."

Bob Young

MAUREEN AND SHAUNA WALSH

"Off the cuff, from the heart"

Maureen Walsh and her daughter, Shauna Walsh, share a gift for speaking directly and humbly, from the heart, with twists of humor. Maureen's most famous example came when she rose on the floor of the State House of Representatives during 2012 debate on a bill to legalize same-sex marriage. Without prepared remarks, Walsh delivered four minutes of homespun wisdom on enduring love, discrimination and a mother's pride. A Republican from Walla Walla, she would be one of just two GOP House members to vote on February 8th for marriage equality.

Walsh's 593 words that day made her, in the words of *The New York Times* columnist Timothy Egan, "a hero to many people around the world." Walsh heard that her speech went viral. "And I said, 'Oh gosh, I'm sorry.' I thought that meant that I put a virus in it," she says.

Waves of calls and emails swamped her office and devices. She heard from irate conservatives; others praised her gumption. And she heard from young people who felt scorned, even by their parents, because of their sexual orientation. One asked to be adopted by her.

Because Maureen made her daughter central to her speech, Shauna was also bombarded by messages—some nasty, others poignant. Shauna, a lesbian, had influenced her mom's thinking on marriage equality, persuading her that domestic partnerships weren't enough. They weren't equal. In her speech, Maureen said domestic partnerships sounded "like a Merry Maids franchise."

Mother and daughter were soon invited to a swank LGBTQ fundraiser in Los Angeles, where Maureen followed Betty White on stage. Shauna chatted with Chaz Bono and they complimented each other's mom. Maureen appeared in a TV ad for marriage equality when it landed on the November ballot as Referendum 74, after the bill signed by Governor Chris Gregoire was challenged by opponents.

Facing page: Shauna Walsh, left, at her 2015 wedding ceremony with her mother Maureen. *Shauna Walsh*

ESSB 6239 • MARRIAGE & DOMESTIC PARTNERSHIPS   2/8/12
REP. MAUREEN WALSH (R)

Maureen's 2012 speech reinforced a key point: people tend to get their values from their families not school teachers, as Christian conservatives have claimed. *TVW*

But back to that speech, which had 1.5 million views on YouTube within a week.

In a 2022 phone interview from her winter retreat, an RV park in Mexico, Maureen Walsh, a relaxed retiree, said it wasn't a difficult decision for her to support marriage equality, despite the political peril. "I was just raised with wonderful parents, who just didn't discriminate. And, you know, the reality is, if you love someone, you love someone. So, it really was pretty simple for me."

Shauna, speaking from her home in Minnesota, also in January 2022, with the temperature hovering around you-don't-want-to-know, said she had an inkling her mom might make a stand. "She had called me ahead of time and said, 'I'm planning on speaking to a bill that's going on the floor,'" Shauna recalls. "And was it OK if she referenced me? Because I was essentially the closest gay person to her and she needed that personal interest piece to tie in to her speech."

Shauna watched her mom's plea for House Bill 2516 on her computer via a live feed from TVW, Washington state's version of C-Span. "What surprised me was how far it reached. People all over the world were looking at this. And even today, in Minnesota, people talk about it at work sometimes. They're like, 'Oh, my gosh, your mom is the one that made that speech.'"

MAUREEN LUCILLE Katherine Stewart Walsh started by saying she didn't want to scold anybody. She did not want to be perceived as throwing other Republicans "under the bus." That was very much a priority. She began:

> *I don't wax as eloquently as most of the people on the floor here, but I've allowed my heart and my mind to guide me in decisions that I've made on a lot of different issues that have been before us in the legislature. And I think sometimes that's what we have to do. I too don't want to wag my finger at anybody about which way you should vote on this.*

Nothing she says was written out, Walsh says. "I've never rehearsed a speech in my life. I do everything off the cuff and from the heart. And I think that's kind of one of my strengths—that when I did give a speech it was always from the heart." Yes, she was from a conservative district and she might pay a severe price. "But on the other hand," she says, "what kind of integrity do you have as an individual if you allow something like that to sway your conscience?"

At one time, she thought her very Catholic parents back in Ohio might object to her support for same-sex marriage. But her mother, a registered nurse, and her father, who worked in public relations for Procter and Gamble, just smiled. Walsh recalls her mother saying, "Well, honey, that's alright, it's the human genome." Her father mentioned a nice lesbian couple who lived down the street with two cute kids. "And I was almost like, 'Where are my parents? Who are you people?'"

Quite personally, she resumed:
> *I was married for 23 years to the love of my life. He died six years ago, and you know, I'm a lonely old widow right now. I'm 51-years-old, looking for a boyfriend. Not having much luck with that.*

Some of her colleagues tittered at her frankness:
> *And yet, when I think of my husband, and I think of all the wonderful years we had, and the wonderful fringe benefit of having three beautiful children, I don't miss the sex. You know? And to me that's kind of what this boils down to. I don't miss that. I mean I certainly miss it.*

More titters.
> *But it is certainly not the aspect of that relationship—that incredible bond I had with that human being—that I really, really genuinely wish I still had.*

WILLIAM "KELLY" WALSH died at 51 from a heart attack in April 2006. His death made the front page of the *Walla Walla Union-Bulletin*, where he was described as the area's "Sausage King," a multi-faceted character who said "Peace," when he parted company with someone, and a savvy entrepreneur who owned a building at the city's busiest downtown corner.

"They truly had a partnership marriage," said Lorie Mastin, a friend of Kelly and Maureen Walsh.
Shauna Walsh

His persona was as bold as his huge handlebar mustache. "He was just a big, gentle bear," said Maureen's legislative aide Marge Plumage. "He had no airs about him. What you saw was what you got."

What Shauna saw: "He was this big brawny huge-shouldered guy who wore coveralls covered in sheet rock dust his whole life. He did not look like the husband of a state senator. [After 12 years in the House, Maureen moved up to the Senate.] He never did. Never would have in his whole life. He felt like your appearance had nothing to do with anything important."

He grew up in Walla Walla where his parents owned Blue Mountain Memorial Gardens cemetery. He dug graves. That's how he got his broad shoulders, Shauna says. He owned a concrete business. He had been bullied in school and his undiagnosed dyslexia made learning a challenge. "I think he never forgot where he came from and being bullied himself really opened his eyes to what that looked like and how that made people feel."

If you knew him well, Shauna says, you could detect him crying quietly, emitting barely audible "pfff" sounds, while watching tragic news stories. "I considered myself to be a pretty emotional person. But yeah, he just felt stories from other people so powerfully."

While in college, Kelly had begun making sausage as a hobby. "And then he really started turning it into something," Shauna says. At first, it meant the family getting up at 5 a.m. on Saturdays to load the truck and set up a stand at the Walla Walla farmer's market. Shauna sold lemonade. Mom ran the cash box and dad worked the grill. One of Shauna's brothers kept the coolers iced; the other was too young then to help.

The family affair led to "Onion World," a downtown brick-and-mortar restaurant, named after the state's official vegetable, the Walla Walla sweet onion. Kelly had helped wrest the title from the powerful potato lobby by bringing his sausage to the Capitol; Maureen did the rest.

Kelly died just as construction was completed on Onion World at First and Main Streets. No one knew the secret behind his "Walla Walla sweet onion sausage." But Shauna's brother Patrick discovered his dad's little red journal on spices and recipes. "We were all very much in the grief-and-love process where we felt it was important. So, we opened the restaurant later that year," she says. She managed it for a few years.

Maureen married Kelly when she was 22. Her parents, Bob and Mary Stewart, left, were married 67 years. Kelly's parents Virginia and William "Paco" Walsh are on the right. *Shauna Walsh*

Wistful, but profoundly grateful about the 23 years she shared with her husband, Maureen Walsh said:

> *So, I think to myself, How could I deny the right to have that incredible bond with another individual in life? To me it seems almost cruel.*

ALMOST TWO MINUTES into her talk, she introduced Shauna:

> *Many of you have met my daughter. She's a fabulous girl. She's wonderful. My boys are great too, but my daughter is just something special. She was the light of her father's eyes.*
>
> *And she went to school and there was a whole group of kids just picking on another kid. And you know, my daughter stood up for that kid. Even though it wasn't the popular thing to do, she knew it was the right thing.*

Shauna was in 8th grade, she recalls, when her friend Shaun, who was new to the school, was getting hassled and hazed in the hall. "I just sort of screamed at a bunch of boys right outside the locker room and explained it is not OK to harass him. He can be whoever he wants and this is bullying plain and simple. It's wrong." School officials called her parents. "I don't know all the words I chose," Shauna says. "But I know they weren't all school-appropriate. So, my mom I'm sure was aware of that one." She was more than aware. She was inspired:

Shauna and her friend Shaun Gray before 9th grade homecoming. Shaun announced his engagement in 2022 to his partner Steve. *Shauna Walsh*

I was never more proud of my kid, knowing that she was speaking against the vocal majority on behalf of the rights of the minority. To me, it is incumbent upon us as legislators in this state to do that. That is why we are here.

I shudder to think that if folks who have preceded us in history did not do that, frankly I'm not sure I would be here, as a woman. I'm not sure other people would be here due to their race or their creed.

Shauna credits her parents for her defense of her friend Shaun, who later came out as gay.

"I never cowed to anyone else's belief or listened to anybody else tell me who I thought I should or shouldn't be. My mom was very strong and she was the career woman in our family and I come from a long line of feminists on both sides, maternal and paternal, of the family. I always stuck up for the underdog and I learned that from my dad. He was always sticking up for people that maybe weren't as fortunate, or faced inequities for broader reasons whether they were born into poverty or based on their race or ethnicity. "Both of my parents believed in judging a person by who they are as a person, their merit."

Monitoring her mom's speech from her workplace in Minnesota, Shauna, then 26, was surprised at what came next:

Someone made the comment that this is not about equality. Well, yes, it is about equality. Why in the world would we not allow those equal rights for those individuals who truly were committed to one another in life? To be able to show that by way of a marriage?

"To me, my mom has always been this larger-than-life person," says Shauna. *Shauna Walsh*

Maureen's words were evidence she listened to her daughter. She had said to Shauna years earlier that she didn't think there was much difference between marriage and domestic partnerships, or civil unions, other than religious ceremonies. "And I had made my counter arguments," Shauna says. "We had political debates all the time, and I was never really able to sway her and she was never able to sway me. It was fine and we moved on and it was good."

But hearing her mom talk in the Capitol about marriage equality was different. "That was really nice and a personal thing for me when she said, 'No, domestic partnership isn't good enough.' " Maureen not only voted for marriage equality; she was the second sponsor to sign on to Seattle Representative Jamie Pedersen's bill. From either party. She then outed Shauna to the world:

> *My daughter came out of the closet a couple of years ago. And you know what, I thought I was just going to agonize about that. Nothin's different. She's still a fabulous human being, and she's met a person that she loves very much, and some day, by God, I wanna throw a wedding for that kid. I hope that is exactly what I can do. I hope she will not feel like a second-class citizen involved in something called a "domestic partnership" that frankly sounds like a Merry Maids franchise to me.*

Shauna, who graduated from Walla Walla High School in 2004, eight years earlier, said she had not come out in the sense of a grand unveiling—despite the impact of others doing so.

"It is really interesting how that has evolved too in recent years. Because it used to be this big thing with Ellen DeGeneres. I remember watching her show, her sitcom growing up—before the talk show—and when she came out it, was just all over, this huge thing. It was so important to come out and state who you are and what box you fit into.

"For me, it was never that I felt like I had to sit people down and say, 'Listen, here is the thing: I'm a lesbian.' So, I never did that. My very close friends knew that I had interests in that area. It wasn't something that we put in the forefront of importance."

Her mom then wrapped up:

Thank you, Mr. Speaker, that's all I want to say. Thank you for the civil, wonderful debate today. It's been great.

"I REALLY KNOW how to poke them in the eye," Maureen says 10 years later with a laugh. "Don't I? 'Oh, you think domestic partners is a big deal—watch this.' Yeah, it was just the right thing to do. I probably cried every night of that session, realizing that that bill was coming up. And the only other person to support that in the [GOP House] caucus was Glenn Anderson (from Fall City in King County) because he had a gay brother.

"Now, let me tell you something else. All those people that voted 'no,' I had several of them come up and put their arm around me, and say, 'You know, I would've voted 'yes' too except I'm afraid I would've been un-elected.'

"And, in some regards, yes, you're there to represent your district. But this isn't talking about water rights. This isn't talking about natural resources. This is talking about an issue of conscience that we all live with. And the only way I can live with myself, is if I'm honest with myself. That was my choice."

Reactions rolled in from all over. Soon, her office assistant Marge Plumage "was just about pulling her hair out." Messages were backing up like I-5 traffic around JBLM. Walsh pulled in extra staff to help. "That's when I understood the power of the internet, let me tell you."

She was pretty sure she'd lose her next election. Her district had voted over-whelmingly against the state's "everything-but-marriage" domestic partnership law when it was on the 2009 statewide ballot.

Back at home, she went to a county GOP meeting. "They were not happy," she recalls, "and by God, I need to be representing their interests.

"I looked at them, and said, 'How dare you? You can't tell me how to feel. You can't tell me what my conscience dictates to me.' So, I defended myself. But I really got beat up at that meeting.

"And I came home, and on my answering machine—see how far we've come? —the little light was blinking. And so I went, 'Oh God, here we go.' I hit the ma-chine and I heard, [imitating a man's gruff voice], 'Hey, this is Jim Smith'—or whatever his name was— 'I'm 92 years old and I don't like gay people. But girl, you got cojones to stand up and talk about what you believe in. And for that, I respect you. And you've got my vote.' "

MOM JUST LOST her job. That was Shauna's reaction. "I had concerns about that because my mom was a single parent then, her income supporting my brothers who were still living at home at the time. So, I had a little bit of guilt that she had done this for me as a show of support and she was really going to pay the price for it with her career."

Then Shauna, a Democrat, saw that her mom was being lionized on "The Young Turks," a YouTube channel popular with progressives. When she saw other liberal platforms hailing clips from the "speech-of-the-year," she thought, "Oh, this is serious here."

Strangers found her email address and Facebook profile.

"That was really wild. And some of the emails were lovely and some weren't so lovely. But a lot of people, even if they weren't on board necessarily with marriage equality, they would still say something like clearly you mean a lot to your mom. So that was at least nice. They were acknowledging the parental love portion of the whole speech."

She also received deeply emotional emails, including from people who said they hadn't spoken to their gay child in years, but her mom changed their thinking.

"Or there was a young person, like a 19-year-old guy who had struggled with suicidal thoughts and he was from this very evangelical household and he felt like my mom—because of her political affiliation—speaking out just made him have hope for the future. Where he had felt there was none before. And I thought that was really powerful."

BUT SHAUNA wasn't expecting a detour to Hollywood.

Soon, she and her mom were invited to the GLAAD (Gay & Lesbian Alliance Against Defamation) Media Awards in

At the GLAAD Media Awards in Los Angeles, Shauna told Chaz Bono she loved his mom. He replied, "Your mom is pretty cool herself." *Shauna Walsh*

Los Angeles. Maureen was asked to speak. Honorees and guests included Ellen DeGeneres, Jesse Tyler Ferguson and Benecio del Toro.

"And it was hilarious, because I was a nobody," Maureen says, "and they told me, 'Go to the Green Room before you go on stage.' So that evening I was all dressed up in my basic black dress, and I went to the Green Room, and there were police officers surrounding it."

She said "excuse me" and tried to go in. They said, "Sorry, ma'am."

She persisted: "No, I'm supposed to go here because I'm up on stage after Betty White and the gals from *Hot in Cleveland*."

The officers wouldn't budge. They grabbed her a chair to sit in backstage. When Betty White came off and said "hello," Maureen told her how much she liked White and her work. Then the lawmaker stepped up to do her part and drew a deep breath.

"And I'm staring out at this room with thousands of people; I presume predominantly gay people. And I said, 'You're probably wondering who this overweight, middle-aged woman is, standing up here on the stage, following the likes of Betty White. My name is Maureen. Maureen Walsh. And I'm a legislator from Washington state—a Republican legislator—and I gave a speech on marriage equality.'

"And everybody in that room stood up on their feet and applauded me. I was in absolute shock."

Shauna was sitting at a beautifully decorated round dinner table in the ball room, dazzled by "star-struck-y" feelings.

"It was amazing. It was surreal. There was a silent auction and people were pulling out their checkbooks and donating to certain causes. There was a man at our table who ended up bidding $30,000 on a trip to Thailand and just pulled out a checkbook and wrote a check for that. I'm like, 'good lord, that's what I make in a year.' And seated to my left was Chaz Bono."

Bono was receiving an award from GLAAD for a documentary he had done about his transition. Former Congresswoman Mary Bono, his stepmoth-

After her speech was praised by liberals, Maureen Walsh drew a Republican challenger in 2012. Walsh won re-election with 58 percent. *Shauna Walsh*

er, was on stage with him when out strode a surprise guest.

"Take one guess," Maureen says.

The woman who needs only one name. She was the reason for the strict security around the Green Room.

"We're in this group," Maureen continues, "and I'm telling you, you talk about rising to their—they were jumping on the tables. Everybody was so thrilled to see Cher. She had an Afro that was as big as a beachball on her head. And she's rockin' some leather outfit, or something. It was just a hoot."

From there, Maureen and Shauna went to Washington, D.C., for a wonky event called the Commitment Summit. It focused on history, policy and the push in states for marriage equality. It was Shauna's first time in the nation's capital and she relished touring the landmarks she had only seen in movies. Everyone went home with a proclamation by President Obama making June LGBT Pride Month. "I still have it in my house," she says. "It's framed up in our bedroom."

The whirlwind next dropped them into a segment of Lawrence O'Donnell's show on MSNBC. Shauna appeared from Minneapolis. A town car whisked her to a local TV station where they did her hair and makeup. It was that kind of a year.

AND THAT WEDDING Maureen wanted to throw for her kid? "She got to throw me four actually. Because I'm just that extra," Shauna says with a laugh.

After Washington, Maine, Maryland and Minnesota all voted in favor of marriage equality in 2012, other states followed. On Shauna's birthday in January 2015, Florida approved marriage equality. She had recently proposed to her partner Amy. Her mom asked what she wanted to do about a wedding ceremony.

Shauna wasn't sure. Her family was in Washington. Her mom's family was in Ohio. She also had a group of people in Minnesota who meant a lot to her. She didn't want people to have to travel long distances to the wedding, and she didn't want to exclude anybody.

"It's really hard to plan a wedding like that without inviting 5 million people and having it at a banquet hall that everyone can teleport to. So, impossible. We toyed around with the idea of doing a vacation destination wedding. My mom was excited about that idea because we were in the middle of winter and session had just started, I think, for her in Washington."

She and Amy thought about getting married in Florida. They'd celebrate with a Disney Cruise because Amy's son Tanner Calverley was eight years old then. "We wanted to do something that would be fun for him, also fun for us. So we took a cruise to the Bahamas from Florida."

Maureen got her wish in 2015. Not only did Shauna and her partner Amy have a wedding ceremony in the Bahamas, above. They also celebrated with friends and family in Ohio, Minnesota and Washington. *Shauna Walsh*

Shauna and Amy were legally wed in a Florida court before departing.

"The ceremony, just for show, was on the beach in the Bahamas which was great," Shauna says. "There were only eight of us total including Amy and Tanner. It was a very private, intimate wedding. My brothers were there and my mom was there. Amy's dad and one of Amy's sisters came and was our photographer as well."

They later had a big party in Ohio with her mom's family. And then they threw a bigger party in Minnesota. And they followed up with a summer bash in Washington. "We kind of had this wedding tour for six months to a year after our wedding actually happened. It was a really fun way to do it. And it kind of pieced it out so it wasn't this huge, stressful situation. I feel like we did our wedding perfectly."

THERE WAS A STRIKING prescience to Walsh's speech. As advocates pushed for marriage equality in 2012, they had adopted a new strategy. Sophisticated research pointed out better ways to sway voters who weren't adamantly opposed to same-sex marriage, but also weren't sure why the LGBTQ community wanted it.

For years, advocates had argued about issues such as hospital visitation rights and military service that didn't quite resonate with many Americans.

By 2012 they had learned to shift the focus from the head to the heart; to center the debate on love and white-picket-fence commitments, and how gay couples wanted the same as folks like Maureen and Kelly Walsh. Without coaching, Maureen had instinctively highlighted that touchstone months before it would appear in TV ads and other pillars of the 2012 election campaign.

"It does really boil down to relationships and love," she says, looking back at a tipping point in history. "And I think that's how things turned around."

BY 2021, Maureen was ready to leave the Legislature. She'd been an aide for 12 years to her mentor Dave Mastin, who switched from Democrat to Republican during his tenure representing Walla Walla and the state's 16th District. She had spent another 16 years trekking to Olympia for her constituents. "And frankly, I had a new person in my life. I was 11 years without anybody in my life," she says.

She joked that it was time to move on before she had people pushing her out. She left when her term ended in January 2021.

She got way "out-out" of partisan politics. She and her partner Jim bought a travel trailer. They spend winters in Mexico. "And then, when it gets hotter than hell, we head up north and travel around. So, I'm not getting ensconced in politics anywhere other than the politics of RV parks."

Beat.

"And let me tell you, there's enough politics in travel-trailing."

Deep in Mexico, Maureen Walsh remains off the cuff, from the heart.

Bob Young

CHRIS GREGOIRE

WITH A LITTLE HELP FROM HER DAUGHTERS

In 2004, just 31 percent of Americans supported same-sex marriage. As public opinion started to edge upward, LGBTQ campaign researchers came to realize the journey many voters were on. With more co-workers, fellow parishioners, and family members coming out, people were taking a longer look, and asking: Why *did* gay couples want to marry? What was the harm in their commitment? How was it American to deny them that right?

Another powerful force was at work: demographics. By 2011, 70 percent of younger Americans, 18 to 34 years old, supported same-sex marriage. That was almost twice the level of acceptance among folks 55 and older.

Those two factors—straight people looking anew at marriage equality and generational change—converged in Chris Gregoire's household. The governor was on a self-described "journey," trying to reconcile her faith and her sense of fairness and justice. She had been married in the Catholic Church. Her two daughters were baptized in the Catholic Church. Her faith did not support marriage equality.

Over her 12 years as the state's top lawyer, Gregoire had also backed anti-bullying and hate crimes legislation. She knew that hostility aimed at sexual orientation could have devastating consequences. Tragedy had hit close to home. Yet, when Gregoire was elected governor in 2004, she said Washington wasn't ready for marriage equality. Fully legal marriage in the U.S. existed then only in Massachusetts. And in the Evergreen State it seemed about as far away as Boston Common.

The governor felt more education was needed.

Gregoire always encouraged her girls, Courtney and Michelle, to stand up for fairness. Family values came full circle when they urged her to see marriage

Facing page: Courtney, Chris and Michelle Gregoire on holiday. Their huddle during Thanksgiving 2011 sealed the former governor's support for marriage equality. *Christine Gregoire*

equality through the same lens. They equated LGBTQ struggles to the civil rights rallies their mother joined when she was young. In dinner table debates and late-night phone calls, they said it was their generation's civil rights movement. Their passion for fairness deeply resonated with their mother.

"We obviously argued a lot," the former governor recalls. "But there was no argument that they could see for allowing others in the country to discriminate. I thought, 'God, it's exactly how I felt [in the 1960s], and said to my own mother, I don't understand how our country can discriminate against race?' So, that's how it came about. Not me seeing myself in them. But *them* raising the issue."

When Gregoire came around, she did so with full conviction. She introduced legislation to legalize same-sex marriage. She vowed to get it passed. Her mediating skill with lawmakers was unsurpassed, says Ed Murray, who was Olympia's preeminent LGTBQ advocate as a state legislator. Murray called her the best "closer" he had ever seen.

HOW DO YOU ARGUE with your mom when she's a three-term Attorney General, never mind one who stared down Big Tobacco and got it to cough up a $206 billion settlement to 46 states?

It's one thing if you were trying to extend your teenage curfew, Michelle Gregoire says. Good luck with that. But when it came to LGBTQ rights, Michelle and Courtney said it helped that gay and lesbian family friends visited their Olympia home, and their parents talked about rights and equality at the dinner table. Their mom also wanted to hear from her daughters and their peers on a range of issues. And she listened.

When Gregoire entered the Legislative Reception Room on February 13, 2012 to sign marriage equality into state law, chants of "thank you, thank you" erupted from the crowd. *Legislative Support Services*

She was very engaged and "present" with her children. Michelle has memories of kitchen-table conversations going back to when her mom had the family vote on whether she should make her initial run for attorney general.

That kind of attention left an impression, Michelle says. Looking back, she says she felt empowered.

Courtney's advocacy for the LGBTQ community dates to Olympia High School. Five years older than her sister, she was part of a 1995 committee that wanted to raise awareness about sexual orientation. The Student Activist Club invited Colonel Grethe Cammermeyer of the Washington Army National Guard to speak. A decorated combat nurse, Cammermeyer had been discharged for admitting she was a lesbian. She challenged the Pentagon's ban that kept members of the military closeted, winning reinstatement in 1994.

Her talk to a voluntary assembly of 600 students raised complaints. A group of state lawmakers scolded the school. One corner store handed out free soft drinks to students who boycotted Cammermeyer's appearance. Two weeks later, two Olympia students were assaulted by teenagers from the nearby town of Rochester. One of the students was openly bisexual and still recovering from an earlier assault. The second attack sent him into profound depression and he took his own life.

Courtney Gregoire, with husband Scott Lindsay at Seattle Pride 2013, has worked for U.S. Senator Maria Cantwell, President Obama, the Port of Seattle, and Microsoft. She has two daughters. *Scott Lindsay*

After a wave of weddings that followed college, Courtney found herself thinking of her LGTBTQ friends. She had watched straight couples exchanging vows, and being recognized by friends, family, and the law. She thought about friends who were comfortably out and wondered: what's their path going to be?

On her own journey, she went to Harvard Law School in 2002 and began gathering tools to build her case.

MARRIAGE DEBATE started to spread. Vermont opened the barn door, with its practical, secular civil unions, which some called "marriage lite." That was in 2000. Four years later, King County Superior Court Judge William Downing ruled that Washington's ban on same-sex marriage was unconstitutional—setting the stage for an appeal to the state Supreme Court. That same year, 2004, Massachusetts became the first state to legalize same-sex marriage. The conservative backlash was swift. President George W. Bush called for a U.S. Constitutional ban on same-sex marriage. His chief strategist Karl Rove orchestrated bans in 11 states.

That was the landscape when Chris Gregoire said Washington wasn't yet ready for marriage equality.

Courtney felt compelled to speak up. She called her mom from her law school dorm. "I definitely remember that late night phone call, 1 or 2 in the morning my time, where I felt I have to say this now: 'This is not fair. And we're clearly not going to see action at the federal level. What can happen? This has to happen at the state level.' "

It was a tense conversation, she says, and it didn't help that Courtney probably said "the Catholic Church got a few things wrong along the way."

Courtney got her law degree in 2005. The Washington Supreme Court ruled against same-sex marriage the next year, overturning Judge Downing's decision in King County. That began a new patchwork strategy.

LAWMAKERS LED by Ed Murray in the state Senate, and Jamie Pedersen, in the House, embarked on a long game. With Gregoire's support, they sought to pass domestic partnership rights in phases, while moving public education down the road toward marriage.

A tragedy in Seattle propelled the plan. A fierce tempest hammered Western Washington on December 16, 2006. Kate Fleming, an audiobook narrator, was trapped in her basement studio by a flash flood for dangerously long before she was rescued. Her partner, Charlene Strong, was told at the hospital she couldn't see Kate unless she got one of Kate's relatives to approve. Strong eventually reached an out-of-state sister, and was at Kate's bedside when she died.

"Beyond belief. *Beyond* belief," Gregoire says about the stark denials same-sex partners faced. They couldn't marry and they couldn't have rights conferred only by marriage. "It ends up educating everyone," Gregoire says of Strong's willingness to publicly share the Catch-22 she faced. "How can anybody can say that's OK?"

Strong's grief became determined advocacy. She was at Gregoire's side, when the governor signed the first of the partnership rights bills.

Wanting to ride the momentum, leading LGBTQ advocates met with Gregoire in late 2007. Some pushed for marriage equality in 2008. Hard. Gregoire calls the meeting "challenging."

When the question was called, Senator Ed Murray said he didn't think his colleagues were ready. Up for re-election in 2008, Gregoire agreed. Some saw her decision as raw politics.

"I couldn't respect more those who said, 'Go now, because we're sick and tired of the discrimination.' But I'm a pragmatist," Gregoire says, "And I'm sitting there, thinking to myself, is that going to get to where we want? Or is there a better route? Where we can actually bring people along and get to a better answer?"

AFTER WINNING the closest governor's race in state history by 129 votes in 2004, Gregoire glided to re-election in 2008 on a cushion of 195,000 votes. She signed bills earlier that year and the next, rounding out the incremental approach to Washington's version of civil unions. It may have been fortuitous to forgo marriage equality. Californians passed a constitutional ban on same-sex marriage in 2008. At the same time, they favored Barack Obama—not yet on-board with marriage equality—for president by 3.2 million votes. They were ready for some changes, but not others.

Michelle Gregoire, with her mom at Seattle Pride 2008, was a collegiate soccer player and worked for King County Executive Dow Constantine and state Senator Jeanne Kohl-Welles before becoming a prosecutor. She has two sons. *Michelle Gregoire*

Michelle and Courtney celebrated domestic partnerships as a great step forward. "You can't say it wasn't," Michelle says. "Reflecting back, I thought that was such a wonderful moment when we had domestic partnerships. But that was not right. That wasn't enough."

Michelle was soon at UW Law School, assembling her own tools of persuasion.

Gregoire's daughters leaned into 1960s racial-equality arguments with their mother. Brimming with law-school knowledge, Courtney even dropped *Loving v. Virginia* on her mom. That was the 1967 U.S. Supreme Court decision overturning laws in 16 states that banned inter-racial marriages.

In that case, Virginia resident Mildred Jeter, a Black woman, and Richard Loving, a white man, were married in the District of Columbia. The Lovings returned to Virginia and were charged with breaking the state's statute against inter-racial marriages. They were sentenced to a year in jail. The trial judge said he'd suspend the sentence if they left Virginia for 25 years.

By a unanimous vote, the Supreme Court held that Virginia violated the Equal Protection Clause of the 14th Amendment.

Gregoire's daughters brought up the arguments that had been made about race to allow discrimination. "Which were wrong," Gregoire says, "and I found them all being applied with regard to marriage,"

The similarity or "pattern matching" that struck Courtney was the role of the younger generation in pushing for change in both civil-rights eras.

It would culminate in a meeting at the Governor's Mansion.

THE FAMILY was reunited in Olympia for the Thanksgiving 2011 holiday. Courtney was back from her job in Washington, D.C., at the U.S. Department of Commerce. Michelle took a break from law-school studies in Seattle and came down.

The governor clearly recalls a meeting in the mansion's main bedroom. Courtney says she talked about her friends who were forgoing a civil commitment ceremony because they were waiting for their moment to get legally married. Michelle recalls they had a "kind of huddle." Courtney said she believed older generations were ready to accept full marriage equality. "I can remember mom listening poignantly and then a big hug between us," she says.

Her daughters had prevailed. Their generation was right. "And I remember the three of us embracing and all three of us crying. And saying, 'We need to do something about this,' " Chris Gregoire says. And off she went.

"I don't know if you got the flavor of what was really happening to me," she says. Her daughters had underscored America's journey to address racial inequality. "I related so well to them and their generation, which doesn't see why in the world you would deny marriage to a loving couple who happen to be the same sex. They just don't see it. I go back to myself at their age, and I was of exactly the same mind. Why in the world do we discriminate? Why do we say you have to be in a separate school? Why do we say you can't marry?"

GREGOIRE ANNOUNCED her change of mind on January 5, 2012. She rejected the idea she was finally backing same-sex marriage because she was not seeking re-election. Tapping her chest during a news conference, she said, "It's right here that frees me up to do this. I have not liked where I've been for seven years. I have sorted it out in my head and in my heart."

She admitted she had been struggling with her religion. "I have always been uncomfortable with the position that I have taken publicly," she said. "And then I came to realize the religions can decide what they want to do but it is not OK for the state to discriminate."

Josh Friedes, director of marriage advocacy for Equal Rights Washington, said he respected Gregoire's path. "Her journey was very much like so many other people's journey. But she's taken it publicly. I think this is going to help other people move in the direction of support for marriage equality."

While many people might have assumed politics was behind the governor's conversion, Michelle disagrees. "I would say at the end of the day, again, it comes back to this core belief that my mom has, that she's instilled in my sister and I to do what's right and fair. She knew it was the right thing to do."

THE ISSUE SHIFTED to the Legislature, where the vote count in the Senate remained uncertain. Gregoire wanted lawmakers, above all, to debate the issue without rancor. "I knew that this issue was going to get national attention," she recalls.

She began bringing lawmakers with strong feelings, from both parties, into the governor's office. She talked to them about where they were on the issue, and what she had gone through herself. At the end of the conversations, she recalls, she asked that during floor debate, "please be respectful of others who didn't share their views."

With a majority appearing thin in the Senate, she stood close to the floor for the vote. "More as a reminder to those whom I had spoken, 'I'm there for you; I support you. I know you've been on a journey. I respect that you're going to take a tough vote here, but you're doing the right thing.' And to those, who didn't agree, 'Please, be respectful.' "

Marriage equality passed both chambers, and Gregoire signed it into law on February 13, 2012. She heaps credit on the Legislature's civility, saying she had witnessed their "finest hour."

Gregoire says Ed Murray was "unbelievably helpful" to her as they weighed how and when to push ahead with gay civil rights legislation. "And I will forever be thankful for that. Thankful on a personal level. Thankful as a governor, for helping me strategize how to make things happen, where he identified some legislators, and said, 'I think you can make a real difference if you talk to them.' "

The former governor also maintains that the allegations Murray sexually abused several teens years earlier—stories that prompted his resignation as Seattle's mayor in 2017 while insisting "the allegations against me are not true"—

Chris Gregoire on Jamie Pedersen, left, with his husband Eric Cochran and their four boys: "He's just solid. He's very much a pragmatist, a guy you can talk to and say, 'I need your help; how do we get there from here?' " *Legislative Support Services*

should not nullify his achievements as a leader of the LGBTQ civil rights movement. She still wants to "recognize a pivotal and instrumental role [he] played in making things happen."

Jamie Pedersen was instrumental in the House, she says, adding, "You can't assume that all those votes in the Legislature were just by accident." Pedersen and his longtime partner, Eric Cochran, had adorable children. He helped legislators "take the journey," Gregoire says. "How—when you see him, and you get to know him—can you say, 'You can't get married'?"

Representative Maureen Walsh, a Republican from Walla Walla, also personalized matters in a floor speech that went viral. In an unscripted, homespun four minutes, Walsh spoke of the love she shared with her late husband, Kelly, and how she couldn't deny others, such as her daughter Shauna, a lesbian, the right to such a commitment. Walsh had also learned from her daughter that domestic partnerships weren't equal. "Everything she said was just so humanizing," Gregoire says of candid Walsh's tour de force.

In emotional remarks she gave at the bill signing, Gregoire stressed a letter she had received from a 16-year-old who was "coming to grips" with her sexual orientation. In the future, the governor said, she did not want the young woman and others to have to "get on bended knee and ask, 'Will you civil union me?' "

Michelle and UW Law School classmates drove down for the bill-signing ceremony. "It felt like the voice of your youth can really make an impact for change and better. But I would also say my mom raised me to be always looking for how you can strive to make equality in a slew of issues."

Courtney recalls being in her Washington, D.C., office at the time. "And a colleague of mine came running in, in tears, into my office, saying, 'What your mom just did is going to change not just the law, but hearts and minds. She spoke about her evolution, and politicians just don't do that.' "

A DECADE AFTER Washington legalized same-sex marriage, Chris Gregoire

"I'm so thankful my childhood upbringing was robust conversations around the dinner table," says Courtney Gregoire. "Man, I brought that to my kiddos, too. And that differences of opinion are to be respected, and we are all growing and learning from others." *Christine Gregoire*

has four grandchildren; Courtney's two girls and Michelle's two boys. And support for marriage equality was up to 84 percent among Americans, 18 to 34.

Michelle Gregoire Garrison, a senior deputy prosecuting attorney for King County, is trying to instill in her boys the values she learned at home: the importance of standing up for what you believe in, the importance of equality and fairness, and embracing individual's differences. But also reminding them that progress took time, journeys and struggles. And they should protect what's been achieved.

"It's important for my sons that they hear from their parents," she says, "and that conversations are welcome, they're open to share. I want to hear about what the issues are going on with them."

Something similar is happening in Courtney Gregoire's home. One of her daughters wanted to arrive early at school one day for the raising of a Pride flag. Her trans friend was going to be making some remarks and she wanted to show her support.

In her job as Microsoft's Chief Digital Safety Officer, Courtney has handled illegal and harmful content and conduct. She sees levels of harassment and intolerance that make her nervous.

But she sees hope in her daughters' generation and what they can teach us: "I'm there to take care of my friend. My friends might be different than me in many, many ways. But that's what makes friendship meaningful and blossom throughout life. That's the full-circle side. Now as a parent."

Bob Young

MARY YU

"SURROUNDED BY LOVE"

At midnight on December 9, 2012, the first same-sex couples in Washington history were legally married. Emily and Sarah Cofer, two school teachers from Snohomish County, stood before Judge Mary Yu in a Seattle courtroom. Emily and Sarah wanted to be married by Judge Yu because she had presided over the adoption hearing for their daughter Carter.

Yu brought a special touch, a signature style to adoption proceedings that other court officers had carried out in assembly-line, "congrats, next" fashion. Yu kept the necessary legal rigor, but added ceremony. She wanted to ritualize the event in a more dignified manner. That was especially important to LGBTQ couples who had no legal status in the years before domestic partnerships and marriage.

Guests sat in Yu's jury box. Sometimes they didn't all fit. She invited comments. She stressed the joining of family. And care for the beloved child. She told squeamish grandparents: "Love who your child loves."

And she did so in a warm way that blended her religious training, her devotion to the law, and her empathy as a member of the LGBTQ community. "She welcomed us and our family and friends and was adorable with Carter, who was only 6 months old at the time," recalls Sarah Cofer. "We left feeling joyous about our family's rights matching the commitment that goes into planning for and raising a child."

Through word of mouth, Yu became the go-to judge for same-sex couple adoptions. After a full day as a trial judge in King County Superior Court, she'd set aside time after 4 p.m. She oversaw some 1,400 adoptions.

It was especially meaningful to her because her standing as a judge kept her from political activism for LGBTQ civil rights.

Adoptions were her most visible contribution to the cause. And they fit

Facing page: In addition to Mary Yu, Washington artist Alfredo Arreguin has painted portraits of Supreme Court Justices Steven González and Charles Z. Smith. *Alfredo Arreguin*

Yu brought a warm, personal touch to adoption proceedings, particularly for same-sex parents such as Emily and Sarah Cofer. *Cofer Family*

her well. "She shined," says Barbara Wechsler, a Seattle attorney who brought the first adoption cases to Judge Yu. "Because these adoptions were both a celebration of humanity and a legal proceeding. It really let both aspects of who she was shine. And shine expertly."

Yu had found her voice in some ways. Not on a soapbox, or in a spotlight. The adoption hearings were not public and went unpublicized. But in a role more befitting her persona: strong but private, judicious but tender. It was the kind of passionate, yet not flashy commitment Yu would become better known for as she ascended to the state Supreme Court, and became the first openly LGBTQ person elected statewide.

ADOPTION HEARINGS were, and can still be, of particular legal significance to LGBTQ couples. Practically speaking, before domestic partnerships and marriage equality were lawful, a lesbian could be inseminated, carry a baby, deliver it, and be on the birth certificate as a parent. Her partner, however, did not have legal status as a parent. If a tragic accident struck the family while traveling, there was no telling how local law officials or hospitals might view a gay couple, or their child's birth certificate. Even if a non-biological parent was on a birth certificate that was not a guarantee those rights would be recognized in all states.

A court order granted by a judge in an adoption hearing was bulletproof, the gold standard. The U.S. Constitution says court orders from one state, properly rendered, must be observed in other states. If a non-biological parent became part of an adoption decree they would be covered in other states.

It was responsible. It was insurance. "It was really important for military families," Yu says. "It was important for people who might see themselves leaving Washington state. They were scared out of their minds. They were afraid if they took their kids to Disneyland, what did it mean?"

Washington state law did not preclude same-sex parent adoptions. Nor did it specifically allow them. The first adoptions that Barbara Wechsler, a family law attorney, handled in the late 1980s were done quietly. "We really didn't want to

More than a hundred people gathered at Seattle Center for a 2014 reunion with Yu, who had united their families through marriage, adoption or both. *Mary Yu*

get much out in the public or the media, at that point. Because it just wasn't ready for it."

Usually, adoption hearings went before court commissioners, officials a notch below judges who attended to less complicated, often uncontested legal matters. In King County there was no way of knowing which commissioner might preside over a case, Wechsler says. Some might be delightful; some might be wooden; and, in the early years, at least one refused to officiate for religious reasons. All had busy workloads, lines of people waiting and reason to be brisk.

In the best case, Wechsler told clients, their adoption hearing would be nice but brief under a commissioner. In the late 1990s, Wechsler and other attorneys began to "special-set" adoption hearings before King County judges. Shortly after Yu was first appointed a judge in 2000, one of Wechsler's clients said she'd like to have Yu, whom she knew from volunteer work, preside over her child's adoption hearing.

"Judge Yu was special in the way she handled it," Wechsler says. "She just made it a magical experience." For the next 14 years, Wechsler would tell clients that they could see a commissioner or Judge Yu. "Then I would say, 'Judge Yu is a lesbian, and welcomes these, and feels honored—she would always say that she feels honored to preside for these adoptions.' " When clients heard that, most felt Yu's courtroom was a safe harbor.

Other attorneys began favoring Yu. Although adoptions added work to the end of her day, Wechsler believes Yu "wanted to use this precious time for the community she viewed during this historical period as needing more affirmation."

Yu created her own model. It was foremost a legal affair. But she incorporated celebration, even fun.

Wechsler recalls one hearing where everyone in the family wore hats for some reason. Yu let them know their hats were wonderful and she loved them. But there was a rule in court: everyone had to remove their hats. And, to add a flourish to the end of the ceremony, they all celebrated by tossing their hats in the air.

She impacted families in other ways, Wechsler says. In one case, a cli-

Emily and Sarah Cofer, with daughter Carter, were married by Yu just after the stroke of midnight, December 9, 2012. *Cofer Family*

ent's father was uneasy that his daughter was a lesbian and reluctant to attend her adoption hearing. But he came. Yu so changed his viewpoint that when Wechsler's client came back for a second adoption, her father was eager see Judge Yu in action again.

"What I had said," Yu recalls, "was that 'The most important thing is to love who your children love. That would be the most important thing that you could do— to love who your child loves. It's that simple.' "

It was an amazing 14 years, Wechsler said, before Yu became a Supreme Court Justice. Even after she began working at Olympia's Temple of Justice, Yu would commute on Friday afternoons back to Seattle for adoptions.

"It was the most uplifting, satisfying, important time in my legal career," Wechsler says.

MARY ISABEL YU's father was born in China and went to work on a cargo ship while still a boy. When docked in New York, he jumped ship, hoping for freedom. At the time there was no such thing as legal immigration for people of Chinese descent. There hadn't been since 1882's Chinese Exclusion Act, a ban ignited by vicious stereotypes and fanned by ambitious politicians. "We have today to decide whether we shall have on the Pacific Coast of the United States the kingdom of Christ or the kingdom of Confucius," said Senator James G. Blaine, who sought the Republican nomination for president in 1880. Blaine, a future secretary of state, also likened Chinese people to an infectious disease.

Yu's father, Choi Kun Yu, later met his bride, Serafina Gomez, in a noodle factory where they both worked. Yu's mother had come to America from Mexico, where she toiled in fields during her childhood, picking strawberries and asparagus. Yu's father never spoke English well, but that was the family's common language.

Mary and her brother Richard were raised on Chicago's South Side in a predominantly Irish Catholic working-class neighborhood called Bridgeport. Mary liked to read but was not a great student. As she grew into her teen years, she preferred socializing. Her parents didn't want her hands to be as dirty and calloused at theirs. They hoped she could become a secretary in an office.

Yu's parents, Serafina Gomez and Choi Jun Yu, had worked in farms and factories. "My mom would always say she didn't want our hands to look like hers," Yu said. *Mary Yu*

In 1971, she went to a Catholic high school, St. Mary of Perpetual Help. Her parents thought it would be safer, if not academically superior. "I think my parents were convinced that if I went to a public school I probably would've dropped out. And that may have been true, on the South Side of Chicago in those days," she says.

The early Yu crew on Chicago's South Side, where they grew up: infant Mary, her brother Richard and cousin Yolanda. *Mary Yu*

Mary fell in with girls from the school. They drove around, listened and danced to Motown grooves. They went to house parties and drank beer and Boone's Farm wine. "I look back at that era and what I was struggling with was making sure I fit in—that I was part of a group," she says.

A young English teacher, Joan Finnegan, saw potential. Yu calls Finnegan "the most influential person" in her life. Yu didn't know anyone who went to college. In her junior year, Finnegan encouraged her to think about her future, and college. "She could just see I would've been one wasted life if I didn't get out of Bridgeport and go someplace and do something. And she was an incredible mentor and guide. I ended up going to the college that she took me to, which happened to be her alma mater."

While studying at Rosary College (now Dominican University), outside Chicago, she joined a Latin American student group. The church's "liberation theology," and its emphasis on economic and social justice, was thriving. "Central America was on fire," Yu

Cardinal Joseph Bernardin was supportive of Seattle Archbishop Raymond Hunthausen when the Vatican cracked down on him for allowing Mass to be celebrated by gay Catholics in a Seattle cathedral. *Archdiocese of Chicago*

recalls. She became a religious studies major, thinking that might be the best route to doing good. The Dominican sisters affiliated with the college "were revolutionary women way before their time in educating and empowering women."

After graduation, Yu took a job with the Archdiocese of Chicago, starting as a secretary in the Office of Peace and Justice. Chicago's Catholics were soon led by Cardinal Joseph Bernardin, considered liberal by the Vatican's standards.

Yu worked to eliminate poverty and related issues of red-lining in housing and insurance, not with charity, but by Saul Alinsky-style organizing. "We weren't feeding people," she says. "We were actually organizing people to politically have power to change the dynamics." In five years, Bernardin promoted her to director of the office. One of the programs Yu funded was run by an organizer named Barack Obama.

Her altruism and ambition were eventually tested by limits of the gospel. The church tried to convert hearts and persuade people to do good. But it couldn't stop hate. Obama had gone off to Harvard Law School. That got Yu and others in her circle thinking.

"The law provides tools to bring about change," she says. "And I thought, 'Gosh, I want those tools. I want the ability to systemically address these issues and make people do that right thing. And the law makes people do the right thing. You don't have to personally believe it, but you've got to follow the law. So, you're not going to discriminate against this Black family despite the fact that you might be a racist and a bigot.' "

She enrolled at Notre Dame Law School. Her female partner landed a job with Seattle University. Soon Yu was commuting to Notre Dame from Seattle.

"What makes Mary stand out is her high level of passion and commitment to doing the right thing," said Bobbe Bridge, who was Yu's client as presiding judge of King County Superior Court. *Mary Yu*

NOTRE DAME ALUMNI take care of one another. Yu says she's proof. She got an internship in the office of King County Prosecuting Attorney, thanks to a lawyer, Mike Duggan, who reached out. A Notre Dame grad, Duggan said the prosecutors' office was a great place to work, and she should spend a summer there. She did and ended up staying.

She started in the criminal division and later transferred to the civil division, where county agencies were her clients. Employment lawsuits, contracts, construction, public records disclosure—the noncriminal legal matters of the county were her bailiwick. Bobbe Bridge, presiding judge of King County Superior Court, was a client; so was Ron Sims, the charismatic county executive.

She worked 12-hour days. She was energetic and tough. Sims wanted to hire her away. After just five years, County Prosecutor Norm Maleng promoted her to deputy chief of staff in 1999. Maleng once said about his hiring philosophy: "What I want to know is what is in that person's soul or heart." He called Yu one of the "best and brightest people in law" he had ever known.

"Norm was really committed to diversity in the office," Yu recalls, and put gays, lesbians and people of color in positions of power.

But Maleng had also been a lightning rod in the LGBTQ community. His prosecutors

If asked to name the most capable lawyers he knew, King County Prosecuting Attorney Norm Maleng said in 1999, "Mary would be on any list that I would give you." *King County Prosecutor's Office*

FACT SHEET: THE STEVEN FARMER CASE

A Dangerous National Precedent:

Having AIDS is Now a Crime, Punishable with a Prison Term!

Only because he is HIV positive...
they sentenced him to more than 7 years in prison.

Steven Farmer became the first person in Washington forced to take an HIV test, leading to critical headlines and protests. *King County Prosecutor's Office*

went hard after a gay man, Steven Farmer, in the late 1980s, for unlawful contact with two teenagers. As the AIDS crisis was beginning to accelerate, one of Maleng's senior prosecutors, Rebecca Roe, argued that the court should force Farmer to test for HIV, the virus that caused AIDS, before sentencing him on counts of sexually exploiting a minor and patronizing a juvenile prostitute. The health of Farmer, a movie-handsome airline steward, was not a legal issue in those convictions.

Maleng was seeking the Republican nomination for governor against more conservative rivals. Some saw Roe's stance as politically related.

Judge Charles V. Johnson (not to be confused with a Supreme Court justice of the same name) ordered a blood draw for Farmer. He tested HIV-positive. He was sentenced to seven-and-a-half years, far beyond the usual range for his crimes. Protesters accused Maleng and Roe of being "AIDS-phobic" if not homophobic. "AIDS is Now a Crime," said a *Seattle Gay News* headline. The state Supreme Court ruled three years later that Farmer's forced HIV test violated his constitutional rights. Governor Mike Lowry granted him clemency.

Farmer was sentenced years before Yu arrived in Seattle, but she knew the story. She defends Maleng. He gave his prosecutors autonomy, which they respected him for. "He didn't micro-manage how those trial deputies went out and did what they did."

What's more, he had promoted Yu and other LGBTQ people. That "speaks loudly," Yu says. As does the fact he set up a unit to prosecute hate crimes against the LGBTQ community. She calls him a visionary in understanding equality.

In 2000, Governor Gary Locke appointed Yu to a judgeship in King County Superior Court. The first Chinese-American governor in the U.S., Locke wanted to diversify the judiciary. Judge Janice Niemi, considered a leading feminist when she was a state senator, asked Yu to replace her. "Big shoes. Big shoes," Yu says of filling Niemi's seat.

Within months, she was thrust into an election to defend her post. Her opponent tried to float innuendo about Yu's sexual orientation. Most of the press ignored him. Those that didn't, depicted him as an opportunist.

It was true that Yu hadn't tried cases in Superior Court at the time of her appointment. "That was the conversation from those who didn't know her," said Bobbe Bridge, Yu's former client, who became a Supreme Court justice. Yu was elected, and re-elected. In 2005, she was named the state's judge of the year by a group that included both plaintiff and defense lawyers.

A reporter from *The Seattle Times* sat in Yu's court one late Wednesday afternoon. A confused, uncooperative defendant refused to sign routine paperwork, wrongly convinced he would be surrendering his rights. Although most of the courthouse had emptied in anticipation of the Thanksgiving holiday, Yu was in no hurry. "She said 'please' and 'thank you' and took considerable pains to explain everything." Her strategy worked, although it took nearly an hour. But justice was served, with patience and respect.

THE ADOPTION JUDGE became the marrying judge in 2012. Washington's new marriage equality law took effect on December 6. The state mandates a three-day waiting period between the issuance of a marriage license and a wedding to legally consummate the bond.

Yu's bailiff, Takao Yamada, here on December 9, 2012 with Carter, Sarah and Emily Cofer, implored the judge to start officiating marriage ceremonies at midnight. The Yu crew worked until 7 a.m., marrying 12 couples. *Barb Kinney*

Bailiff Takao Yamada suggested that Yu start officiating ceremonies at midnight. The idea came to Yamada because his parents could not be married in Virginia before a 1967 U.S. Supreme Court decision struck down the state's ban on mixed-race marriages. "He's a young man who is Japanese and white, and he said, 'You know, judge, we should do this at the stroke of midnight because people should not have to wait to be married,' " Yu recalls. Court officials approved the idea. Yu says some courthouse staff volunteered to work without pay.

Yu's team didn't want to give celebrities preferential treatment. The Yu crew decided that the first couple to call would be the first to wed.

Hello, Sarah and Emily Cofer.

When marriage became legal in Washington, Sarah and Emily wanted to get hitched right away. "Judge Yu had made Carter's adoption a beautiful day and we wanted the same experience for our legal wedding," Sarah Cofer says. They contacted Yu's office. They heard her plan. They said they'd be up for midnight matrimony. They booked a hotel room close to the courthouse and walked there with friends and family.

"When we first arrived in the courtroom," Sarah recalls, "[Judge Yu] ushered us into her chambers where she ran us through what to expect, and we laughed and relaxed as she told us to ignore the camera clicks." Anne Levinson, a back-stage LGBT community-leader for decades, had orchestrated a series of midnight ceremonies around the state. Levinson volunteered to hold Carter, then 9-months old, during the ceremony. With their motor drives whirring, photojournalists snapped away at the historic occasion.

"Carter did great for it being the middle of the night," Sarah says. "Judge Yu was warm and welcoming, she presided over the ceremony with comfort and joy that made it feel like a personal event even in such a public setting." Sarah and Emily left with the feeling they were "surrounded by love."

Daphne Draayer & Vanessa Williams met while skating for the Rat City Rollergirls. "This beats a championship any day," Draayer said about getting married in Yu's courtroom. *Barb Kinney*

Images from Yu's courtroom went national, including a picture of her upraised hands gently on the wedding couple's faces, an almost priestly posture. Some photos conveyed solemnity. But Yu wasn't feeling that during one of most magical moments in her career. "Because it's pure joy to celebrate that commitment between two people and to have the law sanction it. It meant so much to these individuals."

And yet, Yu has mixed feelings about marriage. For herself, she isn't sure the institution really defines love and commitment. For the sake of justice, she's wary of deciding equal rights at the ballot box. "I just am not persuaded that civil rights, or human rights, is something that occurs by popular vote," she says, "because popular vote assumes the majority, right? And it just can't be that endowed rights are up for a vote in that way."

LESS THAN TWO years later, Governor Jay Inslee appointed Yu to a vacancy on the state Supreme Court. In May 2014, Yu replaced Jim Johnson, a conservative who had come under fire, along with Justice Richard Sanders, for racially insensitive comments. In the court's 2006 decision against gay marriage, Johnson wrote that gays and lesbians already had a right to marry—someone of the opposite sex.

Standing with Yu at her 2014 swearing-in at the Temple of Justice were mentors Anne Levinson, Ruth Woo and Phyllis Gutierrez Kenney. A leader in the marriage equality campaign, Levinson said Yu was the first judge she called about officiating the first marriages. *Mary Yu*

It sounded cruel. "Just mean-spirited," Yu says.

News about Yu focused on her barrier-breaking. She was the first openly LGBT justice, the first Latina, and the first of Asian descent. (Unlike Amy Coney Barrett, the first U.S. Supreme Court justice to receive her law degree from a Catholic university, fellow Notre Dame alum Yu joined three justices in Olympia from Gonzaga Law School. Mary Fairhurst, Barbara Madsen and Debra Stephens all received their degrees from the Catholic school.)

She avoided criticizing her colleagues' marriage-equality ruling. But she did announce her presence in lower-key fashion at Christmas, giving all of her fellow justices a coffee-table book by B. Proud, a lesbian photographer .

Soon, Yu, the daughter of a farmworker, was writing the court's unanimous decision in a 2015 case, *Demetrio v. Sakuma* Brothers Farm. It affirmed that farmworkers have a right to paid rest breaks.

She had been a bit reticent about filling a Supreme Court seat, knowing that she would have to run for election statewide in 2016. "I wondered if people would vote for someone like me—an Asian, Latina, openly gay woman. But I realized that if I didn't say yes, how was I going to encourage young people of color to step forward every time an opportunity presents itself?"

She won her election with 57 percent of the vote, although none of the counties east of the Cascades. She carried on with her mentoring activities. For 14 years she served as a judge for mock trials at Seattle Girls' School, a middle school that serves mostly students of color. "This is the time when they're developing the habit of either sitting back or standing up and doing things for themselves," Yu says. "It's important to see a minority female judge."

She's also traveled to schools around the state, planting encouraging words. After one visit with college students and high schoolers in Spokane, Gonzaga student Sanskruti Tomar said, "To see another queer woman of color in that position is so inspiring. I've looked up to her for years."

Yu's compassion ran afoul of the state Commission on Judicial Conduct in 2018. Yu had posted messages on Facebook encouraging people to support two charitable organizations, including one that benefits homeless people. The commission ruled that such "solicitations" did comport with the state's Judicial Code of Conduct "no matter how noble the case." Yu agreed to the commission's least severe, cautionary sanction.

Erin Lewis, inaugural winner of Seattle University's Mary Yu Scholarship, called Yu "not just a trailblazer but all of our wildest dreams come true." *Laura Anglin*

In 2021, Seattle University Law School honored Yu, its "Distinguished Jurist in Residence," with the creation of a $100,000 endowed scholarship in her name. The first recipient, Erin Lewis, a nonbinary person of color, said Yu inspired her and "stands as a promise of what can be for those who live authentically."

Annette Clark, dean of the law school, said Yu's dedication to students went above and beyond. While on vacation, Yu took time to speak at an orientation for first-year law students by Zoom. What Clark didn't know until Yu later posted a picture of her setup was that the justice addressed students from a friend's condo bathroom which she had rigged with several ring lights and a background image of a stately courtroom.

Clark then unveiled a portrait of Yu by Alfredo Arreguin, who compares his painting style to jazz. Chief Justice Steven González told the Seattle University crowd that Yu initially said "no" to a portrait; he suggested she also added some saltier words.

The Cofers send Yu a holiday card every year so she can see how Carter, 9 years old here, has grown since Yu presided over her adoption when she was 6 months old. *Cofer Family*

"You can't take the Chicago kid out of me," she says.

She relented to the Chief's request. She was also mindful that a recent former president had breathed life into anti-Chinese sentiments. "It so surprised me how quickly we could slip back to being the worst of ourselves," she says.

Looking at Arreguin's colorful portrait, Yu envisioned her ancestors and the dreams that led her parents to America. "It represents something bigger than me. It represents an immigrant story. It represents opportunity."

And glancing back at her own career, the history-making judge who changed the face of Washington's judiciary had no problem pointing to a peak—those 1,400 adoptions she presided over. "I can't say enough about how much each of those individuals and families and children really matter to me. When I look at the hierarchy of joy and what I've gotten, it would be those adoptions. They're at the top."

Bob Young

"I not only have my secrets. I am my secrets. And you are your secrets. Our trusting each other enough to share them with each other has much to do with the secret of what it is to be human."
   –Frederick Buechner, theologian and award-winning writer

COMING OUT

DAVID AMMONS TOLD A SECRET

N o cub reporter in the checkered history of the Olympia press corps likely made a more lasting first impression than the AP's 22-year-old David Ammons when he arrived at the Capitol in the summer of 1971. He wrote so quickly and so well that his beat soon seemed boundless. He covered the Washington Supreme Court, interviewed up-and-comers like freshman State Senator Booth Gardner, a boyish millionaire from Tacoma, and explored trends, visiting Pasco to profile a WSU horticulturist who predicted great things from Washington's expanding vineyards.

The practice then at many newspapers was to remove bylines from wire service stories, giving prominence instead to their staff writers. Sometimes the copy desk would even "localize" a few paragraphs and label the story "Daily Herald and AP reports." Ammons' stories were so brightly written his byline invariably stayed put. They were longer than usual, too—so interesting they were harder to cut. When the AP gave him a column—"Ammons on Politics"—it often filled two full columns on weekend editorial pages from Port Angeles to Pullman.

Along the road to becoming the longest-serving capitol reporter in state history, he covered seven governors, more than 40 legislative sessions, the eruption

Facing page: Ammons interviews Brian Ebersole, D-Tacoma, the House majority leader, in 1990.
Washington State Archives

of Mount St. Helens and the search for skyjacker D.B. Cooper. Dixy Lee Ray, Washington's first female governor, initially took a liking to Ammons, misjudging his niceness as timidity. Before long, he was as persona non grata as the other reporters. "She named the pigs on her Fox Island farm after us, then presented each of us a neatly wrapped package of sausage when she had them slaughtered," he remembers with glee. "It was like, 'See, I can grind you up!' "

Ammons was fastidious about ensuring quotes were accurate and in context. Aside from the mercurial Dixy, politicians of all persuasions and press secretaries trusted him. His disarming smile and wry, contagious laugh opened doors for 37 years. When he retired from the Associated Press in 2008 to become communications director for the Office of the Secretary of State, Dino Rossi and Chris Gregoire—adversaries in the most contentious gubernatorial election in state history—stood practically side by side to wish him well.

His collection of AP press passes. *David Ammons*

In an abrupt role reversal, Ammons was soon fielding reporters' questions about a lawsuit against Secretary of State Sam Reed. His new boss maintained that the state's landmark public disclosure law mandated the release of the names and signatures of voters who had signed a petition for a controversial ballot measure. The sponsors of Referendum 71, Protect Marriage Washington, hoped to block implementation of a law dubbed "everything but marriage" because it expanded the rights of same-sex domestic partners. Opponents asserted the Public Records Act cited by Reed was being applied unconstitutionally "because there is a reasonable probability that the signatories … will be subjected to threats, harassment, and reprisals."

Ammons handled Protect Marriage Washington with the same professionalism he accorded gay rights supporters. An article of faith in journalism is that good reporters never let their biases show. Ammons had opinions, of course. But he never shared them indiscreetly, even when other reporters were blowing off steam after a long day.

What no one knew—or at least only a few suspected until 2015 when he surprised even himself by deciding to tell his secret—is that he is gay.

Ammons at a joint session of the Legislature in 1973. *Washington State Archives*

Ammons' life story italicizes that coming out is complicated. Sometimes the journey says as much about the inertia of inner conflict as courage.

For the record, Ammons believes his job with the AP wouldn't have been in jeopardy had he come out years earlier. He believes his objectivity would have defined him more than his homosexuality. However, when he became Secretary Reed's chief spokesman and senior political adviser, he knew being out could cause grief for the agency. Exhibit A being the controversy over the identities of the petition signers. Referendum sponsors could have questioned whether the agency's gay press secretary was being even-handed. Ammons knew Reed, without hesitation, would have defended him vigorously. It was still worrisome. He kept his secret.

AMMONS' CAREER as a journalist, historian and press secretary dovetailed with landmark Northwest moments in LGBTQ history. He covered disheartening setbacks and resounding victories.

In 1972, his second year with the AP, managers of a roller rink in suburban Seattle called the police because two gay skaters were holding hands. The cops handcuffed the miscreants and booked them for disorderly conduct.

Marriage equality was first litigated here in 1974 when gay activists argued that Washington's Equal Rights Amendment prohibited the denial of a marriage license to same-sex couples. When the Court of Appeals denied their claim, the state Supreme Court declined to review the decision.

One of Ammons' most memorable interviews was with Colonel Margarethe

Ammons' 1991 column photo. *Associated Press*

Cammermeyer, the Chief Nurse of the Washington State National Guard. She was discharged in 1991 after revealing she is a lesbian. "I was shocked that they could cashier a decorated Vietnam veteran whose patriotism was beyond reproach," Ammons says.

In 1997, Washington voters soundly rejected a ballot measure to prohibit job discrimination based on sexual orientation.

Slowly at first, the tide began to turn.

Ammons was on hand in 2006 when Governor Chris Gregoire signed a law prohibiting, on the basis of "sexual orientation," any discrimination in employment, housing, lending or eligibility for insurance. He was also in the press house adjacent to the Capitol that summer when the fractured Washington Supreme Court released a decision that's still reverberating: On a 5-4 vote, it upheld the Legislature's 1998 Defense of Marriage Act.

Unsettling as it was, Ammons says the court's split-decision defense of DOMA proved to be more of a bump than a fork in the road. Today, he marvels that Washington's high court is the most diverse in America, with two lesbian justices.

A widely-read column Ammons wrote in the summer of 2007 summed up a turning point in the struggle:

> After three decades of controversy and contention, Washington has quietly adopted back-to-back gay rights laws with little pushback from critics and no blowback from the voters.
>
> Starting Monday, same-sex couples can sign a domestic partner registry that triggers some of the key benefits of marriage. That follows on the heels of a gay civil rights measure that gives gays and lesbians the full protection of the state's anti-discrimination laws.
>
> Neither law was challenged on the ballot, as both sides had originally predicted. Independent pollster Stuart Elway says the

once-radioactive issue of gay rights has mostly fallen off the radar screen and was scarcely mentioned in the last election. ...

The state's first openly gay legislator, Cal Anderson, and other lawmakers struggled for nearly 30 years to get the civil rights bill through Olympia last year. Democrats padded their majorities in both houses and came right back to pass marriage-like rights this year.

On Monday, Senator Ed Murray, Anderson's successor in the Legislature and in leading the charge, and his 16-year partner, Michael Shiosaki, will line up at the Secretary of State's counter in Olympia to register their domestic partnership.

Then Murray will drive home and get started on the next phase of the battle that has sometimes consumed him.

What's next? The gay community isn't much interested in civil unions but plans to seek full marriage equality. How long that takes, say the advocates, will depend on how quickly public opinion continues to turn their way. "I believe we will get there in a decade, if not sooner," says Murray, the senior of five gay men in the state Legislature.

They got there in only five years. On November 6, 2012, nearly 54 percent of Washington voters endorsed same-sex marriage. Opponents had attempted to overturn a legislative mandate signed into law by Governor Gregoire. The first same-sex marriages in Washington took place a month later.

DAVID AMMONS' background will come as a surprise to many. He was born in 1948 in Appalachia, the grandson of a Methodist preacher who often rode a horse into the "hollers" of the mountains of western North Carolina to share the gospel. "That was Grandpa Stevens, my mother's father," Ammons says. "My mother was one of five children. The family was pretty poor all the time. People would pay the preacher in chickens, eggs and cantaloupes. My earliest years were spent there in Waynesville, Haywood County, N.C., not too far from Asheville. That was the big town near us. We were also near Chimney Rock, where Carl Sandburg was from. My father's people, originally from Massachusetts, had homesteaded that area. They were mica and coal miners, literally living off the land.

"My dad was blue collar his whole life. He was absent quite a bit early on. I didn't know if that was due to a divided marriage or just him off earning mon-

Young David in bib overalls in North Carolina. *David Ammons*

ey, the story we were told. In my earliest years I was raised by my mother, an absolute angel devoted to her children. My sibling, Marilyn, came along five years after I was born. We lived in a little house—one of three or four in a family compound of sorts. It was a life of cold running water, with an outhouse out back. A coal stove heated the four rooms. My father would send checks, but I know my mother struggled. She was a brilliant person; valedictorian of her class; hired by the FBI during the war right out of high school. She had come back to the Asheville area to take care of her ailing mother."

Ammons' earliest memories are of learning to read on his mother's lap. Their meager circumstances did nothing to damper her intellect or appetite for literature. "She was my first and best teacher," he remembers fondly. "There was no kindergarten at Allen's Creek School, a two-room schoolhouse. My mother made up for that. I was reading and doing my numbers and all of that by the time I started school. I liked to write stories, too. My grandpa, the preacher, was well read in the classics and all the other books he could get his hands on. He was a wordsmith with his sermons. Writing seems to be in my gene pool."

The seeds of Ammons' abiding Christian faith were planted by his devout mother and grandfather. "Even though they were conservative theologically, the churches I went to were like a warm blanket," he remembers. "If I appeared different in any fashion it didn't matter. I was Free Methodist when I was in college, and Seattle Free Methodists are a little more liberal than a lot of the more fundamental folks. So as I've reflected, I don't recall it [being gay] ever being castigated from the pulpit, or even mentioned. Those churches were about getting you ready for heaven, and following the precepts of the 10 Commandments and all of Christ's teachings. It's the subtext I think of from my childhood years. Growing up in the racist South, I could clearly see that blacks and whites were treated differently. I grew up hating all forms of hate."

When he was in the third or fourth grade, David, his sister and mother moved from North Carolina to Wilmington, Delaware. His father had found work in a

Chrysler plant. The family was reunited for the rest of his childhood.

"Then, all of sudden, just before I was to enter 10th grade, we moved across the country to Vancouver, where a lot of my father's brothers and sisters had migrated during the war to work at Vanport, the big Kaiser shipyard between Vancouver and Portland, or other blue-collar jobs. It was like the Joads' trip out west in *The Grapes of Wrath*. My father traded the family Chevrolet for a huge truck. All that could fit of our worldly possessions were in the back under a tarp. We happily headed off to our adventure!" Ammons chuckles, marveling at the memory of their rag-tag migration.

"When we arrived, an aunt and uncle let us use their double-car garage, which smelled like fish because my uncle was a fisherman! Eventually my father found some property with a little cabin on it in Orchards, on the outskirts of Vancouver. Mount St. Helens was practically in our back yard."

Vancouver's Evergreen High School was a revelation. With his sunny disposition, the handsome new kid in the sophomore class fit in quickly, becoming a standout member of the school newspaper staff. Ammons' writing stood out for its clarity. "I had known since junior high that I wanted to be a journalist," he remembers. "At Evergreen, I received a scholarship to Pacific Slope, the University of Washington's summer training institute for high school journalists and advisers. That cemented everything. I loved every minute of that experience."

David Ammons as Spring News Editor for the *UW Daily* in 1969. *University of Washington*

WHEN HE matriculated at the University of Washington on scholarships in the fall of 1966, Ammons immersed himself in a journalism program on the rise from an influx of talented professors with real-world newspaper experience. William F. "B.J." Johnston, the award-winning managing editor of Idaho's *Lewiston Morning Tribune*, had joined the faculty as publisher of student publications in 1965. The former Associated Press correspondent and editor was a Phi Beta Kappa graduate of the University of Idaho, where he rose quickly from reporter to editor of the student newspaper. At the *Tribune*, Johnston's editorials drew national attention, notably his withering attacks in the 1950s on the red-baiting demagogue, Wisconsin Senator Joseph McCarthy. Johnston was a patient teacher and a demanding editor. What Ammons remembers most are his high expectations, especially an insistence on even-handedness. A prominent Idaho politician whom Johnston often took to task once observed, "Bill is the fairest editor in Idaho. He gives me better treatment [in the news columns] than do some of the papers that support me."

Ammons checks a row of AP teletypes in the 1980s. *David Ammons*

The adviser to *The Daily,* the UW's student newspaper, during Ammons' senior year was Bill Asbury, another standout former managing editor. A UW graduate, Asbury modeled integrity and chutzpah during a staff revolt over conflicts of interest by the paper's left-wing editor. Six staffers resigned, saying their editor had become a mouthpiece for the anti-war movement. One was David Horsey, a future two-time Pulitzer Prize winner for his *Seattle Post-Intelligencer* editorial cartoons. Asbury was frustrated, too. He wanted his name removed from the masthead. To make his stand perfectly clear, he also submitted an opinion piece about the controversy. When it was rejected, he paid to have it printed as an ad. "That was classic Asbury," says Ammons, who as luck would have it, missed the fireworks. He was student teaching at Seattle's Queen Anne High School when the dispute erupted in the spring of 1970, his final quarter of college.

Ammons acquired another mentor in Jim King, the avuncular editor of *The Seattle Times.* King was adviser to the UW chapter of Sigma Delta Chi, the society of professional journalists, when Ammons was chapter president. King's long remembered advice to young journalists is that good reporting is more than just the time-honored "5-W's"—Who, What, When, Where and Why? There were three more, King said: So what? What if? What next?

Ammons' stories for *The Daily* also caught the attention of Wick Temple, the AP's Seattle Bureau Chief. Ammons had considered becoming a teacher or enrolling in law school. But when Temple offered him a job, Ammons says, "I jumped all over it in about 10 seconds!" He collected his diploma, married a bright and pretty Seattle girl and gleefully reported for duty as a reporter for the world's largest newsgathering network. The AP was fond of citing Mark Twain's 1906 ob-

Ammons writes an AP dispatch on a video display terminal in 1981. *Washington State Archives*

servation, "There are only two forces that can carry light to all the corners of the globe—the sun in the heavens and the Associated Press down here." And "I may seem to be flattering the sun."

When a slot opened in Olympia in the summer of '71, Ammons grabbed his dream job—covering the capital. That meant "every sort of story imaginable," from legislative politics to the corridors of the state Supreme Court, and dozens of state agencies. "Imagine covering a gubernatorial press conference at the age of 22, or interviewing the chief justice," he says.

Ammons and his wife soon had two charmingly inquisitive children, a son and a daughter. The AP routinely offered promotions. He was content to be a star reporter rather than a bureau chief who had to spend more time wooing publishers and putting out fires than doing journalism.

Ammons says everything in his life—overtly at least—seemed so, well, *normal*: "Looking around me growing up, and all through my college years, I saw what the definition of 'being a man' looked like—a 'successful man.' The script said: You get your degree. You date. You get married. You have children. There wasn't really another option that seemed apparent to me, even though I was probably attracted to my own gender back when I was a boy. I can remember that first happening when I was 8 or 9 years old. It was something I compartmentalized. It's called 'impression management.' Putting on what the world wanted to see and what I decided to be. That was a bargain I was willing to do. I had some good years in my marriage, especially early on. But certainly, if I had known that [coming out] was an option; if it felt like an option; if I had had a love relationship—which I never did—with a man, should I have done that? I have tried never to get into the area of regret, in part because of my children, who are amazing human beings. And I wouldn't have had them. They wouldn't exist, at least not with me as their dad.

"My marriage fizzled in 1991 after 21 years. When it wasn't working anymore, we had a friendly divorce. The fact that I had been in a marriage and that children were there, it was like I had cover for as long as I wanted it, in the press

With Ammons in his accustomed front row seat, Gov. Booth Gardner fields questions during a packed press conference in 1986. *Tacoma News Tribune*

house or the Legislative Building. If people assumed anything differently, they were kind enough not to make an issue of it or invade my privacy. At that time, it would have felt that way.

"Most of the press corps were just fabulous people. Were and are. I don't think coming out would have hampered my profession. I had wonderful relations with both sides of the aisle. I'm a people pleaser, but a lot of that was my nature. I was brought up to be kind and gentle. And ironically, that's part of the feminine side of us. I was able to embody that kind of treatment of people so that everyone I talked with felt respected, whether it was a firebrand conservative or an arch-liberal from Seattle. I could talk with anybody. I also learned empathy, I think feeling at my core a little bit marginalized."

Ammons had a front row seat for emotional debates over gay rights—from repeal of the state's sodomy law in 1976 to passage of the landmark gay civil rights bill 30 years later. The judgmental things said during the debate over funding to combat AIDS—that the disease was divine punishment for "the sin of homosexuality"—were deeply troubling. Then, in 1995, Cal Anderson died of non-Hodgkin's lymphoma, a complication of AIDS. How did Ammons cope with those emotions? "It was definitely part of processing things," he said, voice quavering at first. "I was trying to keep my head about me while others were losing theirs.

"But the cost was going to be too high to tear off that mask. I was good friends with Roger Nyhus, another AP reporter who was openly gay. And some of the press secretaries and others over the years were gay. I would go to lunch with them and it's like, I wanted to say, 'You know, *me too.*' It was a hard façade to crumble."

MANY COLLEAGUES and friends were baffled by Ammons' decision to leave reporting after 37 years to go to "the dark side"—as reporters like to refer to public relations and speechwriting, as opposed to the noble calling of low pay and long hours. "Sam Reed was a long-time friend and news source," Ammons says. "I'd known him since his days as a young 'Dan Evans Republican' and Thurston County auditor. He was a smart political scientist, with academic credentials, too. So he was on my speed dial. Steve Excell, Sam's assistant secretary of state, was also a friend since our days together at the University of Washington. We were in the same dorm. When they double-teamed me with a heavy pitch to leave the press corps and be the agency's communications and policy adviser, I went to the beach for a week to think long and

Ammons with Secretary of State Sam Reed, center, and Steve Excell, assistant secretary of state, in 2012. *Washington State Archives*

hard about whether I would leave something I loved so dearly as the press corps. I was also doing the *Inside Olympia* program for TVW, which was tons of fun. But eventually I came to the realization I needed to stir the pot and start something new and different and re-energize myself. So I said 'Yes.' "

In the spring of 2008, they stenciled his name on the frosted door-glass of a cozy office adjacent to Reed's. The in-basket was overflowing and the phone wouldn't stop ringing. The "Top Two" primary Reed championed—with strong support from Washington's famously fickle voters—was now the U.S. Supreme Court's to decide. Before long, battle lines were also drawn over the identities of registered voters who had signed the petition to challenge the "everything but marriage" law. If, in his fresh start, Ammons had any inclination to come out, he kept it in his cupboard of secrets and second-thoughts. Ill-timed, the revelation would have been potentially compromising, he says.

When Reed retired in 2013, his successor as Secretary of State was someone Ammons knew and admired. Kim Wyman, who also had succeeded Reed as Thurston County auditor, was a centrist Republican with a big heart and a rarely

With Secretary of State Kim Wyman. *Washington State Archives*

closed door. She asked him to stay. So he did. He had been closer to Reed, "but 95 percent of the time we had a really warm relationship."

Wyman, now a top elections security official with the Biden administration, is a cheerfully self-described "crier" moved to tears by a kindergartner's Mother's Day poem or the introduction of a junior-varsity girls' basketball squad. Ammons wasn't the least bit surprised one day in 2015 when he entered her office and found her emotional.

"Is everything OK?"

She was worried about the pain LGBTQ people were feeling when they decided to come out. Worried, too, about their parents and friends—and the conservative backlash against the growing acceptance of gays.

"I was so struck with how sweet that was. I went back to my office and couldn't get it out of my head. So, half an hour later, I went back into her office and closed the door.

"I said, 'I have something to tell you: I'm gay.'

"Kim was the first person I came out to. She jumped up, hugged me, kissed my cheek and said, 'I'm so happy for you. Thank you for sharing that.'

"Then, at 66, I decided, 'In for a penny, in for a pound.' I went up and down the hallway. Mark Neary, her assistant secretary of state, and some of the other staff were in a pow-wow, so I just told all of them, not knowing what the reaction was going to be. They're like, 'That's wonderful, David!' Everyone I talked to that day was supportive. Some said, 'You know this doesn't change my feelings one way or the other.' I knew that was a vote of confidence, but I thought, 'Well, it shouldn't!' " He laughs at the memory.

Looking back, Ammons says the tenacious "incremental" approach to LGBTQ civil rights pursued by the state's first two openly gay legislators, Cal Anderson and Ed Murray, carried the day, despite galling setbacks. When the voters bluntly rejected the gay civil rights ballot measure in 1997, "we had a culture that was still living in yesterday's understanding of what was appropriate," he says. "The Defense of Marriage Act was another stopgap."

AN ACTIVIST PRESBYTERIAN for decades as a member of his church's board of elders, Ammons is in the thick of what he describes as "an internal, long slog battle over equality."

"There were national votes against the appointment of gay and lesbian pastors, with studies on the psychology and sociology of the issue, as well as the biblical narratives," Ammons says. "The overriding message, of course, is 'Love God. Love your neighbor.' No exceptions, period. That subsumes everything else.

"I credit the young people of America for teaching us important lessons. At our church in Olympia, the youth group was the first to say, 'Hey, let's join the Pride Parade and have a banner that says 'Westminster Presbyterian loves all.' That was very scandalous at the time. But a year later we did exactly that. A younger, more tolerant generation is rising.

"Our pastor at that time was David Kegley, a wonderful, loving man of God. He had preached three powerhouse sermons on why the church is getting it wrong on gay rights and why it's required that we love all our spiritual siblings. It was really powerful stuff. He had been training with the Mennonite Peace Institute in Chicago on dispute resolution and is now doing that professionally. He led a year's worth of conversation to let everyone in the congregation have their say. The framework was 'Shall we become open and affirming?'

"I told David, 'I'd like to bring this conversation to a head in The Session,' which is what we call the board of elders, in a nod to our Scottish forebears. I had three motions: One, that we become open and affirming. Two, that our pastors be authorized to use our facilities to perform same-sex weddings, if they choose. And third, that we would proclaim our stance on our website, on our reader board, and any other way that seemed appropriate to spreading the news. All of those passed our Session, with two dissents on same-sex weddings. The Session makes the rules. It's not a plebiscite among the congregation. We lost a few members, but now every new class of people that comes knows what we stand for. There's a rainbow flag on our welcome sign. If you're not looking for a church that's open and affirming, that would be a deal breaker right from the start."

Eventually, through a series of votes, the General Assembly of the national church decided there should be no outright prohibition on Presbyterian churches appointing gay pastors, or ordaining elders and deacons. "That essentially leaves it to local control right now," Ammons says. "Still, could a church in backwoods USA ever appoint a woman pastor, a person of color or a gay person? Unlikely. But acceptance of gays has moved in church culture quicker than I thought, just as it has in the national culture. That's what gave me the energy and the final courage.

"I didn't think I'd ever come out," Ammons says with a small sigh. "It was just baked into me. My upbringing was not anti-gay, but I could read the tea leaves as to what being an upstanding person looked like. So I lived that script until age 66. It was just a long journey for me, from it being my secret, from it being no-body's business; not wanting to carry any of that baggage of homophobia.

"I came out to my choir, which was like a separate little family in the church, and then just around the coffee hour after church. There was no blowback, although there were a few families that left just before I came out that winter."

Ammons says his daughter and son were "wonderfully supportive" of his decision. Jennifer Ammons is an attorney with the Northwest Justice Project. Jonathan Ammons is a records management analyst for the State Department of Children, Youth, and Families.

"My mother was one of the last calls to make. She said, 'You know what the Bible says, right?' And I said, 'Yes, Mom, I've seen those verses. I've also seen verses that talk about the love of Christ for all of us. All means *all*. I'm the same man I was an hour ago before you got my call.' That kind of stopped her in her tracks. Finally, I said, 'Well, at the very least, let's agree to disagree on the theological aspects of this.' For the rest of her life she went out of her way several times to say 'I love you so much.' That was as close as she could come to welcoming my news. I thought she might want to talk about it some more. But I didn't bring it up. So she never said anything more, and our relationship was as warm as ever. Perhaps more. She died at 93 in 2021."

AMMONS RETIRED from the Office of the Secretary of State in January of 2017. One of the first calls he received was from Governor Jay Inslee, offering an ap-

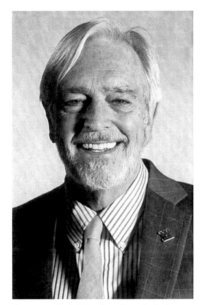

Ammons in 2019 when he was induct-ed into the UW Department of Com-munication Hall of Fame. *University of Washington*

pointment to the Washington State Public Disclo-sure Commission. It was a full circle moment. As a cub reporter, Ammons covered the birth of the PDC after passage of a citizens' initiative in 1972. Backed by 72 percent of the voters, I-276's goal was to ensure transparency in campaign financ-ing, promote access to public records, and mon-itor the activities of lobbyists and the financial affairs of elected officials. "I had seen first-hand what an important role the PDC plays in open government," Ammons says, "so it was a perfect way to begin a new career as a citizen activist." He also represented the public on the 2018 Legislative Public Records Task Force, and in 2019 was cho-sen chairman of the PDC. That same year, he was named to the University of Washington's Depart-ment of Communication Alumni Hall of Fame.

Now chairman of the board of directors of the Washington State Parks Foundation, a do-nor-driven nonprofit, Ammons is also a volunteer and board member with *Side-Walk,* a robust Thurston County program to combat homelessness and hunger. After several terms as a trustee of the Washington State Historical Society, he is now part of a group hoping to create a new Olympia historical museum.

He has had a front-row seat for a half-century of Washington history.

As he reflects on the 10th anniversary of marriage equality in Washington, Ammons says he has never had a serious relationship with another man. "But the fact that I could, felt so affirming and so freeing. Not only did coming out feel like a 5,000-pound weight lifted off my shoulders, the realization that the culture has moved enough to not only empower LGBTQ+ people to be in a relationship—even marriage—is wonderful. Even if I haven't used that opportunity as a lot of people have, just that affirmation feels delightful!

"There's still lots more to do along the road to equality—on race, poverty, and indigenous people. But I think we've come a long way. I didn't expect to see marriage equality happen, really, in my lifetime. It's amazing, isn't it?"

John C. Hughes

J. MANNY SANTIAGO

Keeping the Faith

At home in Tacoma, Manny Santiago only drinks Puerto Rican coffee. In the morning, with milk and sugar. He grew up on a coffee farm in Puerto Rico's highlands, where the volcanic soil produces arabica beans once favored by the Vatican. He started doing what he could at 5 years old to help his family with the crop. He's a proud *jibaro*, a son of the island's rural culture. Urbanites tend to view *jibaro* as simple, poor and uneducated. "When you get out of the mountains," rural people are "looked down on," Santiago says.

Not only poor, he was Protestant on an island where Catholicism predominates. And he was deeply uncomfortable with Puerto Rico's reigning machismo. Bullied in elementary school and junior high, Santiago dreamed of studying stars and planets. He was pulled back to earth by the gravity of political activism—and then religion. The church had held a place in his heart after a parish patriarch, Don Tito, gave his own worn Bible to young Manny as a gift of gratitude.

The first openly gay Latino pastor ordained by his Baptist denomination, Santiago carried Don Tito's old Bible to New York where he ministered to immigrants and homeless people. He brought it to Seattle where he sermonized about civil rights and was active in Washington's 2012 marriage equality campaign—but struggled with his progressive-on-paper parishioners at University Baptist Church.

The marriage cause was very personal for Santiago. His partner, Ferneli Hernández, had been living in Washington for a decade without proper documentation. Legal marriage might allow Hernández to live with more freedom and security. Santiago's parents—from whom he was estranged after he came out—have since warmly embraced their only son and his husband.

"Now we are the same family that we were before," he says about his parents.

Facing page: Santiago at a reception welcoming him as the first executive director of the Washington LGBTQ Commission. *Manny Santiago*

"They love my husband. Like every mother-in-law, my mom loves my husband more than me. And he's always right and I'm always wrong."

In his transition from the pulpit to nonprofit leadership, Santiago became executive director of Tacoma's Rainbow Center in 2017. He was one of the community leaders who helped shape the job description for the first executive director of the state's LGBTQ Commission. The day before applications were closed in 2019, his husband suggested that Santiago should apply; he seemed a great fit. Governor Jay Inslee agreed and appointed him to the post.

The mission of the commission—a 15-member advisory board—is to identify community needs, and advocate for LGBTQ "equity in all aspects of state government." Its members represent identities from "an unapologetic fa'afafine" (a nonbinary gender in Samoan culture), to a tribal police chief, to a policy guru for the Greater Seattle Business Association.

Three years into the job, Santiago is combining his passions for helping the disadvantaged and shepherding a flock.

"I love seeing my folk—my folk being gay folk and people of color and Latinos and immigrants and whatever—I love seeing them happy and achieving their goals and just thriving. I love that. And that's what I go for. Does it pay? I don't know. But that's not my primary concern. I'm seeking the happiness of my community. That is my primary goal."

JUAN MANUEL Santiago Rodríguez was born in a hospital founded by a pacifist religious order. His father's side of the family had been in the Caribbean since the 1500s, Santiago says. They were of Moorish heritage—Muslims from Spain—and some were lightly complected and blond. His mother's side was more diverse. "It's like all colors, all textures, very mixed."

"My dad's side of the family had some resources," Santiago says. Enough to buy shoes for his father to wear to school. "While my mom's side of the family didn't. They had to go barefoot. To the same school."

His family lived in west central Puerto Rico. He grew up in Adjuntas, which remains one of the poorest communities in Puerto Rico by U.S. Census Bureau ranking, with a poverty rate above 60 percent.

Puerto Ricans are U.S. citizens at birth. And yet islanders have long faced an existential question: to stay under the colonizer's umbrella or seek independence?

After Columbus came ashore on Puerto Rico's west coast in 1493, Spain ruled the island for 400 years. That reign ended with the Spanish-American War in 1898, after which the United States seized Puerto Rico. Roughly the size and pop-

A view of the area Santiago grew up in barrio Guaybo Dulce of Adjuntas. Lake Guayo is in the background. *Manny Santiago*

ulation of Connecticut, Puerto Rico became neither a state or its own country, but a U.S. territory, with limited rights.

Santiago's home turf was once dedicated to haciendas, or plantations, of coffee and sugar. His birthplace, Lares, is renowned for supplying the spark of a peasant rebellion against Spanish control in 1868. (*El Grito de Lares*, or "The Cry of Lares," is akin to "Remember the Alamo.") Although the rebels were subdued by the better equipped Spanish militia, the colonizers made concessions, such as ending slavery.

"THERE'S LITERALLY coffee everywhere," Santiago says of the hillsides flanking his hometown. Beans, known for their low acidity and sweet tones, are sown at altitudes above 1,800 feet and grown under abundant shade. In the 19th century, Puerto Rican coffee was served in the cafes of Paris, Madrid and Vienna, as well as the Vatican. But exports plummeted after 1898, "partly because the United States was already buying coffee from Brazil and saw sugar, not coffee, as the island's most potentially lucrative crop."

Santiago's parents owned a small farm. "It's not a big corporation. It has to be you and your family," he says. At harvest time, if kids were missing from school their teachers understood why. Some teachers were themselves toiling in the fields on weekends. The crops didn't pay enough to fully support Santiago's family; his father took odd jobs and the family received food stamps at times.

His parents managed to scrape up enough money to buy encyclopedias for

Manny and his sister. The first book he owned was a gift from a friend of his mom's, who also employed her as a nanny. It was a biography of "El Maestro," Pedro Albizu Campos, the leader of Puerto Rico's independence movement. Campos spoke six languages, finished at the top of his 1921 Harvard Law class, and was later jailed by the U.S.

Santiago with his sister and parents. *Manny Santiago*

Young Manny was raised in a household very respectful of women. "I grew up with women pastors in church. In my head, I just couldn't conceive of talking about women like the way teenagers talk about women," he says.

He was hassled in school for mannerisms that weren't macho enough. He fell in with a group of nerds. One of the boys took an interest in him. "And he kind of started, like approaching me, this teenage romance kind of thing. I didn't know what to do. He was my first kiss. But because I was in church, I was fighting that."

His parents saw his attitudes changing with his new friends. They made him go to therapy with a pastor—"from a more conservative church than ours. "I had to endure several sessions of what would be considered reparative therapy. And that was hard."

Santiago told the Washington State Legislature about his own experience, in support of a 2014 bill aiming to ban conversion therapy for LGBQT minors. The pastor tried shaming him, Santiago recounted, saying he would never be whole in the eyes of God if he continued to feel attracted to men. "It takes years to overcome the shame, to overcome that feeling of unworthiness," he testified. "Conversion therapy, whether it's physical or mental or spiritual or psychological, is damaging to a kid."

A "fantastic" change awaited. Before 11th grade, he was accepted to a boarding school for students who excelled in math and science. It was in Mayagüez, a coastal city, about three hours from his parents. Selected through competitive testing, students received free tuition, rooms, and meals. They treasured learning and were more tolerant of others. And "you could be a little more you," he says.

As a young activist, Santiago joined protests against the U.S. Navy's use of Vieques Island for bombing practice. *Manny Santiago*

Santiago wanted to study astrophysics. Using the top of his parents' bureau as a writing surface, he filled out an application to Ohio State University. He was accepted, but his parents seemed distraught at the idea of him leaving home. He went to the University of Puerto Rico in Mayagüez instead. In his second year of college, in 1997, he came out—and became more outspoken. He protested the U.S. Navy's use of the island of Vieques as a bombing range and munitions dump, and joined other causes.

His passion shifted from the celestial to the terrestrial. He changed his major to sociology. "And I could then explain things to myself in a different language that I didn't know before. I knew religion. I knew science. I didn't know social science. I came out then because I had the language to define what it was."

His ties with a campus religious group were severely strained. His parents threw him out of the house.

"And the only community I had was my friends who were queers or allies," he recalls. "They became my chosen family."

THE DAY AFTER graduating from college in June 2000, Santiago moved to New York City. He landed a research job at the Mellon Foundation and enrolled in an English immersion program at Columbia University. He was in the Bronx for 9/11. It was particularly traumatic, he says, because he didn't have a support network in New York.

He returned to Puerto Rico, where people said his fluency in English would help him in job-hunting. But his first interview, for a government position, ended abruptly, he says, because of his pro-independence politics.

He was drawn back to religion after learning that an underground network of LGBTQ clergy existed in Puerto Rico.

Santiago's family had long been religious, even if his parents were not regular churchgoers. His father's side, once non-practicing Muslims, had been Protestant for generations. At the turn of the 20th century, his great-grandfather helped found the First Baptist Church of Adjuntas. His mother's side were spiritists, dev-

otees of a movement started by French philosopher and scientist, Allan Kardec.*
"They were pure Kardecians," Santiago says. They didn't concoct potions, or cast
spells, or create reality. But his maternal grandfather held a weekly séance.

He and his sister started going to the local Baptist church. Then, one Sunday,
when he was an adolescent, the church had a special ceremony for Father's Day.

His Sunday School teacher asked him if he'd be willing to walk one of the
older men in the parish, Don Tito, to the altar where fathers would be recognized.
Santiago's father didn't attend church, and neither did Don Tito's family; they
were Seventh-day Adventists.

Santiago gladly accompanied Don Tito
Feliciano. On the following Sunday, the old
man thanked the young man for his "beautiful" gesture with a gift—Don Tito's own Bible.

Manny's simple act had such profound
results.

"And that basically sealed the deal right
there," he recalls. "That sort of connected me
to the church in a way I did not expect."

He still has Don Tito's Bible, held together by tape.

The Bible that changed Santiago's life. *Manny
Santiago*

HE WANTED more. He wanted to go to seminary. His local congregation was
part of the American Baptist Churches, one of the many Baptist denominations.
(The largest, the evangelical Southern Baptists, split from their northern counterparts over slavery. Southern Baptists tend to be more conservative and Caucasian
than other Baptists.) Considered moderate in their theology, the American Baptist Churches were not then welcoming to LGBTQ parishioners.

Santiago began a process of reconciling his identity with his faith. A friendly
minister had recommended that Santiago study divinity at the oldest seminary
in the United States, Andover Newton Theological School in Massachusetts, just
outside Boston.

He was accepted. But before starting studies he had a crisis of faith—not un-
common among aspiring clergy. A friend, a gay Presbyterian minister, had given
him some theology books. "And all of the sudden, I realized 'I don't believe any
of this. This is ridiculous and I'm going to seminary. What am I going to do?'"

* Allan Kardec was the pen name of Hippolyte Rivail, 1804-1869, who defined spiritism as the
science of spirits and their relation to the material world.

His Presbyterian friend said not to worry. It happens all the time. He invited Manny to a meeting of Amnesty International. The president of Amnesty's Puerto Rico chapter was an ordained minister, Margarita Sánchez de León.

A Black Puerto Rican lesbian, Sánchez de León was acclaimed for challenging Puerto Rico's criminal law prohibiting sodomy. While she was testifying against an anti-same-sex marriage bill, a legislator had interrupted her to ask if she was a "practicing lesbian." She bravely replied "yes." She went to the Justice Department to confess she had violated the sodomy law. She then led a coalition to overturn the law.

Santiago sought her advice, pouring out his problems.

"And she smiled," he recalls, "and said—and I will never forget— 'Manny, I'm so happy for you because what you're going through is that the building that has been given to you has been shattered. And now it's your turn to take those bricks and find a way to build the building that works for you.' "

Sánchez de León said the faith handed down by his family was theirs. And it was not the faith that would sustain him. He had to find what worked for him.

"That actually re-framed the whole thing," Santiago says. "I went to seminary, still with a lot of questions, still with lot of doubts, still with a lot of gaps,

While a seminary student, Santiago sampled other faiths before returning to the American Baptist Churches denomination. *Manny Santiago*

but committed to finding a denomination that would affirm who I was in my quest."

He experimented with other faith traditions, visiting churches to see how they felt. "And I didn't find myself in any of them," he says.

What he was seeking was waiting just around the corner.

Running late one Sunday for a service he planned to attend in Boston, he went instead to the nearby First Baptist Church in Newton Centre. The senior minister was a woman, Meg Hess, as was the associate minister, Mindi Welton-Mitchell.

Welton-Mitchell was bluntly pro-LGBTQ, having grown up in the Church of the Covenant in Palmer, Alaska, one of the first "welcoming and affirming" U.S. churches in the Baptist denomination. Years later, Santiago joined the board of Welcoming and Affirming Baptists.

But his struggles continued. "I often say I went to seminary because I had so many questions that I wanted to answer, and then I came out with even more questions."

A mentor and friend, the Rev. Mindi Welton-Mitchell says of Santiago: "I was always telling him, 'We need your voice. You are needed in the church.' " *Manny Santiago*

HE WAS CALLED to pastoral service by a church in the Elmhurst neighborhood of Queens, New York. Queens itself has a diverse population of more than 2 million; only one-quarter of the borough is white. Santiago's first assignment, Primera Iglesia Bautista de la Comunidad, was a church of immigrants. Roughly half of the congregation was from Ecuador. Others came from Puerto Rico, Cuba, Colombia, Bolivia and Peru. He welcomed the chance to help marginalized communities. "Of course, I was going to be there," he says.

There was, however, one major complication.

"I knew the Latino church that I was about to start serving was more theologically conservative than the church that was sending me off," he says. "So, I had to make the conscious decision to go back into the closet."

His people were in need. "Not only for spiritual and moral support, but literally for letters to immigration and visits to the detention center," he says. "Or just crying with them because they were about to be deported."

He introduced his congregants to a more "liberating lens" through which to read the Bible. He started with the *Book of Revelation* and comparing the persecution of immigrants and refugees to that of early Christians. He hoped his congregants would take away a message of hope, not fear.

But being closeted was taking a toll on Santiago. "At some point I had to recognize that it was affecting my health, my mental health, my physical health, so I started searching for other jobs," he says.

He landed one as an associate pastor at the Church of St. Paul and St. Andrew, a progressive United Methodist church on Manhattan's Upper West Side. There, he'd see a symphony cellist serving meals alongside a homeless woman who slept on the stairs of the church. Although he enjoyed the special privilege he was granted to officiate at a Methodist church, he wanted to come back home to the American Baptist Churches.

And 2010 offered an opportunity in Seattle's University District.

HE HAD NEVER been to Seattle. But he liked what he gleaned while interviewing at University Baptist. The previous pastor was openly gay. The church had a progressive reputation. And indeed, Santiago would use the pulpit to talk about women's rights, immigration reform, LGBTQ issues and marriage equality. "I did a whole series of sermons about anti-Blackness and how the church was complicit in the narrative about a Black person being inferior," he says.

As a tax-exempt nonprofit, the church could not endorse candidates or ballot measures. Santiago, though, participated in the campaign for marriage equality as a voice of the religious community.

He had met Ferneli Hernández at a club in Seattle, on a Latin night. They

Santiago with two fellow Baptist pastors who supported marriage equality in Washington, Rev. Chris Boyer of Lynnwood, left, and Rev. Craig Darling of Seattle, right. *Manny Santiago*

started dating. Hernández was born in Mexico; a descendant of the Yucatec Maya people. He had come to the U.S. because he did not feel safe as a gay man in southern Mexico, where indigenous Mayas had long faced discrimination, poverty, even slaughter.

Hernández had lived in Seattle's Eastside suburbs since 2001, when he was 19, but lacked proper immigration documents. At the time Santiago proposed to him—

in bed, after watching Governor Chris Gregoire advocate for marriage equality on TV news—federal agents had recently raided farms and restaurants in King County.

"So, there was some urgency in that sense," Santiago recalls. "But my pastor heart also said this is not something to take lightly. It's a commitment and something to take seriously."

They were married in May 2013 at University Baptist, which had nevertheless disenchanted Santiago. In his first year as pastor there, someone told him about what happened behind the scenes when church leaders were making the decision to hire him. One of the church members said they had somewhat enjoyed his sermon, but found it difficult to follow because of his accent. "In the mind of this woman, my accent made my theology unsound and weak," he says.

He was told a retired minister who attended the church said they could pay

Santiago proposed to his husband Ferneli Hernández one night in 2012 after they saw Gov. Chris Gregoire on TV advocating marriage equality. *Manny Santiago*

for Santiago to get speech therapy.

Coming from New York, where his accent didn't stand out, never mind incite criticism, Santiago felt demeaned by racism.

"And had I known about that, I would've declined the offer to come to Seattle to be their pastor. It was very painful to hear that. And after that, it was just downhill."

Questions, concerns, and doubts about faith were creeping back. "And I was looking to transition to something else."

HIS NEXT STOP was Madison, Wisconsin, where he was hired as executive director of a non-denominational ministry on the campus of the University of Wisconsin. He would be more administrator than pastor. That would be a good chance to show lay people he could do more than preach and pray.

Santiago loved his job and the liberal Madison community. But his husband missed Washington. And after Donald Trump was elected president in 2016, Hernández experienced racism in the private club where he worked as a server. "It just made sense for us to leave that and come back to Washington where his family is," Santiago says.

It felt like their destiny to return—and where else, but to the City of Destiny?

In its list of the "Gayest Cities in America," *The Advocate* magazine ranked Tacoma #1 in 2013. *The Advocate*'s criteria were both serious and cheeky. Cities had to have at least 150,000 residents and they received points for electing LGBTQ public officials and enacting non-discrimination policies. They also scored for "fabulous shopping" and having a roller derby league. Marriage equality was

Tacoma Mayor Victoria Woodards gave Santiago the city's LGBTQ Pride Month proclamation in 2018. *Manny Santiago*

heavily weighted in that year's rankings, which helped Spokane and Seattle make the top 15. Washington was the only state that year with three of the gayest cities.

The Advocate encouraged visits to Tacoma in July when the city celebrated Pride at "Out in the Park."

The city's Pride Festival is produced by the Rainbow Center, South Puget Sound's leading LGBTQ2S resource center. (Lesbian, gay, bisexual, transgender, queer, questioning, and two-spirit.) It educates community members and allies, and advocates for policy, as well.

In his two years as executive director of the Rainbow Center, one of Santiago's proudest moments was when the rainbow flag was raised over the roof of the Tacoma Dome for the first time. It culminated a 10-year effort that started with a letter-writing campaign by trans women activists.

NOW RECOGNIZED as a community leader, Santiago joined a percolating movement to create a formal LGBTQ voice in state policy-making. Other minority communities were represented by the state African American Affairs Commission and the Hispanic Affairs Commission.

Governor Jay Inslee was receptive to the idea, as were members of the state Legislature. Claire Wilson, Washington's first openly lesbian state senator led the push to create a LGBTQ Commission in 2019, along with Senator Marko Liias (whose proposed bans on conversion therapy had been supported by Santiago's testimony.) Skyler Rude, the state's first openly gay Republican legislator, was instrumental in gaining GOP support for the commission, Santiago says.

The final vote in the Senate was 30-16, with nays from GOP Senate Leader Mark Schoesler and his successor, John Braun.

Several midwives aided the commission's birthing. When draft legislation was ready, legislators brought it to community leaders for feedback. Santiago and others also were asked for input on the job description for the commission's executive director. "You're talking about someone who is going to be part of the governor's cabinet, whose job description is getting feedback from the community that the position is going to serve. What a

Santiago was on hand when Gov. Jay Inslee signed a bill in 2018 banning conversion therapy. *Manny Santiago*

wonderful way of being a democracy," Santiago says. "Right?"

It made the commission seem like more than window dressing. It was a collaborative product, with its creators willing to seek community expertise, evidently in an ongoing fashion.

Santiago says he was gushing to his husband over dinner about "all the wonderful things in the process," and said, "I hope we find someone good."

His husband said, "Well, why can't it be you?"

Hours before the window closed, Santiago submitted his application. Again, the Governor's Office was intentional about getting community response. Santiago was one of four finalists invited to a public interview, town-hall style. The finalists presented their visions and forum participants were able to submit questions. The LGBTQ community could also offer assessments of the candidates.

Asked to evaluate Santiago in a 2022 interview, Marsha Botzer, the state's most renowned trans activist, points back to the hiring process and the ownership stake she felt in it. "Well, since I selected him," she says, "I think he's pretty good."

Why?

"I had known him before for his work in aspects of the community," says Botzer, who became a co-chair of the commission. "I thought that he would have the best energy, background, and ability to do the job."

INSLEE APPOINTED Santiago in August 2019, praising him as an "activist and administrator." Santiago started in late October. His pronouns are he, her, they. He doesn't have a problem with whichever one you use.

He explains:

"Obviously, language and culture go hand-in-hand. In Spanish speaking countries, one of the ways of defusing the *machista* (male chauvinist) and misogynistic society in which we live is by breaking down the barriers of gender and sex and that sort of thing.

"In order for us to break with those stereotypes and things, gay men use female pronouns when we are interacting with each other and lesbian women use masculine pronouns. In Spanish, my closest friends and I refer to each other as *ella*, her, or she and her.

"Again, it's just a cultural thing for me in Spanish; you want to stick it to the man."

He identifies as "queer" for similar reasons:

" 'Queer' was something imposed on us as an insult. And the community had to reclaim it. So, I'm reclaiming it. So, I do identify as both a gay man and a

Washington LGBTQ Commission officers and staff in 2020, left to right: Santiago, Jac Archer (vice-chair), Marsha Botzer (co-chair), Agaiotupu Viena (co-chair), Alvaro Figueroa (secretary) and Omar Santana-Gomez, (executive assistant). *Washington State LGBTQ Commission*

queer person, queer being my political identity and gay being my sexual orientation.

"I also use some of the slur words in Spanish to identify myself—and in a shocking way for Spanish speakers. Like I want them to be shocked. I want them to know your machismo didn't break me. It tried. But it didn't. And I'm not going to let it. And if you call me *maricón*, which is equivalent to 'fag' in Puerto Rican Spanish, if you call me *maricón*, well, yes, I am Manny Santiago and I am *maricón*. I'm very proud of it."

SANTIAGO WORKS with 15 volunteer commissioners appointed for three-year terms. They come from Walla Walla, Skagit and Okanogan counties; they're descended from Apaches, Guatemalans and Scandinavians. One thing they have in common? "We're all from activist-world," says Botzer, founder of the Ingersoll Gender Center in Seattle. "I'd say we're all equals in that respect."

Rounding out the panel are four members of the Legislature, two from each chamber and each party.

Why is the commission needed?

"From my perspective, our minority types are underrepresented precisely because we are not part of the policy-making processes," Santiago says. "And there needs to be a bold way of having our opinions, our realities, our ideas as part of the process."

Hatched shortly before the Covid pandemic and meeting remotely through much of it, Santiago and the commission have focused on two broad areas: reaching out to learn about community problems in all corners of the state; and remedying gaps, blind spots, and obstacles—down to the syntax of state government.

Through panels, presentations, or meetings with individuals or grass roots groups, the commission may hear about a problem between a queer family and a state agency. Santiago will explore it further, from his vantage in the governor's cabinet. "I don't go to a case worker or front desk person to complain," he says. "I go to my colleagues in the cabinet to let them know about systemic issues happening within an agency so they can actually make some changes."

Santiago and the commission have become go-to sources for some in state government. In one case, an agency was developing a training manual for people who provide services for housebound folks. The agency realized they lacked expertise about the some of the clients they serve. They turned to the commission. Santiago had the opportunity to review and revise the manual to make sure its language was inclusive and accurate about LGBTQ identities and experiences.

The commission also amplifies the viewpoints of community members who have lacked a voice in policy-making. Santiago points to a work-group that Inslee

Santiago's work involves speaking to groups and communities, such as Somos Seattle, one of the state's organizations for LGBTQ Latinos. *Manny Santiago*

put together to advise him on reducing poverty. With the commission's help, it gained perspectives about unhoused youth—who are disturbingly over-represented in surveys of the homeless. "We were able to bring in more voices," Santiago says, "especially of trans people of color who are experiencing poverty and problems with housing and challenges accessing health care."

It's not always easy. Commissioners have heard about school boards adopting guidelines preventing LGBTQ visibility, he says, such as removing books from schools and preventing trans students from engaging in sports.

The state doesn't have jurisdiction in those matters unless the local policies are unconstitutional. Santiago says the commission has been able to prevent some actions by sending letters, and reminding school boards of their educational duties. He also works with the Office of the Education Ombuds in the Governor's Office, which may facilitate talks with administrators and faculty to protect students facing attacks in school.

"I am very transparent about not being able to change government overnight," he adds. "We are in a system that moves slowly and we need to understand that and play within those rules, while, at the same, changing the system. And those two things work hand-in-hand.

"I think we do have influence because we're visible. But at the same time, I

Santiago was estranged from his parents after he came out. "Now we are the same family as before," he says about their reconciliation. "They love my husband." *Manny Santiago*

cannot change someone's heart just because I'm director of the commission."

The Reverend Mindi Welton-Mitchell has known Santiago for 20 years, back to when he was a seminary student and she was associate minister at the church he attended outside Boston. Welton-Mitchell and her husband, J.C., consider Santiago and his husband, Hernández, family. Santiago is godfather to the couple's son A.J. who has autism. Manny babysat for A.J. so his parents could go on date nights. "He's not afraid of the challenges that come with disabilities," Welton-Mitchell says.

She sensed long ago that a traditional church would be a difficult fit for Santiago. "He's creative. He wants to change the status quo. He wants to transform the world."

She sees his current job as ideal. Being a voice at the state level for inclusion and equality, "is one of the highest ways to live out Christ's call to love our neighbors as ourselves in the world. I think he's settled into what he wants to do. I see him leading the call to justice by being in that position."

WHILE URGING patience, Santiago lives with urgency. He was diagnosed with a heart condition at 13. He also has cancer—a kind of sarcoma that is not curable but is manageable, he says. He sees his oncologist every six months and gets treatments "off and on."

"So I know that my time is limited. Now does that mean that I have 50 more years, or five more years, or five more seconds? I don't know. Therefore, I'm going to do as much for my community, for the people that I love, for my country, for my adopted country, for as long as I can."

He wants the community to keep pushing, sending emails, making calls. To show its needs.

"Their mobilization is one of the tools I have to change the system. I'm always telling the community, 'Keep doing that. Even though it's a slow process that's the only tool that I have.' "

The cadence of a Latino Baptist pastor kicks in.

"And that doesn't mean I'm always right in the final decision. Or that I always understand the complexity of the issue. But I try my best to not see the urgency and desperation of the community as an attack on me and my work.

"It is a tool that I use. The desperation, and the pain, it is also my pain, my desperation.

"Because I am a queer, gay Latino man in Washington."

He pauses, then smiles.

"There's some preaching there," he says.

Bob Young

Washington's Journey

1909: Washington's 1893 sodomy law expands to make certain sex acts illegal for consenting adults, whether heterosexual or homosexual, with the penalty up to 10 years in prison.

1978: Two Seattle police officers launch an initiative to repeal the city's anti-discrimination law; 63 percent of voters reject their ballot measure.

1973: Seattle City Council makes it illegal to discriminate in employment based on sexual orientation. It is the first mention of gays and lesbians in city law.

1996: President Bill Clinton signs the Defense of Marriage Act (DOMA), which says no state is required to recognize another state's same-sex marriage. Only one member of Washington's congressional delegation votes against it: Jim McDermott of Seattle.

1975: State Senator Pete Francis pushes to repeal the sodomy law. A conservative foe says that would "repeal the Ten Commandments." But Francis secures the needed votes. Gov. Dan Evans signs the new criminal code into law.

2004: King County Superior Court Judge William Downing finds the state ban on same-sex marriages unconstitutional in a case featuring eight couples, including a firefighter, cop, and nurse. This sets the stage for a state Supreme Court ruling on marriage equality.

1971: John Singer and Paul Barwick go to the King County auditor's office and demand a marriage license. The county had never received such a request and denies them an application. State courts back the county's decision.

1993: Gay-marriage debates ignite after Hawaii's high court rules that a ban on same-sex marriage violates the state constitution. The Hawaii Legislature redefines marriage as between one man and one woman. Mainland Christian conservatives start to rally against marriage equality.

to Marriage Equality

2006: In January, Governor Chris Gregoire signs a law adding "sexual orientation" and "gender identity" to existing prohibitions on discrimination in jobs, housing, lending, and insurance. It culminates a 27-year effort to win equal rights in state law.

2006: In a July 5-4 decision, the state Supreme Court upholds the state ban on same-sex marriage, finding a "reasonable basis" in the law for the sake of procreation and good-parenting. In dissenting, Justice Mary Fairhurst flays the majority's logic as flawed and discriminatory.

2012: With public opinion shifting, and strategy stressing love and commitment, legislation is passed in Olympia, along party lines. Conservatives mount a repeal effort via R74. The November statewide vote is 53.6% in favor of marriage equality, 46.3% against.

Dec. 9, 2012: The first same-sex marriages are performed. In Seattle, Superior Court Judge Mary Yu officiates from midnight until 7 a.m. Two matriarchs of the movement, Jane Abbott Lighty and Pete-e Petersen, exchange vows at Benaroya Hall that afternoon. The crowd whoops when Judge Anne Levinson pronounces "by the power *now vested* in me ..."

2009: Christian conservatives try to repeal the state's third domestic partnership law with Referendum 71. In November, Washington voters become the first in the nation to ratify domestic partnerships (also known as "civil unions") for same-sex couples.

2007-2009: Gregoire signs three incremental laws creating domestic partnerships and conferring benefits to couples—both straight and gay—such as hospital visitations and inheritance rights that married heterosexuals enjoyed.

2019: Governor Jay Inslee appoints J. Manny Santiago to head the state's new LGBTQ Commission. Its mission is to identify needs of the community and advocate for equity and inclusion in all aspects of state government.

BIBLIOGRAPHY

Atkins, Gary L., *Gay Seattle, Stories of Exile and Belonging*, University of Washington Press, Seattle and London, paperback with a new introduction by the author, 2013

Buechner, Frederick, *Telling Secrets*, HarperSan Francisco, 1991

Cammermeyer, Margarethe, with **Chris Fisher**, *Serving in Silence*, Viking Books/Penguin and AuthorHouse, revised edition, 2016

Cervini, Eric, *The Deviant's War, The Homosexual vs. the United States of America*, Picador, Farrar, Straus & Giroux, New York, 2020

Hughes, John C., *Julia Butler Hansen, A Trailblazing Washington Politician*, Legacy Washington/Gorham Printing, Centralia, Wash., 2021

Ingersoll, Robert G., *The Works of Robert G. Ingersoll*, Volume 12, Miscellany, Dresden Publishing, New York, 1900 via Gutenberg.org

Irons, Peter, *A People's History of the Supreme Court*, Viking/Penguin Putnam, 1999

Issenberg, Sasha, T*he Engagement, America's Quarter-Century Struggle Over Same-Sex Marriage*, Pantheon Books, New York, 2021

Lepore, Jill, *These Truths, A History of the United States*, W.W. Norton & Co., New York, 2018

Mauro, Tony, *The Supreme Court Landmark Decisions*, Fall River Press, New York, 2016

Smith, Martin J., *Going to Trinidad: A Doctor, a Colorado town, and Stories from an Unlikely Gender Crossroads*, Bower House Books, Denver, 2021,

Stein, Mark, *Rethinking the Gay and Lesbian Movement*, Routledge, London & New York, 2012

SOURCE NOTES

PETE FRANCIS

"pushy jerks," quoted in *Gay Seattle*, p. 125

"discrimination against anyone," quoted in "Marriage license denied," *Seattle Times*, 4-4-2006

"a bunch of closet cases," quoted in *Gay Seattle*, p. 125

"government out of private lives," quoted in *Gay Seattle*, p. 221

"enter into any marriage contract," Engrossed Senate Bill 27, 41st Legislature, Second Extra Session, RCW 26.04.010

"infamous and detestable crime," quoted in *Gay Seattle*, p. 14

"for not more than 10 years," quoted in *Gay Seattle*, p. 24

"half as much time in jail," *Gay Seattle*, p. 24

distaste for "queers," Moore oral history, OSOS web site, p. 227

"silence would be acquiescence," Francis to author, 7-21-2022

"will remain men and women," quoted in "U.S. Rights measure ratified," *Spokesman-Review*, 3-23-1973.

"I also thought to myself," Francis to author, 7-21-2022

"clearly dispels any suggestion," *Singer v. Hara*, 11 Wash. App. 247 (1974) https://scholar.google.com/scholar_case?-case=5576229373244357890&q=singer+v.+hara&hl=en&as_sdt=6,48&as_vis=1

"as old as book of Genesis," *Singer v. Hara*

"apparent that state's refusal," *Singer v. Hara*

"We are not unmindful," *Singer v. Hara*

"I'm not going to sit back," quoted in "Senate approves new crime code," *News Tribune*, 6-5-1975

"no fan of victimless crimes," *Gay Seattle*, p. 224; also to author, 8-15-2022

"major advance for gay people," quoted in *Gay Seattle*, p. 224

"to perpetuate their lifestyle," quoted in "Homosexuality rejected," *Centralia Daily Chronicle*, 3-17-1977

"expressed between consenting persons," quoted in "Homosexuality rejected"

"looked on women with lust," quoted in "Gay rights plea is made by educator," *Spokane Daily Chronicle*, 3-22-1977

"impact would be stunning," "Homosexual civil rights bill hotly debated," *Olympian*, 3-24-1977

"Do you ask why he's black?" "Homosexual civil rights bill hotly debated"

"unnatural, anti-social deviant conduct," quoted in "Homosexuality rejected"

"wasn't willing to answer that question," Francis to author, 7-21-2022

"a bright, articulate legislator," quoted in "A citizen legislature?" *Columbian*, 11-29-1977

"ranked him one of most effective," quoted in *Gay Seattle*, p. 372

"put gay people on earth," Francis to author, 7-21-2022

CAL ANDERSON

"We want in!" quoted in "Crowd packs hearing," *Seattle P-I*, 3-3-1993; *Gay Seattle*, p. 360-361

Brydon and Moreland counseled Anderson, Murray to author, 8-23-2022

"an unprecedented location," "Insults, hisses flow," *Morning News Tribune*, 3-3-1993

"School of Hard Knocks," quoted in "Rookies making impact," *Spokesman-Review*, 1-24-1993

"chance at American dream," quoted in *Gay Seattle*, p. 361

Chamber grew quiet, Murray to author, 8-25-2022

"Get out of here, you freak!" quoted in *Gay Seattle*, p. 361

"Read Leviticus," quoted in "Insults, hisses flow"

"When's next train to Auschwitz?" quoted in *Gay Seattle*, p. 361

"hatred was palpable," Kessler to author, 8-18-2022

"Isn't it Leviticus?" quoted in "Cal Anderson's was a voice of courage," *Tri-City Herald*, 8-13-1995

"what next?" quoted in "Insults, hisses flow"

"never lost his cool," Kessler to author, 8-18-2022

"not want to be hurried," quoted in *Gay Seattle*, pp. 363-364

"a stunning reversal," *Gay Seattle*, p. 364

"needed to regroup," Murray to author, 7-19-2022

"Call him right now!" Murray to author, 7-19-2022

"probably without proper respect," Ehlers to author, 8-18-2022

"Cal felt positive," Murray to author, 8-23-2022

"seemed like we were so close," quoted in *Gay Seattle*, p. 365

"queer AIDS activists," quoted in "Vandals target lawmaker," *Seattle P-I*, 3-3-1993, and "Legislator's home vandalized," *Olympian*, 3-3-1993

"don't have the guts," quoted in "Legislator's home vandalized"

"Well, come on over!" Murray to author, 7-19-2022

"Cal was a politician," Murray to author, 7-19-2022

"always present," Murray to author, 7-19-2022

"fell to Ed to carry on," Kessler to author, 8-18-2022

"had to boil the frog," Kessler to author, 8-18-2022

statewide poll results, "Voters support reform, not anti-gay measures," *Spokesman-Review*, 5-26-1994

"immediately became a tension," Murray to author, 7-19-2022

"caught media's attention," Murray to author, 6-22-2022

"Anderson never imagined," Murray to author, 7-19-2022

"boxed in by opponents," quoted in "Why Bill Clinton signed DOMA," Richard Socarides, *New Yorker*, 3-8-2013

"God never intended," quoted in "Moving the fence around marriage," Julie Gunter, National Catholic Reporter, 9-5-2012

"How would you feel?" quoted in "Same-sex marriage role in procreation, *Bellingham Herald*, 2-11-1996

"weren't going anywhere," quoted in "Moving the fence around"

"since statehood," quoted in "Same-sex marriage role"

"What about folks?" quoted in "Same-sex marriage role"

"wouldn't pass muster, either," quoted in "Lowry takes parting shot," *News Tribune*, 1-10-1997

"incredible moral victory," quoted in "NW gay-rights advocates jubilant," *Spokesman-Review*, 5-21-1996

"seen as extreme by some," quoted in "Lowry takes parting shot"

"insult to hard-working citizens," quoted in "Ban on same-sex marriages heads to first vote," *Bellingham Herald*, 2-5-1997

"besmirches sacred institution," quoted in "Ban on same-sex marriages"

"remains progressive state," quoted in "Gay Marriage ban in works," *News Tribune*, 2-4-1997

"divide, disrespect or diminish," quoted in "Locke vetoes gay marriage ban," *News Tribune*, 2-22-1997

fearing more gay-bashing, "Legislative aftermath," *Columbian*, 5-5-1997

"unlike any already on the books," quoted in "Washington gay rights measure has new twist," *S.F. Examiner*, 10-16-1997

"still want your kids," quoted in "Washington gay rights measure"

"I-677 isn't about fairness," quoted in "I-677 gay rights issue loses," *Seattle Times*, 11-5-1997

"sending powerful message," quoted in "gay rights issue loses"

"bring out conservative voters," "Marriage Equality and Gay Rights in Washington," *HistoryLink.org*

"Republicans have the votes," quoted in "Gay-marriage ban coasts into law," *Seattle Times*, 2-7-1998

"it was like I was 'Ellen,' " quoted in "Openly gay legislator sees 'caucus' expand," *Longview Daily News*, 2-9-2003

"eliminate the mystique," quoted in "Openly gay legislator"

"top priority creating jobs," "Senate avoids gay rights vote," *Olympian*, 3-6-2004

"stepping stone," "State Senate strikes down gay-rights bill," *News Tribune*, 4-22-2005.

"poised to do so again," "Microsoft caves on gay rights," *Stranger*, 4-21-2005

"external factors," quoted in "Microsoft backs off gay-rights support," *News Tribune*, 4-22-2005

"absolute lie," Murray to author, 7-27-2022

"vanguard institution," "Microsoft caves on gay rights"

"looking at question from all sides," quoted in "Microsoft backs gay rights bill, *Olympian*, 5-7-2006

"Republican Fink," "Republican Fink," *Stranger*, 4-14-2005

"a number of conversations," quoted in "New ally joins gay rights side," *Olympian*, 1-10-2006

"political football by both parties," quoted in "Swing vote now says he'll vote yes," *Seattle Times*, 1-9-2006

"Sounds like we've got 25 votes," quoted in "New ally joins gay rights side"

"hopeful but cautious," quoted in "New ally joins gay rights side"

"heart chooses who it will love," quoted in "Gay rights bill passes," *News Tribune*, 1-28-2006

"really smiling down on us," quoted in "Washington gays win anti-bias fight," *Louisville Courier-Journal*, 1-29-2006

"will not allow discrimination," quoted in "Washington gays win anti-bias fight"

"Before you reach for a pen," quoted in "Washington gays win anti-bias fight"

"It's through God's eyes," quoted in "Gay rights get state guarantee," *Olympian*, 1-28-2006

"That's called tough love," quoted in "Gay rights get state guarantee"

"sense of sadness," Finkbeiner to author, 8-3-2022

"just a different time," Finkbeiner to author

"I felt conflicted," Finkbeiner to author

"Cal would be proud," quoted in "Partner of state senator," KING5, 2-2-2012, https://www.king5.com/article/news/local/olympia/partner-of-late-state-senator-cal-would-be-proud/281-330890839

"always knew in our heart," quoted in "Partner of state senator

"people hereby permit," quoted in "Want to discriminate?" *Spokesman-Review*, 2-3-2006

"Legislature entitled to believe," quoted in "State's high court upholds ban on gay marriage," *Seattle P-I*, 7-25-2006

"The issue is in play," quoted in "Washington court upholds ban on gay marriage," *New York Times*, 7-27-2006

"Today we hurt," quoted in "Justices uphold same-sex marriage ban," *Spokesman-Review*, 7-27-2006

"between two people and their faith," quoted in "Justices uphold same-sex marriage ban"

"Most don't give up a powerful job," Murray to author, 7-19-2022

"letting the culture collapse," quoted in "Domestic partner registry," *Olympian*, 4-11-2007

"**Therefore I beg of you,**" quoted in "Domestic partner registry"

"**Why fight battle you can't win?**" quoted in "Domestic partnership expansion set," *Bellingham Herald*, 5-17-2009

"**It's historic,**" quoted in "Washington supporters of gay rights confident of win," *Tri-City Herald*, 11-5-2009

"**can't be single-issue legislator,**" Murray to author, 7-27-2022

"**been on my own journey,**" quoted in "Governor supports gay marriage bill, *Kitsap Sun*, 1-5-2012, and "Gregoire backs gay marriage," *Spokesman-Review*, 1-5-2012

"**Without Chris in the mix,**" Murray to author, 7-27-2022

"**never seen a better closer,**" Murray to author, 7-27-2022

"**will never forgive me,**" quoted in "Same-sex bill hinges on five state senators," *News Tribune*, 1-23-2012

"**never asked me for my vote,**" Haugen to author, 7-20-2022

"**racist**" and "**homophobe,**" quoted in "Same-sex bill hinges on five state senators," *News Tribune*, 1-23-2012

"**It was Mary Margaret's family…,**" Murray to author, 7-19-2022

"**neither here nor there,**" quoted in "Haugen's announcement," *Seattle Times*, 1-24-2012

"**very strong Christian beliefs,**" quoted in "Faith-based tolerance," *L.A. Times*, 2-5-2012

"**probably other factors, too,**" Haugen to author, 7-20-2022

"**Their lives are just fine today,**" Haugen to author, 7-20-2022

MARGARETHE CAMMERMEYER

"**despised, stigmatized minority,**" *Serving in Silence*, p. 263

"**chains of prejudice,**" p. 5

"**just need to shoot straight,**" quoted in "Ban on gays senseless attempt to stall inevitable," Barry M. Goldwater, *Washington Post* and *L.A. Times*, 6-11-1993

"**I am still amazed,**" etc., "Ban on gays senseless"

"**very first military operation,**" *Serving in Silence*, p. 9

"**too tall, too shy,**" p. 32

"**most important job in the world,**" p. 37

"**eyes that say goodbye,**" p. 37

"**completely rejected**" might be gay, p. 43

"**as shocked as I,**" p. 86

"**absolutely dumbfounded,**" p. 93

"**immobilized by the horror,**" p. 55

61 percent younger than 21, US. Wings, https://www.uswings.com/about-us-wings/vietnam-war-facts/

"**helping them get well,**" p. 145

"**colonels can cry, too,**" p. 154

"**on a continuum,**" p. 212

"**last, connecting piece,**" p. 261

"**continued not to believe it,**" etc. quoted in "Panel recommends discharging veteran," *Spokesman-Review*, Spokane, 8-24-1991

"**the same argument,**" "Panel recommends discharging veteran"

"**one of the great Americans,**" Panel recommends discharging veteran"

"**I can't do this to her,**" www.survivingthesilence.com

"**sorry I had to do that to you,**" www.survivingthesilence.com

"**based on the assumption,**" quoted in "From the Publisher," *Madison County Record*, Huntsville, Arkansas, 8-22-1991

"**second-class armed force,**" quoted in "Emotions high on military gays," *Atlanta Constitution*, 5-12-1993

"**a person can say, 'I am a homosexual,' **" quoted in "Many don't get 'Don't Ask, Don't Tell,' " *Corpus Christi Caller-Times*, 7-24-1993

"**People are not allowed,**" quoted in "Many don't get"

"**substantial advance,**" "Many don't get"

"**beginning of exoneration,**" "Many don't get"

"**scream in outrage,**" "Many don't get"

"**convincing evidence,**" etc., "Many don't get"

"**have to prove I'm unfit,**" "Many don't get"

"**rationales offered,**" quoted in "U.S. judge reinstates gay colonel," *Washington Post*, 6-2-1994

"**absolutely ecstatic,**" quoted in "Judge orders lesbian colonel reinstated," *Times-Leader*, Wilkes-Barre, PA., 6-2-1994

"**so powerful, so vindicating,**" quoted in "U.S. judge reinstates"

"**had a loss of privacy,**" quoted in "Cammermeyer keeps speech subdued," *Olympian*, 4-1-1995

"**leaders of tomorrow,**" quoted in "Cammermeyer keeps"

"**platforms to educate youth,**" quoted in "Legislators scold school board," *Olympian*, 4-1-1995

called "fags" and assaulted, quoted in "Rally to support assaulted teens," *Olympian*, 4-12-1995

"**into severe depression,**" quoted in "Crimes occur in atmosphere of hate," *Olympian*, 8-9-1995

"**compelling" and "extraordinary gifts,**" quoted in "Cammermeyer has chance to oust Metcalf," *Olympian*, 10-2-1998

"**spokesperson for lesbian lifestyle,**" quoted in "Cammermeyer has chance"

"**not a politician,**" quoted in "Lesbian activist targets congressional barrier," *Olympian*, 7-26-1998

"**as if to make a toast,**" *Serving in Silence*, pp. 267-268

"**Far, please pass the salt,**" *Serving in Silence*, pp. 267-268

"**nothing more needed to be said,**" *Serving in Silence*, pp. 267-268

Valerie Mariano

Mariano to author, 10-19-2022, and email to author, 11-9-2022

"**strength of her smile,**" https://www.youtube.com/watch?v=jigauxLQUmU

Rand survey of LGBTQ service members, https://www.rand.org/pubs/research_reports/RR4222.html

Podcast with LGBTQ soldiers and former soldier, Raven Communications, 6-11-2021 https://podcasts.google.com/feed/aHR0cHM6Ly93d3cuZHZpZHNodWIub mV0L3Jzcy9wb2RjYXN0LzMxMA/episode/aHR0cHM6Ly93d3cuZHZpZHNodWIub mV0L3BvZGNhc3QvZG93bmxvYWQvNz kyNTEvRE9EXzEwODM5NTA3MC5tcDM?sa=X&ved=0CAUQkfYCahcKEwigmsjro7D4A hUAAAAAHQAAAAQCg&hl=en

Marsha Botzer

Brussels to Beijing, Botzer to author, 3-31-2022

life-changing words, Botzer to author, 2-21-2022

Schneider set records, "Amy Schneider's Record-Breaking Jeopardy! Streak Ends," jeopardy.com, 1-26-2022

rose to top, Kevin McKenna, "Marsha Botzer," Seattle Civil Rights & Labor History Project, University of Washington, 8-6-2014

400 hours of electrolysis, Sherry Stripling, "Crossing Over," *Seattle Times*, 8-3-1986

2,516 consecutive weeks, Botzer to author, 2-21-2022

"**time to be happy,**" *Robert G. Ingersoll, The Works of Robert G. Ingersoll, Volume 12, Miscellany,* Dresden Publishing, New York, 1900 via Gutenberg.org

describes gender dysphoria, American Psychiatric Association, "What is Gender Dysphoria?" *psychiatry.org*, November 2020

"**ideological and harmful misrepresentations,**" "Rand Paul criticized for trans 'genital mutilation' remarks in Rachel Levine hearing,"

NBC News, 2-26-2021

they pivoted, Isaac Chotiner, "Why Marriage Equality Movement Succeeded," *New Yorker*, 6-10-2021

historic wave of bills, Kimberly Kindy, "GOP lawmakers push historic wave of bills," *Washington Post*, 3-25-2022

"bete noire" to many, Botzer to author, 2-21-2022

appeared to be, Rishika Dugyala and Melanie Zanona, "Can the Republican Party Save One of Its Last Latina Congresswomen?" *Politco*, 12-11-2019

A reporter for The Chronicle, Claudia Yaw, "At Centralia Event, Kent Further Solidifies his Position as Furthest-Right Herrera Beutler Challenger," *Centralia Chronicle*, 8-13-2021

classic "wedge issue," Jeff McMillan and Marc Levy, "In trans people, GOP candidates find latest 'wedge issue,' " *apnews.com*, 2.25.2022

Dr. Oz was attacked, "In trans people, GOP candidates find latest"

Twitter also suspended Hartzler's, AP, "Twitter suspends U.S. Senate candidate for hateful conduct," *Seattle Times*, 3-1-2022

Greene put up a sign, Janine Santucci, "Marjorie Taylor Greene faces backlash," *USA Today*, 2-25-2021

rallying point around Putin, David D. Kirkpatrick, Maggie Astor & Catie Edmondson, "Trump praises Putin, putting GOP leaders in a bind," *New York Times*, 2-24-2022

Botzer's parents met, Botzer interview, 2-21-2022

"I had never seen," Botzer interview, 2-21-2022

"be the male the world," Marsha Botzer interview, 3-31-2022

"Nothing was very clear," Botzer interview, 2-21-2022

outed in 1976 by Carlson's father, Kelefa Sanneh, "Tucker Carlson's Fighting Words," *New Yorker*, 4-10-2017

Army veteran from Bronx, Victor Salvo, "Christine Jorgensen, 1926-1989, Inductee,"

The Legacy Project (Chicago), via https://legacyprojectchicago.org/person/christine-jorgensen

"seeing my mom," Botzer interview, 2-21-2022

She read *Helix*, Botzer interview, 2-21-2022

learned about commitment, Botzer interview 2-21-2022

On to Paris, Botzer interview

"things were getting messy," Botzer interview

"Now I can't claim," Botzer interview

"drawing room," Margaret D'Evelyn, "Piazza San Marco: 'The most beautiful drawing room in Europe,' " *Christian Science Monitor*, 4-26-1988

"I don't want to put too glowy," Botzer interview 2-21-2022

"I'm not alone," Botzer interview with Shaun Knittel, *The Legacy Project* (Seattle), posted 4-3-2020 https://www.youtube.com/watch?v=qpvNttJle1s

90-pound jackhammer, Botzer to author, 2-21-2022

"Notes from the Underground," Bob Young, "Mark Twain with an Illegal Smile," *Legacy Washington*, April 2018

"Make No Mistake," Digital Collections, "KRAB-FM Lesbian-Feminist Radio Program Recordings," University of Washington, https://content.lib.washington.edu/krabfmweb/index.html

considered outdated, GLAAD Media Guide 11th Edition, "Glossary of Terms: Transgender," https://www.glaad.org/reference/trans-terms#gcs

"I just about drove," Botzer to author, 2-21-2022

saw 13 therapists, Sherry Stripling, "Crossing Over," *Seattle Times*, 8-3-1986

3 o'clock in the morning, Kevin McKenna, "Marsha Botzer," Seattle Civil Rights & Labor History Project, University of Washington, 8-6-2014

Compressors used in construction, Botzer interview with Shaun Knittel, *The Legacy Project*

(Seattle), posted 4-3-2020

Sermon about freedom, Botzer interview with *The Legacy Project* (Seattle)

Founded in 1969, Seattle Counseling Service, "About us," https://seattlecounseling.org/about/

"If it doesn't exist," Botzer interview with *The Legacy Project*

In 1969, Biber started performing, Martin J. Smith, "Made this town world's 'sex-change capital,'" *L.A. Times*, 9-12-2019

"Satan's physician," "Made this town world's 'sex-change capital'"

revered John Wayne, Martin J. Smith, *Going to Trinidad: A Doctor, a Colorado town, and Stories from an Unlikely Gender Crossroads*, Bower House Books, Denver, 2021, (excerpted in 5280 magazine April 2021) https://www.5280.com/2021/04/the-visionary-surgeon-who-put-trinidad-on-the-map/

good for business, Nicole Brodeur, "New book highlights Seattle's role in transgender movement," *Seattle Times*, 4-15-2021

"foundational figure," *Going to Trinidad*, p. 147

Botzer had introduced Bowers, Nicole Brodeur, "New book highlights Seattle's role"

"One reason I'm public," Sherry Stripling, "Crossing Over," *Seattle Times,* 8-3-1986

"I will forever praise," Botzer to author, 2-21-2022

"I want to see us like that," Botzer interview with Shaun Knittel, *The Legacy Project* (Seattle), posted 4-3-2020

"Sometimes it would take years," Botzer interview with Dr. Evan Taylor, "Trans Activism Oral History Project," 2.19.2020 https://vimeo.com/478929224

chapters across Washington, "Hands Off Washington Records," Western Washington University, August 2018, https://library.wwu.edu/node/19457

crushed at polls, David Ammons, "Gay Employment Initiative Fails Across State," AP, 11-5-1997

Undeterred, Washington ACLU, "Bill of Rights Dinner Features Award Winners and Comedian Jessica Williams, 11-2-2016, https://www.aclu-wa.org/story/bill-rights-dinner-features-award-winners-and-comedian-jessica-williams

only the third major U.S. city, "Transgendered People Protected," *Seattle Times*, 8-31-1999

summarizes them neatly, *Going to Trinidad*, p. 60-63

Her study found, *Going to Trinidad*, p. 98

most trans-inclusive, Kevin McKenna, "Marsha Botzer," Seattle Civil Rights & Labor History Project, University of Washington, 8-6-2014

most visible early leader, Louise Chernin, "The Passing of Charlie Brydon," *Seattle Pride*, 2-12-2021

gave spirited speech, "Marsha Botzer National Gay and Lesbian Task Force Board co-chair, National Equality March (video)," 10-13-2009, https://www.youtube.com/watch?v=WEMu_p_Lg3I

atop the Space Needle, "Pride Flag Flies High Above Space Needle," National Gay and Lesbian Task Force, 6-25-2010 https://www.thetaskforce.org/pride-flag-flies-high-above-the-seattle-space-needle/

for the first time, Lornet Turnbull, "Gay groups ask Space Needle to fly gay-pride flag," *Seattle Times*, 4-25, 2013

she went to China, Shaun Knittel, "Exchange Program Brings Seattle Transgender Activist to China," *Edge Media Network,* 11-7-2011, https://boston.edgemedianetwork.com/story.php?126504

"My job was to work," Marsha Botzer interview, 2-21-2022

ban "sissy men," Joe McDonald (AP), "China bans 'sissy men' from TV to encourage more masculinity in young men," *USA Today*, 9-2-2021

CNN headline, Ben Westcott & Steven Jiang, "China's LGBTQ community fading from rainbow to gray," *CNN.com*, 7-9-2021

Israel's pioneering LGBTQ group, Robert Nagler Miller, "Proud to be part of Pride in Israel," *Jewish News of Northern California*, 6-26-2015

painting over problems in Israel, Zari Weiss, "Mayor Murray's trip to Israel not 'pink-washing,' " *Seattle Times*, 5-26-2015

"I was there," Botzer interview, 2-21-2022

paused for a moment, Botzer interview, 2-21-2022

oppressive institution, Diane Targovnik, "Spousal Rape: Washington Has Only Limited Protection," *Seattle Times*, 5-18-1997

wasn't until 2013, Anna Minard, "Washington Closes Troubling Marital Rape Loophole," *Stranger*, 5-2-2013

have been intertwined, *Going to Trinidad*, p. 70

Jedi knight or weather vane, Scott Horsley, "Not Always A 'Thunderbolt': Evolution of LGBT Rights Under Obama," *National Public Radio*, 6-9-2016

Obama filled in gaps, German Lopez, "We Were Heard for the First Time," *vox.com*, 1-17-2017

"That was quite a big deal," Botzer interview, 2-21-2022

Schneider streamed and beamed, Martha Ross, "The Amy Schneider Effect," *Mercury News*, 3-14-2022

"appealingly wonky," "The Amy Schneider Effect"

Conservatives targeted them, Adam Serwer, "The Republican Party Finds a New Group to Demonize," *Atlantic*, 4-13-2021

opposition grown more sophisticated, Botzer interview, 2-21-2022

worst year on record, Martha Ross, "The Amy Schneider Effect"

nearly 200 state bills, Kimberly Kindy, "GOP lawmakers push historic wave of bills targeting LGBTQ teens, children and their families," *Washington Post*, 3-25-2022

Cox stood up, Utah Governor Spencer Cox, "Why I'm Vetoing HB11," 3-22-2022, https://governor.utah.gov/2022/03/24/gov-cox-why-im-vetoing-hb11/

Harrell's transition team, Paige McGlauflin, "Harrell announces transition team: LGBTQ+ leaders to work directly with four committees," *Seattle Gay News*, 11-26-26 https://www.sgn.org/story.php?ch=local&sc=&id=310870

co-leader of the state, "Commissioners," Washington State LGBTQ Commission, https://lgbtq.wa.gov/about-us/commissioners

"All these advances," Botzer email to author, 4-1-2022

"I love good people," Botzer interview with Dr. Evan Taylor, "Trans Activism Oral History Project," 2.19.2020 https://vimeo.com/478929224

JEFF HEDGEPETH & JOHN MEDLIN

made front page, Mike Lewis, "Seattle gay couple marries in Canada; others expected to follow," *Seattle P-I*, 8-1-2003

rode with naked bicyclists, Jessie Wesley, "How to Ride Au Naturel in the Fremont Solstice Parade," *Seattle Met*, 6-12-2012

"practicing introvert," Hedgepeth and Medlin to author, 7-22-2022

record-bequest, Kristi Heim, "Seattle man who helped launch Microsoft left $65M for gay rights, *Seattle Times*, 2-24-2008

"very much part of community," Hedgepeth & Medlin to author, 7-22-2022

"when the soggy T-shirt," Hedgepeth & Medlin to author,

"just plain" struck, Hedgepeth & Medlin to author

"And yes, I am cut," Hedgepeth & Medlin to author

"expensive lamps," Hedgepeth interview with *The Legacy Project*, 2013, via https://www.youtube.com/channel/UC2M1GhRlhxldrJnFd-FLJ6DA

fish, pick cotton, Hedgepeth & Medlin interview, 7-22-2022

to "colored people," Hedgepeth & Medlin interview

"sitcom by Tennessee Williams," Hedgepeth & Medlin interview

"just occurred to me," Hedgepeth & Medlin interview

"with a vengeance," Hedgepeth interview with *The Legacy Project*, 2013

"whole production," Hedgepeth & Medlin interview, 7-22-2022

out of a hat, Hedgepeth interview with *The Legacy Project*, 2013

"wasn't true me," Hedgepeth & Medlin interview, 7-22-2022

"doing a lot of gay stuff," Hedgepeth & Medlin interview

it was a "seg academy," Hedgepeth & Medlin interview

"And the congregation," Hedgepeth & Medlin interview

starring Divine, Hedgepeth interview with *The Legacy Project*, 2013

teetered on bankruptcy, Kevin Baker, "Welcome to 'Fear City,'" *Guardian*, 5-18-2015

a spiritual crisis, Jonathan Mahler, *Ladies and Gentlemen, the Bronx is burning*, Farrar, Strauss and Giroux, 2006

"You'd go to the post office," Hedgepeth & Medlin interview, 7-22-2022

they lacked the talent for, Hedgepeth & Medlin interview

grilled duck, Hedgepeth & Medlin interview

gardening talents, Valerie Easton, "On Capitol Hill, A Postage-Stamp Garden Bursts With Verve," *Seattle Times*, 8-22-1999

a national publication, Gary Thompson, "Garden Ideas & Outdoor Living," *Better Homes Special Interest Publication*, Summer 2002

"not a person who needs," Hedgepeth & Medlin interview, 7-22-2022

next 17 years, "Retirements," *Library Directions: A Newsletter*, University of Washington, Autumn-Winter 2007-2008

also ran a program, Jon Marmor, "The Road Ahead," *Columns* (University of Washington magazine), March 1999

"Then I land," Hedgepeth & Medlin interview, 7-22-2022

impressed by Audrey Haberman, Hedgepeth & Medlin interview, 7-22-2022

broken by the Pride Foundation, Sarah Kershaw, "Wal-Mart Sets a New Policy," *New York Times*, 7-2-2003

"It was wild," email from Hedgepeth to author, 8-18-2022

coast-to-coast, Greg Giuffride, "Anti-discrimination policy at Wal-Mart extended to gays," *Rome (GA) News-Tribune*, 7-3-2003

"shareholder-activism" push, email from Jeff Hedgepeth, 8-18-2022

employee number-two, Lia Stifler, "The remarkable life and legacy of Ric Weiland, Microsoft employee No. 2," *Geekwire*, 1-25-2017

not a big public speaker, Benjamin J. Romano, "Richard Weiland, low-key champion of causes," *Seattle Times*, 6-30-2006

increasing its endowment, Kristi Heim, "Seattle man who helped launch Microsoft left $65M for gay rights, *Seattle Times*, 2-24-2008

most consequential donor, Nina Shapiro, "Microsoft pioneer Ric Weiland's huge bequest," *Seattle Times*, 1-7-2017

"Ric's imprimatur," email from Hedgepeth to author, 8-18-2022

famously blunt, Sandi Doughton, "George Bakan, longtime editor of *Seattle Gay News*, dies," *Seattle Times*, 6-13-2020

"they can order cookies," interview with Hedgepeth and Medlin, 7-22-2022

discriminated against, Sasha Issenberg, "How Canada brought same-sex marriage to United States," *Globe and Mail* (Toronto), 7-24-2021

Mike Frederickson, interview with Hedgepeth & Medlin, 9-29-2022

openly gay dean, Janet I. Tu, "Taylor resigns as dean of troubled St. Mark's," *Seattle Times*, 3-29.2008

unclear to Canadian officials, Mike Lewis, "Seattle gay couple marries in Canada," *Seattle P-I*, 8-1-2003

"I believe marriage," "Seattle gay couple marries in Canada"

Bush's political guru, Sasha Issenberg, *The Engagement*, Pantheon Books, 2021, pp. 351-352, 368-369, 384

"The Court today pretends," Sasha Issenberg, "How Canada brought same-sex marriage to the United States," *Globe and Mail*, 7-24-2021

"Civil Marriage Trail," "How Canada brought same-sex marriage"

"if Thea was Theo," Issenberg, *Globe and Mail*, 7-24-2021

"thank you, thank you," Lornet Turnbull, "Gregoire signs gay marriage into law," *Seattle Times*, 2-13-2012

did so within hours, "Gregoire signs gay marriage into law"

Jeff was in meetings, Hedgepeth & Medlin interview, 9-29-2022

"If you met a heterosexual," Hedgepeth & Medlin interview, 7-22-2022

"on a contact list," Hedgepeth & Medlin interview, 7-22-2022

didn't jell as well, Hedgepeth & Medlin interview

"anti-homosexual 101 through 501," Hedgepeth interview with *The Legacy Project*, 2013

"just never recovered," Hedgepeth & Medlin interview, 7-22-2022

"This whole ambassadorial thing," Hedgepeth interview with *The Legacy Project*, 2013

"most popular guy there," Hedgepeth & Medlin to author, 9-29-2022

"Even at the gym," Hedgepeth interview with *The Legacy Project*, 2013

opposites began merging, Hedgepeth & Medlin interview, 9-29-2022

They planned an evening, email from Hedgepeth, 8-18-2022

"We had a blast," email from Hedgepeth

"Went to Canlis," email from Hedgepeth

LAURIE JINKINS

"Hopelessly disgusted" and **"just how long,"** quoted in *Julia Butler Hansen, A Trailblazing Washington Politician*, p. 107-108

"demonstrably erroneous decisions," quoted in "Thomas says gay rights, contraception rulings should be reconsidered," CNBC, 6-24-2022, https://www.cnbc.com/2022/06/24/roe-v-wade-supreme-court-justice-thomas-says-gay-rights-rulings-open-to-be-tossed.html

"Nothing should be understood," quoted in "Justice Thomas," *Politico*, 6-24-2022, https://www.politico.com/news/2022/06/24/thomas-constitutional-rights-00042256

"no one should be confident," quoted in "Justice Thomas"

"we'll be a beacon of light," and **"We won't back down!"** quoted in "Pro-choice rally and press conference," TVW, 5-3-2022m https://tvw.org/video/governor-jay-inslee-pro-choice-rally-and-press-conference-2022051079/?eventID=2022051079&startStreamAt=2184&stopStreamAt=2388

"always were speaker of our house!!" quoted in "Jinkins came to Washington," James Drew, *Olympian*, 8-4-2019

"how I learned about community," quoted in "Jinkins came to Washington"

"It took us two years," quoted in "Jinkins came to Washington"

"cornfields, cows and trout streams," Pat Raimer to author, 7-13-2022

Que sera, sera, Raimer to author

"I would always live an out life," quoted in "Jinkins came to Washington"

"of winning up to 28 cents," quoted in Jack Jinkins obituary, Larson Funeral Homes web site, 9-01-2020, https://www.larsonfuneralhomes.com/dr-john-w-jack-jinkins/

"a miserable record," "UPS law school protest planned," *News Tribune*, 4-5-1990

"What we're really asking for," quoted in "UPS law school protest planned"

"a civil war of values," quoted in "Anti-gay activist," *News Tribune*, 9-23-1989

Church groups square off over vote, "Church groups split over gay rights," *News Tribune*, 11-4-1989

"What price do we pay?" quoted in "Economic stresses could be catalyst," *News Tribune*, 11-3-1991

"much less tolerant society," etc. quoted in "Economic stresses could be catalyst"

"oozed across Columbia River," quoted in *Gay Seattle*, Gary L. Atkins, p. 358

"The idea was to say," Anne Levinson to Bob Young, for *Love, Equally*

"What works in Tacoma, or Spokane," Levinson to Young

"We did overarching things," Levinson to Young

"responsible for the end of society," Levinson to Young

"feminist-Chicana-lesbian-activist," quoted in "Goal and effort both remain valid," *Spokesman-Review*, 6-20-1997

"a warmer, safer place," quoted in "Anti-gay initiatives short on signatures," *Olympian*, 12-30-1995

"boxed in by opponents," quoted in "Why Bill Clinton signed the Defense of Marriage Act," Richard Socarides, *New Yorker*, 3-8-2013

"we're not monsters," quoted in *Gay Seattle*, p. 357

"legitimizing homosexuality," quoted in "Gay-rights backers," *Columbian*, 10-14-1997

"still want your kids," quoted in "Gay-rights backers"

"Ed worried if initiative failed," Wayne Ehlers to author, 8-2-2022

"Legislature's blatant animosity," quoted in "Gay marriage issue on table," *Spokesman-Review*, 1-12-2007

"Do not betray Christ!" quoted in "Gregoire signs gay marriage bill," *Kitsap Sun*, 2-14-2012

"wealthiest few to pay fair share," quoted in "Viewpoint," *News Tribune*, 6-7-2015

"a lot more inertia," quoted in "Jinkins lambasts," *Olympian*, 2-8-2020

"no end to learning," quoted in Tacoma Pride interview with Kim Davenport, 7-11-2022, https://www.youtube.com/watch?v=aTEs-MVDF88

Jamie Pedersen

scooped fries, Pedersen to author, 12-15-2021

liked to invite for dinner, Pedersen to author

case of Joseph Steffan, *Steffan v. Perry,* U.S. Court of Appeals, District of Columbia Circuit, No. 91-5409. 11-12-1994

early evangelist for same-sex marriage, Richard Wolf, "For Freedom to Marry's founder, a date with history," *USA Today*, 6-17-2015

"became my life's work," Pedersen to author, 12-15-2021

wildly lopsided, Roll Call 104th Congress, second session, "On Passage of H.B. 3396 (Defense of Marriage Act)," *U.S. Senate*, 9-10-1996

"It was low point," Pedersen to author, 12-16-2021

Pedersen as co-counsel, "Attorneys," *Andersen v. King County,* LambdaLegal.org, 7-26-2006

Concentrated message, Molly Ball, "The Marriage Plot: Inside This Year's Epic Campaign for Gay Equality," *Atlantic*, 12-11-2012

"We are Vikings," Pedersen to author, 12-15-2021

Craig Beetham, "In Memoriam," *Seattle U Lawyer*, Spring 2016

"She got outed," Pedersen to author, 12-15-2021

"lovely" brochure, Pedersen to author

"handwritten Bible verses," Pedersen to author

"I had tried a few times," Pedersen to author

sea-urchin fishing, Pedersen to author, 12-16-2021

"AIDS shattered," Dominic Holden, "Meet The Women Who Won The First Same-Sex Marriage Case 19 Years Ago," *BuzzFeedNews*, 4-27-2015

candlelit dinners, Amy Hagopian, "To Have And To Hold," *Seattle Times*, 10-13-1996

had won medals, Kate Kershner, "Anderson, Cal (1948-1995)," *HistoryLink.org*, 12-26-2012

"gun people in droves," Pedersen to author, 12-16-2021

Davis recruited Pedersen, Pedersen to author repealed its sodomy law, Richard W. Larsen, "Revision of Criminal Code clears Legislature," *Seattle Times*, 6-5-1975

a Texas couple, "Lawrence v. Texas (6-26-2003)," LambdaLegal.org, https://www.lambdalegal.org/in-court/cases/lawrence-v-texas

attended the oral arguments, Pedersen to author, 12-16-2021

"became the foundation," Pedersen to author
future husband Eric Cochran, Eli Sanders, "Boring, Traditional, Religious Marriage," *Stranger*, 6-20-2012

rooted since the 1880s, Pedersen to author
Judge Downing agreed, Sanjay Bhatt, "Judge backs gay marriage; state high-court fight next," *Seattle Times*, 8-5-2004

found a "rational basis," Adam Liptak, "Washington Court Upholds Ban on Gay Marriage," *New York Times*, 7-26-2006

"muddled," David Postman, "9 justices, 6 opinions, no consensus," *Seattle Times*, 7-26-2006

stinging dissent, "Washington Court Upholds Ban"

"dreadful, dreadful decision," Pedersen to author, 12-16-2021

1909 Victorian house, Liz Meyer, "Two Men having a Baby," *Seattle Gay News*, 10-12-2008

switched vote, Andrew Garber, Ralph Thomas, "State gay-rights bill OK'd 29 years after effort began," *Seattle Times*, 1-28-2006

"I had zero, zero," Pedersen to author, 12-16-2021

"He literally yelled," Pedersen to author

Savage lambasted Pedersen, Dan Savage, "Jamie Pedersen's Dirty Punch," *Stranger Slog* (blog), 5-24-2006

"Welcome to politics," Pedersen to author, 12-16-2021

"political earthquake," Andrew Garber, "Murray endorses Pedersen in 43rd District primary," *Seattle Times*, 9-6-2006

"completely aligned on," Pedersen to author, 12-16-2021

14 people would die, David Wilma, "Hannukah Eve Wind Storm ravages Western Washington," *HistoryLink.org*, 12-27-2006

"touched thousands of lives," Charlene Strong, "Add your voice to the chorus calling for equity and dignity," *Seattle Times*, 8-9-2007

ran to emergency room, "Add your voice to the chorus"

compelling voice, Elliott Wilson, "Seattle woman shares story to aid push for domestic-partner bill," *Seattle Times*, 1-26-2007

"came out of Charlene's experience," Pedersen to author, 12-16-2021

"overriding theme," Rachel La Corte, "Partners' law revisited—more benefits sought for same-sex couples," *AP*, 1-22-2008

Gregoire balked, Pedersen to author, 12-16-2021

"chaos," Pedersen to author, 12-16-2021

full-throated, "State should legalize same-sex marriage," *Seattle Times*, 11-15-2011

"fifth edition," Kate Riley, "Same-sex marriage: Getting to 'I do' took patience," *Seattle Times*, 9-16-2012

"wasn't ready," Andrew Garber, "Gregoire's journey on gay marriage," *Seattle Times*, 1-5-2012

"she became beloved," Lornet Turnbull, "Gay Marriage Becomes Legal; Gregoire's signature makes history," *Seattle Times*, 2-14-2012

decisive sponsor, Pedersen to author, 12-16-2021

"one-by-one campaign," Pedersen to author

"commitment I see," Molly Ball, "The Marriage Plot: Inside This Year's Epic Campaign for Gay Equality," *Atlantic*, 12-11-2012

Haugen's role, Andrew Garber, Lornet Turnbull, "Gay marriage has votes," *Seattle Times*, 1-24-2012

rejected 31 times, Molly Ball, "The Marriage Plot: Inside This Year's Epic Campaign for Gay Equality," *Atlantic*, 12-11-2012

"they simply didn't know," "The Marriage Plot"

call it "marriage equality," "The Marriage Plot"

Wolfson was behind Obama's, "The Marriage Plot"

unscripted tour de force, Timothy Egan, "A Widow's Wisdom," *New York Times*, 2-14-2012

hand-on-hip candor, Maureen Walsh to author, 1-11-2022

Walsh was second sponsor, Pedersen to author, 12-16-2021

followed Betty White, Walsh to author, 1-11-2022

"To be very frank," Rebecca J. Rosen, "The Touching Story Behind Jeff and MacKenzie Bezos' $2.5 Million Gift," *Atlantic*, 7-27-2012

early money mattered, "The Marriage Plot"

"something going to go down," Lornet Turnbull, "REF 74 PASSING, Washington voters making history," *Seattle Times*, 11-7-2012

Coontz wrote that matrimony, John C. Hughes & Bob Young, *Ahead of the Curve*, Legacy Washington, Olympia, 2019

"It's one of the fastest," Lisa Pemberton, "Q&A: Evergreen historian Coontz talks about gay marriage ruling," *News Tribune*, 7-5-2-15

"Compared to almost every," Pedersen to author, 12-16-2021

every family stroll, Eli Sanders, "Boring, Traditional, Religious Marriage," *Stranger*, 6-20-2012

"fought about transgender," Pedersen to author, 12-16-2021

"I've been educated," Joseph O'Sullivan, "Sen. Tim Sheldon, Rep. Jesse Johnson won't return to Legislature," *Seattle Times*, 3-10-2022

matronly Dorothy Nelson, Pedersen to author, 12-16-2021

No shortage of marriage licenses, Adam Haslett, "Love Supreme," *New Yorker*, 5-31-2004

ANNE LEVINSON

Using potent, Zach Silk to author, 6-7-2022

She was one of the first, "Who's Who Among Power Gay Leaders," *Seattle Times*, 8-1-1993

arm-twister, Florangela Davila, Lily Eng, David Schaefer, "Deputy Mayor's Departure to Leave Gap," *Seattle Times*, 10-29-1996

want to risk, Levinson to author, 4-1-2022

funeral leave, Robert T. Nelson, "Initiative 35 opponents bracing for a tough fight," *Seattle Times*, 9-7-1990

she coined, Levinson to author, 3-31-2022

"spine of steel," Mark Higgins, "Deputy Mayor Levinson Gives Notice; 'Workaholic' Wants Time," *Seattle P-I*, 10-29-1996

"warm and approachable," Courtney Nash, "Force 10 is with Them," *Seattle Met*, July 2008

"little jock," interview with Levinson, 3-30-2022

"the woman behind," Dominic Holden, "WA's first same-sex marriage," *Stranger*, 12-9-2012

only allows right-handed, Brian Connolly, "Why Are All Field Hockey Sticks Right-Handed?" *sportsrec.com*, 12-5-2018

program's only one, Levinson to author, 3-30-2022

baton-passing relay, AP, "Run for the Money," *Kansas City Times*, 4-4-1978

Within hours, AP, "Women's athletics back in regents [sic] budget," 4-4-1978

caught the eye, Levinson to author, 3-30-2022

Banks told her, "Distinguished Alumni: Social justice and public service are hallmarks of Anne Levinson's career," *KU College Stories, College of Liberal Arts and Sciences*, 6-15-2022 via https://blog-college.ku.edu/

anne-levinson-distinguished-alumni/

Title IX had been adopted, Collin Binkley, "Men, women split on equity gains since Title IX," *AP*, 6-14-2022

effectively end men's sports, "Distinguished alumni," *KU College Stories*, 6-15-2022 via https://blog-college.ku.edu/anne-levinson-distinguished-alumni/

born in Eastern Europe, Levinson to author, 6-27-2022

immersed himself, Claudia H. Deutsch, "Harry Levinson, Psychologist for the Workplace, Dies at 90," *New York Times*, 6-28-2012

largest training center, https://www.britannica.com/topic/Menninger-family

"I had a different accent," interview with Levinson, 3-30-2022

"It was my preferred sport," Levinson to author

"NPR was always on," Levinson to author

But it didn't appeal, Levinson to author

Founded in a YMCA, "Northeastern Timeline," Northeastern University, *Archives and Special Collections*, via https://web.archive.org/web/20150919153632/http://www.library.neu.edu/archives/history_exhibits/northeastern_timeline/

classrooms shook, Levinson to author

Known for producing, Katie Thisdell, "Best Schools for Public Service," *preLaw Magazine, National Jurist,* Winter 2020

28 years before, "A Brief Timeline of Our First Two Centuries," *History of Harvard Law School,* https://hls.harvard.edu/about/history/

Urvashi Vaid, Cody Mello-Klein, "Urvashi Vaid, Northeastern Alum, Remembered as Legendary LGBTQ Activist," *News@Northeastern,* 5-18-2022

"Our Thurgood Marshall," Sasha Issenberg, *The Engagement,* Pantheon Books, New York, 2021, p. 731

first person and youngest woman, Michelle P. Fulcher, "How a Colorado Legal Pioneer Went From 'Ladies Day' at Harvard Law to Supreme Courts (excerpt)," *Colorado Public Radio,* 3-30-2017

early LGBTQ victory, Susan Berry Casey, "Nine Justices and One Colorado Lawyer," *History Colorado,* 5-14-2021

"welcoming city," Levinson to author, 3-30-2022

Cranston's long-shot bid, AP, "Alan Cranston, former U.S. Senator, is dead at 86," *New York Times,* 1-1-2001, https://www.nytimes.com/2001/01/01/us/alan-cranston-former-us-senator-is-dead-at-86.html

bus fare out of Cedar Rapids, Levinson to author, 3-31-2022

making cassette recording, Levinson to author, 3-30-2022

come out to his parents, Kate Kershner, "Anderson, Cal (1948-1995)," *HistoryLink.org,* 12-26-2012

"We called it that," Levinson to author, 3-31-2022

Bobbe Bridge hired, Levinson to author

"There wasn't a dance party," Levinson to author

"I was not expecting," Levinson to author, 3-30-2022

creating domestic partnerships, Robert T. Nelson, "Initiative 35 opponents bracing for a tough fight," *Seattle Times,* 9-7-1990

William Goodloe, Robert T. Nelson, "Former Justice slams mayor at fund-raiser for Initiative 35," *Seattle Times,* 9-27-1990

"workaholic," Mark Higgins, "Deputy Mayor Levinson Gives Notice"

assembled a coalition, Robert T. Nelson, "Domestic Partner Laws Survive Challenge," *Seattle Times,* 11-7-1990

cited their cost, Mindy Cameron, "Initiative 35: The Times' view—and mine," *Seattle Times,* 11-4-1990

detected a pattern, Levinson to author, 3-31-2022

hellfire rhetoric, AP, "Oregon's anti-gay debate: strange times indeed," *Seattle Times,* 9-27-1992

"war going on," Joni Balter, Mary Ann Gwinn,

"It's 'War,' says anti-gay leader," *Seattle Times*, 10-24-1993

Brydon locked up, Levinson to author, 3-31-2022

Plastered on bumpers, Susan Gilmore, "Democrats gather in Richland," *Seattle Times*, 6-11-1994

She asked Seattle Police, Levinson to author, 3-31-202

in that era, Joni Balter, "Police chief parades his explanations," *Seattle Times*, 6-30-1994

conservatives failed, Jim Simon, "Initiatives against gay rights fail," *Seattle Times*, 6-9-1994

"Gay Klux Klan," Susan Gilmore, Jim Simon, "Initiatives 608, 610 opponents confront signature-gatherers," *Seattle Times*, 5-19-1994

"is unsurpassed," *Seattle Times* Staff, "People to watch in '95," 1-1-1995

"first selfish thing," Mark Higgins, "Deputy Mayor Levinson Gives Notice"

"always unflappable," Governor's Communication Office, "Gov. Locke appoints new UTC Chair," *Gov. Gary Locke*, 8-12-1997

"I really missed," Levinson to author, 3-31-2022

Bush's sagging support, Sasha Issenberg, *The Engagement*, Pantheon, New York, 2021, p. 352

campaigns in 11 states, Issenberg, *The Engagement*, p. 384

trying for 29 years, Andrew Garber, Ralph Thomas, "State gay-rights bill OK'd 29 years after effort began," *Seattle Times*, 1-28-2006

"activity in the Capitol," "State gay-rights bill OK'd"

"We don't choose," "State gay-rights bill OK'd"

"Love Is a Battlefield," "State gay-rights bill OK'd"

"dogfight of the year," "State gay-rights bill OK'd"

asked Levinson, Levinson to author, 3-31-2022

112,400 signatures, Andrew Garber, "Eyman files measures to undo gay-rights law," *Seattle Times*, 1-31-2006

"high-octane," Joni Balter, "Eyman's clever word games," *Seattle Times*, 2-2006

"reprehensible," Editorial, "What's 'preferential' about being fair to gays," *News Tribune*, 2-2-2006

others, Editorial, "Eyman's efforts to undo gay civil rights must be defeated," *Walla Walla Union-Bulletin*, 2-1-2006

joined in the berating, Editorial, "See through rhetoric—law simply extends civil rights protections," *Yakima Herald-Republic*, 2-5-2006

"Referendum Sunday," Kristen Millares Bolt, "Church groups preach tolerance; Eyman doesn't turn in signatures," *Seattle P-I*, 6-5-2006

toting plastic light saber, Kristen Millares Bolt, "Church groups preach tolerance"

"Jesus," Eli Sanders, "Reverse Backlash," *Stranger*, 6-6-2006

"maneuvered out," Eli Sanders, "Reverse Backlash,"

"They declined to sign," Editorial, "One less pain on the ballot," *Seattle Times*, 6-8-2006

17th state, Rachel La Corte, "Gregoire signs gay-civil-rights bill," *AP*, 2-1-2006

"terrible" decision, Levinson to author, 3-31-2022

"it couldn't be done," Levinson to author, 4-1-2022

"different than me, Levinson to author

"we laughed," Levinson to author

most difficult transaction, Levinson to author

Levinson was hailed, "The calm that saved the Storm," Washington Jewish Museum, excerpt from *Distant Replay!*, 9-16-2018

Named grand marshals, Lornet Turnbull, "Run and Walk with Pride marks start of gay-pride week," *Seattle Times*, 6-23-2008

devastating turn in 2008, Sasha Issenberg, *The Engagement*, pp. 493-506

website crashed, *The Engagement*, p. 507

"prince married a prince," *The Engagement*, p. 508

voice-over said, Jessica Garrison, Cara Mia Dimassa & Richard C. Paddock, "Voters approve

Proposition 8," *Los Angeles Times*, 11-5-2008

"live and let live," The Engagement, p. 494

"look at the national landscape," Levinson to author, 4-1-2022

Thurston County judge, Lornet Turnbull, "Challenge to R-71 is rejected in court," *Seattle Times*, 9-9-2009

by 1,400 signatures, Janet Tu, "Ref. 71 certified for ballot, but legal battle not over yet," *Seattle Times*, 9-3-2009

"The numbers were not," Levinson to author, 4-1-2022

"One of the reasons," Levinson to author, 3-31-2022

under a new lens, *The Engagement*, pp. 548-554, 585-587, 592-596

turned over her playbook, Silk to author, 6-7-2022

$2.8 million, Phillip Stutzman, "Preserve Marriage Case," No. 13-026, The *State of Washington Public Disclosure Commission*, 5-21-2015, pp. 190, 201 https://www.pdc.wa.gov/sites/default/files/2021-09/13-026%20Preserve%20Marriage%20Washington.pdf

outspent five to one, Issenberg, *The Engagement*, p. 612

"But I was realizing," Levinson to author, 4-1-2022

"We would overwhelm," Levinson to author

first recipients, AP, "Washington same-sex couples get marriage licenses," *USA Today*, 12-6-2012

Lisa Brodoff and Lynn Grotsky, Jonathan Kaminsky, "Washington state readies for same-sex marriage," *Reuters*, 12-5-2012

covered the ceremonies, "Washington state issues first gay marriage licenses," *BBC News*, 12-6-2012

held their nine-month-old, Dominic Holden, "WA's first same-sex marriage," *Stranger*, 12-9-2012

"woman behind the curtain," "WA's first same-sex marriage"

"terrific idea," Levinson to author, 4-1-2022

whooped and whistled, Seattle Men's Chorus Holiday Concert, 12-9-2012, https://www.youtube.com/watch?app=desktop&v=Yue-VSEOSXe8

Edie Windsor, *The Engagement*, pp. 658-660

Obergefell v. Hodges, *The Engagement*, pp. 720-721

"extraordinarily" important, Silk to author, 6-7-2022

"were it not for," Silk to author

Gregoire considered Levinson adviser, Gregoire to author, 10-27-2022

complex matters, Levinson to author, 3-30-2022

"polymath of politics, business," Marley Zeno, "There's a Gun to Your Head: Who's Going to Be Elected Mayor in 2013?" *Stranger*, 8-9-2011

"one of the great civic leaders," Silk to author, 6-7-2022

MAUREEN & SHAUNA WALSH

just two GOP House members, Bill History, SB 6239/HB 2516, https://app.leg.wa.gov/billsummary?BillNumber=6239&Year=2011

"a hero to many," Timothy Egan, "A Widow's Wisdom," *New York Times*, 2-12-2-2012

"Oh gosh, I'm sorry," Maureen Walsh to author, 1-11-2022

One asked to be adopted, Maureen Walsh to author

influenced her mom's, Shauna Walsh to author, 1-26-2022

"like a Merry Maids franchise," Maureen Walsh floor speech, HB 2516, *Washington House Video*, YouTube, 2-8-2012, via https://www.theatlantic.com/politics/archive/2012/02/a-lonely-widows-conscience-helped-gay-marriage-pass-in-washington/252858/

followed Betty White, Maureen Walsh to author, 1-11-2022

chatted with Chaz Bono, Shauna Walsh to author, 1-26-2022

appeared in TV ad, "Freedom," 30-second advertisement, *Washington United for Marriage,* via https://www.msnbc.com/melissa-harris-perry/gop-lawmaker-releases-pro-marriage-equal-msna35432

1.5 million views, Erik Smith, "Maureen Walsh is Celebrity of Statehouse," *Washington State Wire,* 2-14-2012, (w/speech transcribed) https://washingtonstatewire.com/maureen-walsh-is-celebrity-of-statehouse-standout-speech-has-nearly-1-5-million-hits-on-youtube/

RV park in Mexico, Maureen Walsh to author, 1-11-2022

"She had called me," Shauna Walsh to author, 1-26-2022

"under the bus," Maureen Walsh to author

"I've never written," Maureen Walsh to author

"Well, honey," Maureen Walsh to author

made the front page, Sheila Hagar, Vicki Hillhouse, Terry McConn, "Valley icon Kelly Walsh dies," *Walla Walla Union-Bulletin,* 4-27-2006

"just a big, gentle bear," Sheila Hagar, Vicki Hillhouse, Terry McConn, "Valley icon Kelly Walsh dies," *Walla Walla Union-Bulletin,* 4-27-2006

"this big brawny," Shauna Walsh to author, 1-26-2022

He grew up, Shauna Walsh to author

State's official vegetable, Hagar, Hillhouse, McConn, "Valley icon Kelly Walsh dies," *Walla Walla Union-Bulletin,* 4-27-2006

dad's little red journal, Shauna Walsh to author

"I just sort of screamed," Shauna Walsh to author

"made my counter arguments," Shauna Walsh to author

"poke them in the eye," Maureen Walsh to author, 1-11-2022

pretty sure she'd lose, Maureen Walsh to author

district had voted overwhelmingly, Rachel Alexander, "Rep. Maureen Walsh address marriage equality in lecture, *Whitman Wire,* 3-29-2012

"They were not happy," Maureen Walsh to author

"Mom just lost her job," Shauna Walsh to author

"speech of the year," Erik Smith, "Maureen Walsh is Celebrity of Statehouse," *Washington State Wire,* 2-14-2012

Honorees and guests, Megan Townsend, "Modern Family, Beginners Among GLAAD Media Awards Recipients in Los Angeles," 4-21-2012, https://www.glaad.org/blog/modern-family-beginners-among-glaad-media-award-recipients-los-angeles

"it was hilarious," Maureen Walsh to author

"big as beachball," Maureen Walsh interview, (GLAAD awards photos) https://www.flickr.com/photos/glaad/sets/72157629512134214/with/7103465889/

town car whisked her, Shauna Walsh to author

"got to throw me four," Shauna Walsh to author

they had adopted, Molly Ball, "The Marriage Plot: Inside This Year's Epic Campaign for Gay Equality," *Atlantic,* 12-11-2012 https://www.theatlantic.com/politics/archive/2012/12/the-marriage-plot-inside-this-years-epic-campaign-for-gay-equality/265865/

"It does really boil down," Maureen Walsh to author

fired up the state nurses' union, Dan MacGuill, "Did State Sen. Walsh Say Nurses 'Play Cards'?" *Snopes.com,* via https://www.snopes.com/fact-check/maureen-walsh-nurses-cards/

"out-out," Maureen Walsh to author

Chris Gregoire

just 31 percent, "Attitudes on Same-Sex

Marriage," *Pew Research Center*, 5-14-2019, https://www.pewresearch.org/religion/fact-sheet/changing-attitudes-on-gay-marriage/

came to realize the journey, Sasha Issenberg, *The Engagement*, Pantheon Books, New York, 2021, p. 585

70 percent of younger Americans, Justin McCarthy, "Support for Gay Marriage by Age Group—2004-2021," *Gallup.com*, 6-8-2021 https://news.gallup.com/poll/350486/record-high-support-same-sex-marriage.aspx

self-described "journey," Neal Conan (host), "Wash. Governor Discusses Legalizing Gay Marriage," *Talk of the Nation, National Public Radio*, 2-1-2012

backed anti-bullying, Eric Benson, "An Education," *New York Magazine*, 2-24-2012

wasn't ready for marriage equality, Andrew Garber, "Gregoire's journey on gay marriage," *Seattle Times*, 1-5-2012

"We obviously argued," Chris Gregoire to author, 10-27-2022

always encouraged her girls, Courtney Gregoire to author, 11-4-2022, and Michelle Gregoire Garrison to author, 11-9-2022

called her the "best closer," Ed Murray to John C. Hughes, 7-22-2022

stared down Big Tobacco, James Tierney, "The Tobacco Settlement: 20 Years Later," *StateAG.org*, via https://www.stateag.org/initiatives/the-tobacco-settlement?rq=Gregoire

parents talked about rights and equality, Courtney Gregoire to author, 11-4-2022, and Michelle Gregoire Garrison to author, 11-9-2022

felt empowered, Michelle Gregoire Garrison to author, 11-9-2022

Courtney's advocacy, Courtney Gregoire to author, 11-4-2022

a decorated combat nurse, John C. Hughes, "Col. Cammermeyer's War," *Seattle Times*, 12-4-2022

free soft drinks to students, Courtney Gregoire to author, 11-4-2022

took his own life, "Col. Cammermeyer's War"

a wave of weddings, Courtney Gregoire to author, 11-4-2022

"marriage lite," Sasha Issenberg, *The Engagement*, Pantheon Books, New York, 2021, p. 291

Judge Downing ruled, Tracy Johnson, "Gay marriage backed by local judge," *Seattle P-I*, 8-4-2004

"I definitely remember that late night," Courtney Gregoire to author, 11-4-2022

hammered Western Washington, David Wilma, "Hannukah Eve Wind Storm ravages Western Washington beginning on December 16, 2006," *HistoryLink.org*, 12-27-2006

was told at the hospital, Charlene Strong, "Add your voice to the chorus calling for equity and dignity," *Seattle Times*, 8-9-2007

"Beyond belief," Chris Gregoire to author, 10-27-2022

Strong's grief, Elliott Wilson, "Seattle woman shares story to aid push for domestic-partner bill," *Seattle Times*, 1-26-2007

calls the meeting "challenging," Chris Gregoire to author, 10-27-2022

"I couldn't respect more," Chris Gregoire to author

"You can't say it wasn't," Michelle Gregoire Garrison to author, 11-9-2022

Courtney even dropped *Loving v. Virginia*, Courtney Gregoire to author, 11-4-2022

"Which were wrong," Chris Gregoire to author, 10-27-2022

family was reunited, Chris, Courtney and Michelle Gregoire Garrison to author, 10-27, 11-4, and 11-9-2022

"don't know if you got the flavor," Chris Gregoire to author, 10-27-2022

Tapping her chest, Andrew Garber, "Gregoire's journey on gay marriage," *Seattle Times*, 1-5-2012

"always been uncomfortable," "Gregoire's journey on gay marriage"

"Her path was very much," Gregoire's journey on gay marriage"

"She knew it was the right thing," Michelle Gregoire Garrison to author

"I knew that this issue," Chris Gregoire to author, 10-27-2022

Murray was "unbelievably helpful," Chris Gregoire to author, 10-27-2022

In emotional remarks she gave, Joel Connelly, "Gregoire signs same-sex marriage bill," *Seattle P-I*, 2-13-2012

"the voice of your youth," Michelle Gregoire Garrison to author, 11-9-2022

"And a colleague of mine," Courtney Gregoire to author, 11-4-2022

Was up to 84 percent, Justin McCarthy, "Support for Gay Marriage by Age Group—2004-2021," *Gallup.com*, 6-8-2021

"It's important for my sons," Michelle Gregoire Garrison to author

"I'm there to take care of my friend," Courtney Gregoire to author

Mary Yu

first same-sex couples in Washington, Laura L. Myers, "Same-sex couples wed in Washington state for first time," *Reuters*, 12-9-2012

wanted to be married by Judge Yu, email from Sarah and Emily Cofer to author, 2-7-2022

a special touch, Wechsler to author, 1-27-2022

ritualize the event, Yu to author, 1-19-2022

sat in Yu's jury box, Yu to author

"love who your child loves," Yu to author

"She welcomed us," email from Sarah and Emily Cofer to author, 2-7-2022

oversaw 1,400 adoptions, "Lesbian Moms May Soon No Longer Have To Adopt Their Own Kids," Joshua McNichols, *KUOW*, 6-9-2015

"She shined," Wechsler to author, 1-19-2022

of particular legal significance, Yu and Wechsler to author, 1-19-2022

"really important for military families," Yu to author, 1-19-2022

"Judge Yu was special," Wechsler to author 1-19-2022

"What I had said," Yu to author, 1-19-2022

When docked in New York, "Women important in Mary Yu's life," Assunta Ng, *Northwest Asian Weekly* (blog), 5-22-2014

said Senator James G. Blaine, Jennifer Robinson, "The Chinese Exclusion Act," *KPBS*, 5-25-2018

in a noodle factory, Yu email to author, 3-22-2022

picking strawberries, Sheila Cain, "Washington State Supreme Court Justice Mary Yu leads the way," *crosscut.com*, 9-30-2019

never spoke English well, "Women important in Mary Yu's life"

not a great student, Yu email to author, 3-22-2022

didn't want her hands, Sheila Cain, "Washington State Supreme Court Justice Mary Yu leads the way"

"I think my parents were convinced," Yu to author, 12-29-2021

"struggling to fit in," Yu to author

"the most influential," Yu to author

"Central America was on fire," Yu to author

"were revolutionary women," "Mary Yu '79 – Serving as a Role Model for Young People of Color," *Dominican Magazine*, November 2019

considered liberal, David Gibson, "Pope Francis breathes new life into Bernardin's contested legacy," *Religion News Service*, 10-24-2013

issues of red-lining, Maureen O'Hagan, "A special ruling: judge of the year," *Seattle Times*, 11-26-2005

"we weren't feeding people," Yu to author, 12-29-2021

organizer named Barack Obama, Yu to author

"The law provides tools," Yu to author

Yu says she's proof, Yu to author

Worked 12-hour days, Ronald Fitten, "Top Prosecutor is on 'mission in life,' " *Seattle Times*, 6-7-1999

Sims wanted to hire her, Maureen O'Hagan, "A special ruling"

"What I want to know," Ronald Fitten, "Top Prosecutor is on 'mission in life,' " *Seattle Times*, 6-7-1999

"Norm was really committed," Yu to author, 12-29-2021

His prosecutors went hard, *Gay Seattle*, pp. 327-330

"AIDS Now a Crime," "Having AIDS is Now a Crime," *Seattle Gay News*, 6-22-1990

Supreme Court ruled three years later, Rosette Royale, "Farmer, Steven George (1956-1995)," *HistoryLink.org*, 11-19-2021

"He didn't micro-manage," Yu to author, 12-20-2021

asked Yu to replace her, Yu to author, 1-19-2022

"That was the conversation," Maureen O'Hagan, "A special ruling: judge of the year," *Seattle Times*, 11-26-2005

"took considerable pains to explain," "A special ruling"

"He's a young man," Yu to author, 12-29-2021

"Judge Yu had made Carter's adoption," Sarah and Emily Cofer email to author, 2-7-2022

Yu's courtroom went national, Elizabeth Weise, "Same-sex weddings have their day in Washington state," *USA Today*, 12-9-2012

"Because it's pure joy," Yu to author

Yu has mixed feelings, Yu to author

racially insensitive remarks, Steve Miletich, "Two state Supreme Court justices stun some listeners," *Seattle Times*, 10-21-2010

already had right to marry, J.M. Johnson, (concurrence in judgment only) p. 15, 75934-1, *Andersen v. King County*, 6-26-2006, via https://www.courts.wa.gov/newsinfo/?fa=newsinfo.internetdetail&newsid=707

"Just mean-spirited," Yu to author, 1-19-2022

Unlike Amy Coney Barrett, Margaret Talbot, "Amy Coney Barrett's Long Game," *New Yorker*, 2-7-2022

coffee-table book, Yu interview, 1-19-2022

affirmed that farmworkers, Sheila Cain, "Washington Supreme Court Justice Mary Yu leads way," *crosscut.com*, 9-30-2019

"I wondered if people," "Mary Yu '79 – Serving as a Role Model for Young People of Color," *Dominican Magazine*, November 2019

with 57 percent, Secretary of State, Election Results 2016, via https://results.vote.wa.gov/results/20161108/supreme-court-justice-position-1.html

For 15 years, "...Mary Yu leads way"

"This is the time," "...Mary Yu leads way"

"To see another queer woman," Johnathan Curley, "Justice Mary Yu shares her story," *Spokesman-Review*, 9-29-2018

endowed scholarship in her name, Assunta Ng, "Justice Mary Yu's portrait unveiled," *Northwest Asian Weekly* (blog), 11-18-2021

"stands as a promise," "Justice Mary Yu's portrait unveiled"

Compares his painting style to jazz, "Portraits of Justice," Sheila Farr, *University of Washington Magazine*, Winter 2021

Yu initially said 'no,' Steven Gonzalez, "Honoring Justice Yu," Seattle U, via https://www.youtube.com/watch?v=kyaRt7i6du0, 11-12-2021

"You can't take the Chicago," Yu to author, 12-29-2021

"It so surprised me," Yu to author, 1-19-2022

"represents something bigger," Mary Yu, "Honoring Justice Yu," via https://www.youtube.com/watch?v=kyaRt7i6du0, 11-12-2021

"I can't say enough," Yu to author, 1-19-2022

DAVID AMMONS

"subjected to threats ...and reprisals," quoted from SCOTUS decision in *Doe v. Reed*, 6-24-2010, https://www.law.cornell.edu/supct/html/09-559.ZS.html

gay skaters arrested, https://gayseattlehistory.com/chapter-excerpts-to-read/read5-marriage-family/; *Rethinking the Gay and Lesbian Movement*, Mark Stein, Routledge, New York, 2012

Marriage equality first litigated here in 1974, "Marriage Equality and Gay Rights in Washington," Alan J. Stein, *HistoryLink.org* Essay 10255, https://www.*HistoryLink.org*/File/10255

"three decades of controversy and contention," "Gay Issues Lose Their Sting; Is Marriage Next?" *Kitsap Sun*, 7-22-2007

"fairest editor in Idaho," quoted in "Johnston, 73, former Tribune Managing Editor," *Lewiston Tribune*, 7-10-1990

Asbury paid for ad, "He was a classic journalist," *News Tribune*, 3-14-2015

MANNY SANTIAGO

only drinks Puerto Rican coffee, Santiago to author, 7-20-22

favored by Vatican, Abby Goodnough, "Puerto Rico's little secret: coffee," *New York Times*, 7-31-2005

"When you get out," Santiago to author

deeply uncomfortable, Santiago to author

first openly gay Latino, Ross Murray, "Black and Latino Faith Leaders Speak Out in Support of Marriage for Gay Couples and President Obama," glaad.org (Gay & Lesbian Alliance Against Defamation), 5-10-2012

ministered to immigrants, Santiago to author, 7-26-2022

cause was very personal, Santiago to author

"Now we are the same family," Santiago to author, 7-20-22

before applications closed, Santiago to author

The official mission, "Engrossed Second Substitute Senate Bill 5356, LGBTQ Commission," (signed by Gov. Jay Inslee), effective 7-28-2019

"unapologetic fa'afafine," Agaiotupu Viena, "About Us," *Washington State LGBTQ Commission*, 9-23-2022, https://lgbtq.wa.gov/about-us/commissioners

"love seeing my folk," Santiago to author, 7-26-2022

founded by religious pacifists, Santiago to author, 7-20-22

"It's like all colors," Santiago to author

per capita income of $7,117, "Quick Facts, Adjuntas Municipio," *U.S. Census Bureau*, accessed 9-23-2022

Columbus came ashore, Raquel Reichard, "Why Isn't Puerto Rico a State?" *history.com*, 10-4-2021

Roughly the same, Abby Goodnough, "Puerto Rico's little secret: coffee," *New York Times*, 7-31-2005

"El Grito de Lares," Jaquira Diaz, "Let Puerto Rico Be Free," *Atlantic*, November 2022

"literally coffee everywhere," Santiago to author, 7-20-22

served in the cafes, Abby Goodnough, "Puerto Rico's little secret: coffee," *New York Times*, 7-31-2005

"because the United States," Goodnough, *New York Times*, 7-31-2005

teachers were themselves, Santiago to author Pedro Albizu Campos, Jaquira Diaz, "Let Puerto Rico Be Free," *Atlantic*, November 2022

"I grew up with women pastors," Santiago to author

testified to the state Legislature, Max Wasserman, "Legislature bans conversion therapy," *Tacoma News Tribune*, 3-6-2018.

"fantastic" change, Santiago to author

The top of his parents' bureau, Santiago to author

"And I could explain things," Santiago to author

But his first interview, Santiago to author

"pure Kardecians," Allan Kardec, The Spirits' Book (pub. 1857, translated by Darrel W. Kimble and Marcia M. Saiz), *International Spiritist Council*, Brasilia, Brazil, 2006.

known as Don Tito, Santiago to author

split from their northern counterparts, The Editors of Encyclopaedia Britannica, "Southern Baptist Convention," *Britannica*, 5-24-2022

more conservative and Caucasian, Gregory Smith, "America's Changing Religious Landscape," *Pew Research Center*, 5-12-2015

Considered moderate, Human Rights Campaign, "Stances of Faith on LGBTQ Issues: American Baptist Churches, USA," https://

www.hrc.org/resources/stances-of-faiths-on-lgbt-issues-american-baptist-church-usa

oldest seminary, G. Jeffrey MacDonald, "Oldest US graduate seminary to close campus," *Religion News Service*, 11-13-2015

"And all of the sudden," Santiago to author, 7-26-2022

black Puerto Rican lesbian, "Puerto Rico's Sodomy Law Just 'Tip of the Iceberg,' " *The Gully*, 3-14-2003

led a coalition, "Puerto Rico's Ban on Same-Gender Sex Targeted by ACLU Lawsuit," American Civil Liberties Union, 6-22-1968

"And she smiled," Santiago to author

The senior minister, Santiago to author

first "welcoming and affirming," Santiago to author

only one-quarter is white, "Quick Facts, Queens County, New York," *U.S. Census Bureau*, 7-1-2021

Roughly half of congregation, Santiago to author

"to go back into the closet," Santiago to author

previous pastor openly gay, Janet I. Tu, "University Baptist Church building to be sold," *Seattle Times*, 12-14-2007

"I did a whole series of sermons," Santiago to author

participated in the campaign, Ross Murray, "Black and Latino Faith Leaders Speak Out in Support of Marriage for Gay Couples and President Obama," *GLAAD*, 5-10-2012

where indigenous Mayas, Henry Morales, "Meanwhile, Maya Descendants Face Discrimination and Poverty," *Agence France Press*, 12-19-2012

"So, there was some urgency," Santiago to author

"In the mind of this person," Santiago to author

His next stop, Rev. J. Manny Santiago, "The Gospel Call to Cross Borders," *Baptist Peace Fellowship of North America*, 3-15-2015

In its list, Matthew Breen, "Gayest Cities in America, 2013," *Advocate*, 1-9-2013

the roof or the Tacoma Dome, Melissa McCarthy, "Tacoma Dome Dons Pride Flag," *South Sound Magazine*, 7-9-2019

Claire Wilson, "About Us, A Brief History," Washington LGBTQ Commission

Marko Liias, Santiago to author, 7-27-2022

final vote in Senate, "Roll Call, SB 5356, LGBTQ Commission," *Washington State Legislature*, 4.23.2019

"You're talking about someone," Santiago to author, 7-27-2022

he was "super happy," Santiago to author

"Well, since I selected him," Botzer to author, 2-21-2022

"activist and administrator," Gov. Jay Inslee, "Inslee names J. Manny Santiago executive director of the new state LGBTQ Commission," 8-23-2019

"defusing the *machista*," Santiago to author

"all from activist world," Botzer to author, 2-21-2022

"From my perspective," Santiago to author

state doesn't have jurisdiction, Santiago to author

diagnosed with a heart condition, Santiago to author, 7-20-2022

Their mobilization, Santiago to author, 7-27-2022

"There's some preaching," Santiago to author

INDEX

ACKNOWLEDGEMENTS

We are grateful to the many individuals and organizations that lent expertise, artifacts, time and financial support for this project.

Catherine Ahl

ALL Foundation of Washington

David Ammons

Gary Atkins

Gail Basso Girtz

Miriam Bausch

Bayard Rustin Center for Social Justice

Frank Blethen

Randy and Brigitte Bolerjack

Miriam Campbell

Tracey Carlos

Emily Cofer

Sarah Cofer

Carter Cofer

Stephanie Coontz

Scott Douglas

Sandy Deneau Dunham

Carolyn Dimmick

Sandy Dunham

Pat and Susan Dunn

Wayne Ehlers

David Elliott

Candace Espeseth

Jay Fredericksen

Gibbons Lane Winery LLC

Greater Seattle Business Association

Stuart Halsan

Bettina Hansen

Jeffrey Hedgepeth and John Medlin

Ben Helle

Heather Hirotaka

Patsy and John Hughes

Sasha Issenberg

William Jacobs

Yvonne Jump

David Kimball Hansen

Quentin King and Glen Kriekenbeck

Barbara Kinney

Kristie and Allen Kirkpatrick

Carolyn Lakewold

Robert Lane

Renee Lewis

Amy Lin
Ilona Lohrey
Frank Mahood
Laurie P Maricle
Alex McGregor
Kevin McKenna
Victoria Metz
Steve Miletich
Laura Mott
Museum of History and Industry
Patricia Nadolny
Valarie Nelson
Bao Nguyen
Trova O'Heffernan
Jose Oliva
Thomas Oliva
Gabby Oliva
Estela Ortega
Brian and Christine Peck
Aaron Peplowski
Kylie Phillips
Stephanie Prentice
Tom Quigg
Amber Raney
Bill Reader
Cassidy Rehwaldt

Robin Ritterhoff
Aurora San Miguel
Shawn Schollmeyer
Seattle Gay News
The Seattle Times
Zach Silk
Martin J. Smith
Ruth Steel
Mary Thornton
Betsy Vandrush-Borgacz
Sharon Vormestrand
Shauna Walsh
Washington Legislative Photo
Services
Washington State Archives
Washington State Library
Barbara Wechsler
Western Washington University
Center for Pacific Northwest
Mary Whisner
Charlie and Mrs. Nancy Wiggins
Adam Williams
Claudia Yaw
Bob Young

THANK YOU TO OUR SPONSORS

Legacy Washington is dedicated to preserving the history of Washington and its continuing story.
www.sos.wa.gov/legacy

Other Legacy Washington books:

An Election for the Ages: Rossi vs. Gregoire, 2004
Booth Who? A biography of Booth Gardner
Nancy Evans, First-Rate First Lady
Where the Salmon Run, A biography of Billy Frank Jr.
Lillian Walker, Washington Civil Rights Pioneer
The Inimitable Adele Ferguson
Pressing On: Two Family-Owned Newspapers in the 21st Century
Slade Gorton, a Half Century in Politics
Across the Aisles: Sid Snyder's Remarkable Life
A Woman First: The Impact of Jennifer Dunn
John Spellman: Politics Never Broke His Heart
Washington Remembers World War II
Korea 65, the Forgotten War Remembered
1968: The Year that Rocked Washington
Ahead of the Curve: Washington Women Lead the Way, 1910-2020
Julia Butler Hansen, a Trailblazing Washington Politician
Daniel J. Evans, an Autobiography